More Leaders Praise
Building The Master Agency

This book synthesizes the very best solutions to the problems and opportunities of agency building. The Kinders have espoused these systems for many years, and it is great to have them all in one place, so well organized and articulated.

> Stan Benfell, CLU, ChFC, FLMI
> Executive V.P. & CMO
> Beneficial Life

I've been a pupil and fan of Jack and Garry Kinder for 30 years. Their execution of the basics is second to none. Their new book, *Building The Master Agency,* is a masterful and succinct execution of agency building fundamentals.

> Conk Buckley, Jr., CLU, ChFC, FLMI
> Past President - GAMA

The Kinder doctrine has been a positive influence in my career for 25 years. As an aspiring new agent, general agent, and corporate executive, the Kinders have been there as mentors and friends. Learning their concepts can do for you what it's done for me.

> Tony Mazzei
> Vice President – Marketing
> The Guardian

Jack and Garry Kinder have again challenged us to develop world class organizations. This latest book will take you where you want to go, and you'll love every minute of the trip.

> Ralph "Chip" Crews, CLU, ChFC
> Sr. V.P., Career Agency System
> Penn Mutual Life Insurance Company

The Kinders and Val Ivanov have delivered another potent "step by step" solution to *Building The Master Agency* in the 21st Century! Their methodology, unique insights and motivating anecdotes provide a solid foundation to grow an agency to greatness in today's competitive environment. This book will be a gift to every one of our General Agents.

> Tom M. Kochan, CLU, ChFC
> V.P. – Sales
> Signator Financial Network

To arrive at the destination of "high-level success" in today's market requires mastering multiple new skills. The Kinders have skillfully mapped out the path . . . don't miss this journey! A must read.

> Robert Krumroy
> President
> Identity Branding, Inc.

This is a rare book by the Kinders with Val Ivanov. It is both simple and informative. It is a must for every new and experienced General Agent and Manager. I will read it again.

> Bill Pollakov
> President
> GAMA

Jack and Garry Kinder's friendship, encouragement and wisdom have helped guide me for more than 30 years in the insurance industry; as an agent, general agent, regional vice president and now head of a career distribution system. Their energy, insight, integrity and knowledge clearly set a course for success.

> Joe Miller, CLU –
> Sr. V.P. Career System
> National Life Group

Jack and Garry Kinder, teamed with New York Life's "Babe Ruth" of Managing Partners, Val Ivanov, make this book a "don't miss." If you truly want systems that help you build a great agency – they are here! This book is one of the very best on agency building ever written.

> Mike Reeves
> Sr. Vice President
> New York Life

Agency builders committed to growing their agencies big should make this a "night-stand" addition, for easy reference. This is vintage Kinder all the way – their best!

> Mike Cataldo
> Vice President
> Jefferson-Pilot

Jack and Garry continue to stay the course as the two most committed and productive Financial Leaders and teachers in the industry. The systems shared in *Building The Master Agency* will take your organization to leading prominence.

> Ron Price
> Vice President – Life Marketing and Annuities
> American National

For years, the Kinders have been leaders in our industry in providing managers with the systems and tools needed to achieve success. I used their systems when I was a manager, and have witnessed the positive influence they have had on many of our top managers. The Kinders' systems provide the foundation managers need to be on the leading edge in the 21st Century.

> Lynn Wilson
> Sr. Vice President
> Iowa Farm Bureau

Throughout my association with the life insurance industry, the Kinders' systems and procedures have helped me achieve success at every level. I have been privileged to introduce the Kinder systems to international audiences around the world and watch the bottom line results soar. Their teachings are timeless, their systems transferable, and their inspiration is fundamental to personal and organizational success.

> *Terry Schuster*
> *CEO and Founder*
> *The ICMS Group and*
> *The Global Institute*

As always, the Kinders hit the mark! Building an organization is about fundamentals. Not only do they reinforce the fundamentals but lay out the systems necessary to successfully implement the fundamentals. This is a must read for field managers in the Financial Services industry.

> *Chris Noonan, CLU, ChFC*
> *Executive Vice President*
> *AXA Advisors, LLC*

The Kinders have the unique ability to simplify the complex. We are reminded in their latest book, *Building The Master Agency,* to stay brilliant on the basics. I consider this edition to be required reading for all serious managers.

> *Ken Martin, CLU, ChFC, MSFS*
> *President*
> *First Protective-Insurance Designers*

The Kinder Brothers' systems of success have been a major part of my management style for the last 20 years. Our master agency growth is due, in large measure, to their systems and Val Ivanov's inspiration.

> *Burr Anderson*
> *Managing Partner*
> *New York Life*

It motivates, it focuses, it teaches, it inspires, it makes you think, thus providing you with the guide for success.

> *Dick Cleary*
> *President and Managing Partner*
> *Jefferson-Pilot*

The Kinder Brothers have helped us in countless ways over 20-plus years of consultation. Most important, they remind us when we need the courage to change, and when we need the courage to stay the course.

> *Nick Horn*
> *President*
> *Lincoln Financial Advisors*

Many books on agency building contain a couple of strong areas worth reading. Jack and Garry's outstanding work not only covers all the essential areas and draws upon their own cumulative wisdom and practical experience of 40 years, but it also showcases best practice secrets in each of these critical management/leadership areas from many of the industry's best. It's got it all. Bravo Kinders.

> *Bob Littell*
> *Littell Consulting Services*
> *Co-Author of Power NetWeaving*

Here it is – the master agency builders' handbook. The Kinders have delivered, in "user-friendly" fashion, specific tools to implement the core systems necessary for building a master agency. Invaluable to the new agency builder – and essential "back to the basics" refresher for the seasoned veteran.

> *Rich Morasco*
> *Vice President – Sales*
> *MetLife*

Jack and Garry have done it again! They have blessed us with another straightforward, practical tool for agency building based on the Kinder hallmark of strong philosophies and effective systems.

> *George Worley, FLMI, CLU, ChFC*
> *Sr. Manager of Field Development*
> *Modern Woodmen*

At our company – we've made implementation of the ten systems our highest priority. We know this book contains what we need to be one of the premier sales organizations in the country.

> *Andy Martin, CLU, ChFC*
> *Regional Sales Manager*
> *First Protective*

The Kinders and Val Ivanov – what a winning combination! They continue to create value for agency builders who desire to balance fundamentals and new marketing initiatives in order to take their business to the next level. Their systems are specific, transferable and proven effective!

> *Vera Jo Springer, CLU, CLF*
> *Managing Partner*
> *New York Life*

An outstanding step-by-step "blueprint" of proven doctrines and principles for successful agency building, communicated in a style that all field managers will love. Once again, Jack and Garry Kinder have hit a home run.

> *Ken Massey, FICF*
> *Director of Agencies*
> *Modern Woodmen of America*

Every successful athletic team has a common thread: belief in it's teammates and use of team work. As in a professional sports playbook, the Kinders' book gives a clear, practical and useful blueprint of drafting talent, training and communicating with them in winning ways, building pride in the organization and confidence in the coaches. A "need to read" for all levels of agency management.

Angelo Schiralli
General Agent
New England Financial

The Kinders latest book is the most comprehensive book on building a master agency I've ever read. It provides a clear, effective and motivating approach to agency building with real tools and procedures that I can put to use today.

Bob Lyman, CLU, ChFC, CFP
General Agent - Manager
John Hancock

The Kinders provide the essential keys necessary for unlocking the secrets of agency building, agency management and personal development.

Mark Jones
President
Mark S. Jones and Associates

What the Kinders teach us about agency management is timeless. Management fads come and go. This book will help you build a great agency.

Quincy Crawford
President
First Financial Group

You could search the great libraries of the world and dig into the depths of the World Wide Web and you would never find a more practical, a more relevant, or a more systematic guide to building and growing a profitable financial services organization. This book offers ageless wisdom in a fresh and contemporary format that is a must read for all who are associated with the business of production growth, manpower development and profitable operations.

Steve Worthy, CEO
The Carolinas Planning Group, L.L.C.
Charlotte, North Carolina

The Kinders stand alone as teachers and coaches of Master Agency Builders. This book is for anyone aspiring to true leadership.

Kevin P. Kelly
V.P. – Marketing
Michigan Farm Bureau

After 35 years in the financial services industry, I continue to come back to the basics learned from the Kinders. I find it to be my first choice for training new agents and staff.

> Dennis Clark
> Agency Manager
> Kansas Farm Bureau

This book gives you all the insights you'll need to become a dominant agency builder in the 21st Century.

> Brett Davenport, CLF, LUTCF, CLTC
> Managing Director
> Prudential Financial

The Kinders have been instrumental in helping us to develop and implement agency systems that have benefited us immeasurably. Along with Val Ivanov, they have provided invaluable critical insights, a wealth of knowledge and practical suggestions that have fueled our growth and profitability.

> Mark Kostrzewski, CLU, ChFC
> General Agent
> National Life

For any agency to be successful today, it must develop systems that will assure its success. An agency manager can spend untold dollars and years trying to learn by trial and error, or they can learn from others' experience. This book allows the individual to learn from the experience of some of the best in the business.

> David Schulman, CLU, ChFC
> General Agent
> Mass Mutual

Once again in confident simplicity Jack and Garry Kinder along with an industry legend – Val Ivanov, have delivered the fundamentals to building a Master Agency in black and white. Little more is required! This is must reading for all leaders, both new and seasoned alike.

> D. Duane Bartlett
> President
> Baron Financial

Jack and Garry have outlined the basic principles for success in running an agency. Anyone who consistently follows these proven methods will certainly see the success they desire.

> Mark Sutton, CLU
> Managing Director
> Prudential Financial

A vital reference gem for today's field leaders. This collaboration of basic truths from the industry's best transcends time and fully applies to the new era of financial services distribution.

> *Gary Simpson*
> *Strategic Wealth Management*

If a manager aspires to build a truly successful agency, *Building The Master Agency* is a must read. The ten-step approach covers the essentials for success in a concise and interesting fashion.

> *Doug Ferguson*
> *Director, Field Resources*
> *Indiana Farm Bureau Insurance*

Once again, Jack and Garry are "brilliant on the basics." With great systems, talented people will always reach greater heights. This book is a blueprint for both new and veteran agency builders.

> *Rich Snebold, Jr., CLU*
> *Managing Director*
> *The Acacia Group*

This is powerful material . . . a practical book that is a "must read" for all agency builders. The Kinder Brothers have done it again!

> *Tommy Hudgins*
> *Manager*
> *American General Financial Group*

There are no magic bullets . . . only systems that work. This book gives you systems to use in your daily activity that make agency building simple. A must for every agency builder!

> *Albert Hurst*
> *General Agent*
> *Modern Woodmen*

No surprise here! The Kinder Brothers have once again delivered usable and practical systems for achieving superior success as an agency builder.

> *Andy BluestoneCFP*
> *General Agent*
> *Selective Benefits Group*

If I were starting an agency today, this is one of the first books I would put on my reading list. If you are already an agency builder, be sure this goes on your reading list.

> *Jim Pierce*
> *General Agent*
> *National Life of Vermont*

I have been a general agent for over 30 years and I've learned that you can't build a great agency without basic systems. There is no one better at this than the Kinder Brothers.

Walt Cardinet
General Agent
Integrated Financial Services

I have known Jack and Garry Kinder for over 30 years. The materials they have developed for agents, general agents, and managers are crucial to have in every agency. We have successfully used these materials in my agency and encourage everyone to do the same.

Vasil W. Allabashi
CLU, President
V. W. Allabashi & Company

Jack Kinder, Jr. and Garry D. Kinder with Val Ivanov

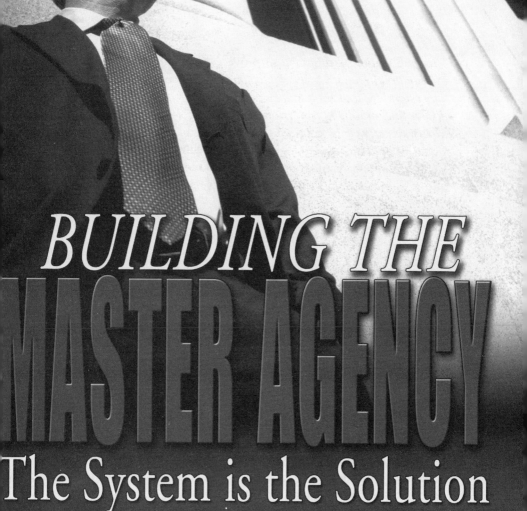

BUILDING THE MASTER AGENCY

The System is the Solution

The National Underwriter Company
PROFESSIONAL PUBLISHING GROUP

P.O. Box 14367 • Cincinnati, Ohio 45250-0367
1-800-543-0874 • www.nationalunderwriter.com

ISBN: 0-87218-613-X

This publication is designed to provide accurate and authoritative information in regard to the subject matter covered. It is sold with the understanding that the publisher is not engaged in rendering legal, accounting or other professional service. If legal advice or other expert assistance is required, the services of a competent professional should be sought. **— From a Declaration of Principles jointly adopted by a Committee of the American Bar Association and a Committee of Publishers and Associations.**

Fifth Printing

Copyright © 2002
The National Underwriter Company
P.O. Box 14367, Cincinnati, Ohio 45250-0367

Printed in U.S.A.

DEDICATION

September 11, 2001 – A day that will live long in all our memories. We were moving along toward the completion of this manuscript when word reached us of the unthinkable terrorist actions in New York City.

Countless millions of lives were changed forever that day. We learned of the young son who received an email from his Dad, who worked in the World Trade Center. It was to the point. It read simply: "I love you. I'll see you on another day . . . in Heaven."

Many families are still clinging to heart-wrenching final words like these, or cherished memories of their lost loved ones.

We dedicate this book to all of those who demonstrated and continue to demonstrate courage, faith and hope.

This book is also dedicated to the agency builders and leaders who have discovered how to stay at their best by educating, encouraging and stretching others. What we have learned from them, we now share with you.

THE CHALLENGE

It has been said that a challenge well defined is a challenge already half-solved. Today's challenge is spelled out for the agency builder – *The situation is still the boss*. And the situation is challenging modern day agency heads to build organizations faster, bigger and better.

The increasing tempo of the times, the escalating pace of technology, the cascade of compliance-driven paperwork, the rapid development of new products and the flood of computer generated information all tend to inhibit communication between managers and producers. In short, it's made agency heads' jobs more complex and demanding.

What's needed to meet and conquer this challenge? We believe it is agency builders who will lead with a systems-behavior. *The system today is the solution*. That's what this book is all about.

Now, with pen in hand, read and inwardly digest these pages. Master the ten systems. When you do, you will be well qualified to meet the challenge. What's more, you will have the satisfaction of heading up a master agency.

Jack and Garry Kinder
Dallas, Texas
March, 2002

INTRODUCTION

By Helen Kooiman Hosier

The American Dream Realized

Vision without action is merely a dream. Action without vision just passes the time. Vision with action can change the world.

– Joel Arthur Barker

When the publisher asked me to write an introduction for this book, it made my day. There are giants in every industry. And then there are Jack Kinder, Garry Kinder, and Val Ivanov. They transcend that, they are more than giants, they are men with fabulous stories that personify the American Dream. They are men who had the courage to put their dreams and visions into action. And while it may be a stretch to say they've changed "the world," I know they have positively changed the lives and careers of countless people over the years.

It's important to know who Jack, Garry and Val are beyond their successes and awards and nationwide recognition. Theirs are tales of survival, perseverance, faith and valuable lessons passed on by their families. Through their stories, you will also come to understand how their visions took shape, how they achieved the American Dream and how they can help you do the same.

While their dreams and visions didn't take shape immediately, they never overlooked an opportunity. They kept the faith and determination. These qualities – and possibly some good timing – have brought them to where they are today. Learn from their stories. Let them lead you to the promised land of more success and fulfillment in your career.

Jack and Garry Kinder: From Humble Beginnings to KBI

Through the example of their parents, Jack and Garry learned that hard work and discipline were necessary to become loyal, trustworthy, successful individuals. The work ethic was clearly defined by the example of their father. Garry made the journey into the world with an older brother near at hand. Together they did the things that brothers do. They disagreed now and then, as all siblings do, but together they emulated the discipline and teaching of their parents. They played, prayed, learned and grew.

At Pekin Community High School, they were members of the National Honor Society. They also pursued their athletic dreams. Jack was All-State in basketball and Garry was All-State in baseball. Both were captains of their football, basketball and baseball teams. "We wanted to be athletes," Garry remembers. They excelled, learning the importance of sportsmanship, rules, and fair play.

At Illinois Weslyan University, Jack became an outstanding college basketball player. Garry was the quarterback on the first undefeated team at the university. However, the brothers encountered some set-backs. Injury cut Garry's athletic career short. Jack, who had set his sights on becoming a college coach, left coaching after three years of high school work. "If I could have gotten a college coaching job, I'd still be coaching," said Jack, who's also quick to admit that God had other plans for him. He had majored in education and minored in business. Business beckoned. Garry majored in business with a minor in education. Both men graduated with honors, and today, they serve as co-chairmen of the alumni association.

The brothers took their disappointments as opportunities. If the promised land couldn't be athletics, it could be something else. That something else was insurance.

Jack was recruited into the business by Fred G. Holderman, the first man inducted into the GAMA Hall of Fame. Jack had found his niche in the insurance business and became licensed at Equitable Life, now known as AXA. Once there, he recruited his brother when Garry was 19 and still a junior in college.

Together, they discovered something that motivated them. Selling was in their blood. Albert Einstein said, "Try not to become a man of success, but rather try to become a man of value." Jack and Garry Kinder were becoming men of value. Self-discipline, imagination, and staying power fueled them. They became peak performers committed to excellence.

Moving up through the ranks, the brothers earned superior selling credentials and became managers. Both have been Equitable's Young Manager of the Year. Both earned the CLU designation in 1962. They have been members of NAIFA for nearly 50 years.

They were managing directors of the Purdue Management Institute for 30 years. They qualified for the Million-Dollar Round Table (MDRT) at young ages, as well as qualifying for the 2001 MDRT in Toronto. They have conducted workshops at the MDRT conventions in Orlando and Toronto.

In 1976, Jack and Garry formed Kinder Brothers International. Building in-depth training programs for more than 300 companies, domestically and internationally, they are still delivering ideas and services to clients through the products they have to offer. Jack and Garry have jointly sponsored training programs with MDRT and GAMA and are recognized leaders in the development of interactive CD-ROM training.

Many of their courses are now available through the Internet. Their materials have been translated into seven different languages. Overseas markets are heavily centered in Singapore, Taiwan, India, China, Malaysia, Thailand, South America, and Europe.

The brothers' strong faith is at the core of everything they do. It guides their thinking and decision-making. They subscribe to the idea that *"Life is God's gift to us, what we do with it is our gift to God."*

Jack and his wife, Mary Sue, have one daughter, Jayne Ann. Jayne and her husband Craig have three children, all of whom are outstanding athletes. Jack is proud of the fact that his two grandsons are Eagle Scouts.

Garry was married to Barbara for thirty-four years before she was tragically killed in 1990. He has since married Janet, who lost her husband to cancer. They have four children and six grandchildren. Garry's son-in-law, David Smith, heads up the software development at Kinder Brothers. His other son-in-law, Curt Ladd, is an 18-year-member of the MDRT, having made Top of the Table for three years in a row.

Had it not been for their vision ...

Val Ivanov: To America by Way of Europe, Africa and Asia

"GIVE ME YOUR TIRED, YOUR POOR, YOUR HUDDLED MASSES YEARNING TO BREATHE FREE, ... I LIFT MY LAMP BESIDE THE GOLDEN DOOR."

– Emma Lazarus

On video, Val Ivanov appears almost bigger than life. While watching the video, I often wondered how one man could survive it all and become what he is today. Weeks later, in Dallas, I had the good fortune of meeting this tall, smiling man whose entrepreneurial spirit and drive for excellence greeted me along with his outstretched hand.

After more than 30 years with New York Life Insurance Company, Mr. Ivanov is still passionate about his career. "I thought about retiring, but decided against it – I love what I do. For me, it's not really work." And so he stays on as Executive Managing Partner, on a scaled back workweek. Like Jack and Garry, the business is in his blood, and seldom out of his thinking.

"I found my true calling," he said. "New York Life turned my life around because I found a way to earn a living, and discovered I could help people at the same time."

"And the keys to your success?" I asked.

"I'm a likeable, energetic workaholic." There is honesty and humility in his blunt response. That is Val Ivanov. A man who survived a harrowing childhood in Europe but never lost sight of the American Dream.

Like Jack and Garry, Val came from humble beginnings. His father was a farmer in the Balkan Mountains near the border of Yugoslavia and Romania. It was wartime. There were only two countries in the European world that didn't allow the Germans to execute the Jews – Denmark and Bulgaria. Val's father helped the Jewish people and was imprisoned. He was a tall, big man, but when he came home he weighed about a hundred pounds.

"There was no high school in our village, so I went away to school. My father had given me a code so that I would know whether we were going to try to escape and, I was to meet him in a certain vineyard. On the appointed day, I met my father and he said, 'We can't stay here anymore. We must cross over the border.' My brother was already in the army and my sisters were both married and had children, thus they could not flee."

The border was ten kilometers away and gunfire was exchanged as they crossed. In Yugoslavia, Val and his parents moved from one place to another, finally settling in a camp that processed fleeing Bulgarians. His parents were sent to a work farm in Novi Bechay, and Val was sent to an orphanage in Stari Bechay for schooling. Already separated from his brothers and sisters, he was now separated from his parents. His one attempt to escape to see his parents resulted in his arrest and a merciless beating.

In 1950, Val's father paid him a visit and told him they were going to escape once more, this time by train to a place near the Austrian border. They were caught and put in prison. Six months later, they succeeded in escaping and landed in Triesta, Italy at another refugee camp. Val lived in the camp along with 10,000 others – Russians, Bulgarians, Albanians, Yugoslavians and some Greeks, all awaiting immigration to anywhere. Val and his father set their sights on America but, on the "quarter system," they had to wait in the camp for five years before qualifying to request immigration to America.

As a teen, Val wondered what the future held for him in such a place. He had bigger dreams. Together, he and a friend decided to make a run for freedom. They knew the international trains came through the free-zone city where the refugees were being detained. Sneaking onto the train at night, they crossed the border into France. At the police station, they kept their refugee status secret, saying they were from Albania.

While in France, Val and his friend worked in an automobile factory. But the urge to move on was strong. After a brief jaunt to Germany, they signed up for the French Foreign Legion, knowing they'd eventually try to escape. They were sent to Africa and then given orders to go to Vietnam where Val served as a paratrooper.

Once again, the two planned an escape, this time as stowaways on a tugboat. They were discovered and turned over to the Sicilian authorities who sent them back to a refugee camp. Three years of running came to an end. The Italians gave an ultimatum. Finish high school or be shipped back to Bulgaria.

In one year, Val completed three grades and received his diploma.

America beckoned. The U.S. Army was recruiting. If you had escaped from Eastern Europe and were between the ages of 18 and 35 you could join the Army for five years and acquire citizenship. He qualified and passed an American intelligence test. He was flown to Frankfurt, Germany and sworn in the moment he stepped off the plane.

A sergeant heard Val speaking to different men and asked him, "You can talk to everybody here?" When he said, "Yeah…" he was made an acting sergeant. Interpreters were badly needed. His entrepreneurial skills began to surface as he sold blankets, toothpaste, and other scarce items the German people needed.

Before long he was on his way to the states for specialized training. He asked for and received a leave to visit his parents who were still in the Italian refugee camp. In Trieste, he went to the Ambassador's office and requested that his parents be allowed to go to America. By Christmas 1958, they found themselves in New York City.

In 1962, after spending six years in the Army, Val Ivanov was an American citizen and settled in New York City. He was reunited with his parents and moved into their tiny Greenwich Village apartment. At 28, he was uncertain about the future but knew he wanted to be successful.

"I had a refugee high school education and an Army equivalent, but I went to New York University and took an entrance exam." His fluency in foreign languages landed him a teaching job that sustained him while he earned his master's degree in Linguistics. He also married during those years.

One day, in utter frustration, he quit his job as a linguistics teacher. "My wife was pregnant. We had a two-year-old daughter. My wife looked at me and said, 'What are you going to do?' and I responded, 'I'm going to New York Life and I'm going to sell insurance.'"

Now, more than three decades later, the name Val Ivanov is synonymous with New York Life. He followed his vision to be a success in America and found his niche. From Bulgaria, to the refugee camps of Eastern Europe, to America, the award-winning, multi-millionaire Ivanov exudes the entrepreneurial spirit that has been his hallmark virtue. He has won an unprecedented number of sales awards from New York Life and a record number thirteen Chairman's Trophies, the highest award New York Life gives.

Follow the Dream, Achieve the Vision

These special men have put in writing for you a "how-to-plan" on building a master agency that can take you to new heights. You can go as fast and as far as your talents and energy will take you. Through their years of experience, through their own personal stories and the tales of others, they have developed a groundbreaking path for you to follow in building a great organization.

You hold in your hands information that can help you become another Val Ivanov, Jack or Garry Kinder. The promised land is yours.

ACKNOWLEDGMENTS

Many of you contributed directly or indirectly to the development of the systems identified in this book. To thank only a few may do a disservice to many. However, we are especially indebted to our colleague of more than 20 years, Lu Ann Fowler, for her enormous editorial assistance and helpful suggestions.

Thanks to Lainie Ridgway for contributing her proofreading skills to make the final manuscript a superior one.

To our associates Jane McDonald, David Smith, Keith McDonald, Melissa Morrow and Shad Spears, thank you for your many contributions to this project.

We are fortunate to be partnering with The National Underwriter Company, a publisher that has been at the forefront of education in the financial services industry for over a century. A special thanks to Steve L. Nieman, LUTCF and Deborah A. Miner, J.D., CLU, ChFC for your unwavering commitment to excellence.

LIFE IS GOD'S GIFT TO US.
WHAT WE DO WITH IT IS OUR GIFT TO GOD.

TABLE OF CONTENTS

Chapter 1 / *PLANNING*

*CREATE NO SMALL BLUEPRINT. DARE TO DREAM THE BIG DREAM. ONCE
A BIG DREAM IS RECORDED, IT WILL NEVER DIE, UNTIL YOU CAN TOUCH
IT WITH YOUR HAND — AND SEE IT WITH YOUR EYE.*

Earl Nightingale

Thomas I. Watson, the founder of IBM, was asked to what he attributed IBM's great success. Mr. Watson said it boiled down to these three things.

1. Have a clear picture of what the final product will look like when it is finished. **Planning comes before the doing.**

    "At the start, we had a model in mind of what IBM would look like when our vision was in place," he said.

2. Decide how the product will act.

    "We created a picture of how IBM would look when the dream was in place, and then how such a company would have to act. We realized that unless we acted that way from the beginning, we would never get there."

3. Measure progress on a regular basis.

    "Each day," observed Mr. Watson, "we asked ourselves how we did. We discovered the difference between where we were and where we were committed to be. The next day we set out to make up for the difference."

Watson's three-pronged approach to building a successful organization all began with the building of a clear-cut vision and a commitment to a model carried in his mind. So must yours!

Exhibit 1.1 / *THREE-PRONG APPROACH*

OUR VISION
A dynamic, profitable
high-performing organization

SUCCESS MODEL
Talent supported by
Structure – Systems – Strategies – Standards

Philosophies to Embrace

❶ **PRIDE IN THE OUTFIT AND CONFIDENCE IN THE LEADERSHIP GOES BEFORE ALL.** Work consistently at building these two morale ingredients.

❷ **QUALITY RECRUITING MAKES GOOD THINGS HAPPEN FAST.** Stay producer-focused and committed to recruiting enough of the right kind of individuals each year.

❸ **IT IS THE PRODUCER UPON WHOM IT ALL DEPENDS.** Build each individual's competence and confidence in the vital selling function.

❹ **KEEPING SCORE IS BASIC TO SOUND MANAGEMENT.** Communicate the score in appropriate ways—it causes the score to improve.

❺ **INDIVIDUAL SUCCESS TAKES PLACE WITHIN THE FRAMEWORK OF HIGH EXPECTATIONS.** Develop the strengths while managing the weaknesses.

❻ **A PERSON'S LOYALTY IS A FUNCTION OF HOW MUCH HE OR SHE IS APPRECIATED.** Promote a program of recognition, inspiration, and morale building.

❼ **HONEST, INTELLIGENT EFFORT IS ALWAYS REWARDED.** Endeavor to make every occasion a great occasion.

❽ **MAKING GOOD IS THE PRIMARY CONCERN OF MANAGEMENT.** Focus on the primary elements of the job.

*Everything we seek to achieve will be predicated
upon the success of the individual producer.*

IF YOUR PRINCIPLES CAN BECOME DATED, THEY'RE NOT PRINCIPLES.

Warren Buffett

UNSPECTACULAR PREPARATION

Surprisingly, most agency builders don't take the time to construct in advance a blueprint for success. They have no five-year plan or operational plan. Why? Because planning is inglorious. It's not exciting. There's seldom instant feedback. Most agency building success stories don't appear suddenly and fully formed; they bloom over the years as intelligently set benchmarks are reached.

We often quote Roger Staubach's reflection used in his response after being introduced at Canton, Ohio, on his selection to the professional football Hall of Fame. Roger stated, "Spectacular achievements are almost always the result of unspectacular preparation!" That's true in life—and in agency building.

PLANNING BEFORE DOING

Planning comes before the doing—and planning is just as important as the doing. Planning focuses on philosophical beliefs, organizational structure, production and producer numbers.

Your attitude and thinking exert an enormous influence on what happens in the organization. You play the dominant role. You provide the directional force that brings about the desired results. Making the right things happen is achieved when you consistently reinforce the basics and demonstrate your belief in them.

Commitment climbs when your associates see your passion. They catch the feeling. Commitment is highly contagious.

The more consuming your commitment, the more your associates will rally to the cause and the achievement of your plan. Your passion and intensity—your focus, drive and dedication—carry the maximum influence over the level of commitment you can expect from associates.

Like it or not, you set the climate. Associates always take a reading on the individual in charge. When it comes to building the plan and gaining total commitment to its fulfillment, you must take the lead.

> *Attitude is the speaker of our present; it is the prophet of our future.*

Make your commitment to a growth plan so exciting that it becomes a cause, and watch your agency come alive. It's worth noting that Martin Luther King shouted, "I have a dream!" and he created a crusade.

Exhibit 1.2 / *ORGANIZATIONAL CHART*

In the center of all we do is serving an ever-increasing number of clients, at a mutual profit.

BUILD A FIVE-YEAR PLAN – KEY QUESTIONS

Carefully study Exhibit 1.3, the Five-Year Model. This simplified format will prove helpful to you when thinking through your answers to the big question: *What do you want your organization to look like at the end of one year? At the end of two years . . . or in 60 short months—five years?*

In order to plan intelligently for the desired results, you'll need to think about your responses to these important questions with respect to the next 60 months.

- What will be your production objectives?

- How many starters will you need each year? What retention rate must you achieve? What must be their per-capita productivity?

- What kind of training program will you need? Will you have sufficient facilities? Will you need a training specialist?

- What kind of support services will you be expected to offer?

- Will you need to develop new markets? Which ones? How? When?

- How large a staff will you require? Administrative? Marketing?

- What size of a management team must you attract, develop and appoint? How many specialists?

- What facilities, equipment and computer support will you need?

- What will be the amount of your budget?

Again, carefully study the example provided in Exhibit 1.3. This was a scratch organization in 1990. Today, General Agent, Lee Harrison, has his sights set on $12 million of FYCs by the year 2005.

Exhibit 1.3 / *FIVE-YEAR MODEL*

Lee Harrison, General Agent   12-01-01
Date of Appointment – 1/1/90   Tallahassee

North Florida Financial
Five-Year Plan

	POPULATION					PRODUCTION (in 000's)				
Class	**'01**	**'02**	**'03**	**'04**	**'05**	**'01**	**'02**	**'03**	**'04**	**'05**
Starters	34	40	45	45	45					
(A)	30	34	38	38	38	550	680	760	760	760
(B)	16	20	26	29	29	500	800	1040	1160	1160
(C)	9	12	15	20	23	550	670	750	1000	1150
(D)	4	7	8	14	18	300	560	640	1120	1440
(E)	17	19	23	27	37	1530	2090	2990	3780	5550
SUBTOTAL	76	92	110	128	145	3430	4800	6180	7820	10060
Sales Mgrs./ MTLs	16	19	22	25	28	3000	3400	3600	3750	4000
Gen. Agent/ Asst.	2	2	2	2	2	150	150	150	150	150
Other						1500	1650	1850	2000	2250
TOTAL	94	113	134	155	175	8080	10000	11780	13720	16460
Percent Gain						31%	23%	19%	16%	20%

	RETENTION RATIOS	PRODUCER PRODUCTIVITY
(A) Class	85	20
(B) Class	65	40
(C) Class	50	50
(D) Class	45	80
(E) Class	90	150

PRODUCER DEVELOPMENT

	'01	'02	'03	'04	'05
Guardian's Club	75	80	90	95	100
MDRTs	40	45	50	55	60
Credentialed	35	40	45	50	55

Kinder Comments

This agency has become an industry showcase. It's interesting to see what a "scratch operation" can become over a ten-year period. Good recruiting with strong retention makes a big difference. Add to the mix a complete commitment to a sales strategy and close monitoring—and good things happen quickly. This outfit is extremely well-managed and led. The Sales Managers and Marketing Team Leaders are strong personal producers. They lead by example.

Jack Kinder, Jr.
12/01/01

RESPECT THE OPERATIONAL PLAN

These are the numbers for the current year and they represent management's responsible commitments. You must find the way to focus everyone's attention on these numbers. They must have visibility; they must be *front and center* with management team members all year long.

We found it helpful to promote the visibility of these numbers by putting them on an attractive plaque, which was then placed on a small tripod. At the plaque's top was the manager's name followed by the posted numbers he was responsible for achieving. At the bottom of the plaque was the all-important philosophy: "A Commitment Made Is a Debt Unpaid." Finally, the plaque was positioned next to the manager's telephone for instant, daily recall.

SET PRODUCER GOALS

The key to effective planning at the producer level lies in guiding the process in such a way that it results in the producer making a responsible commitment. Our popular "Professional's Planning Procedure" is the type of tool that formalizes the process.

I DWELL IN POSSIBILITIES.

Oprah Winfrey

It's important to recognize the essential principles of good planning. Let's review the four principles in our producer goal setting strategy.

1. ### GOALS MUST BE ACHIEVABLE.

    Why push and strive toward a goal when you know it's outside your associate's reach? Properly–established goals are attainable only with a maximum effort. Set them realistically high.

2. **GOALS MUST BE BELIEVABLE.**

This is closely related to the first criteria. Goals must reflect realism, not idealism. They must be things you're convinced can be reached.

3. **GOALS MUST BE MEASURABLE.**

Think about an athletic event. Would you find the contest interesting if there was no scoreboard? What makes the game exciting is knowing the score, and how much time is remaining. Goals become challenging only when they are measurable.

4. **GOALS MUST HAVE DEADLINES.**

Time is a most precious commodity. It can never be replaced. Goals must have deadlines if time is to be used profitably.

Those are the four goal-setting principles—achievable, believable, measurable and deadlines.

I EXPECT TO SPEND THE REST OF MY LIFE IN THE FUTURE, SO I WANT TO BE REASONABLY SURE OF WHAT KIND OF FUTURE IT'S GOING TO BE. THAT IS MY REASON FOR PLANNING.

Charles Kettering

Exhibit 1.4 / *GOAL SETTING GUIDELINES*

WELL-CONCEIVED PRODUCER GOALS	POORLY-DEFINED PRODUCER GOALS
Stated numerically in terms of end results.	Stated in terms of adjectives and adverbs.
Achievable at a specific time.	Are never fully achievable—no specific target dates set.
Definite as to what is expected.	Ambiguous as to what is expected.
Realistically high and practical.	Theoretical or idealistic.
Precisely stated.	Too brief and indefinite, or too long and complex.
Limited to five or fewer areas.	Written with many areas of concentration.

PLANNING STEPS

Step 1 – Self-Assessment

The first priority on the producers' road to sales success is to realistically evaluate where they are currently. Are they satisfied with what they are becoming? This initial step helps producers examine and answer this question. They should be assisted by management in evaluating where they are professionally, personally, physically, financially and spiritually. Our planning process does this most effectively.

Step 2 – Compile a Master Dream List

Potential lies dormant until aroused by the belief that dreams can be made to come true. It's important for producers to dream of what they want to do. They will be motivated to do what they decide and commit to do.

Producers make their dreams—and then their dreams make them. "The research of neuroscience has proven that what you determine for yourself, what you conceive and give your energies to, will create or call upon a life force which will turn the dreams you dream into a touchable reality." So says Dr. Shad Helmstetter, Ph.D., in his book, What to Say When You Talk to Yourself.

Precise yet perceptive is the Proverb that states, "Without vision, the people perish."

I CAN NEVER STAND STILL. I MUST EXPLORE AND EXPERIMENT. I AM NEVER SATISFIED WITH MY WORK. I RESENT THE LIMITATIONS OF MY OWN IMAGINATIONS.

Walt Disney

Step 3 - Establish This Year's Goals

Yearly goals bridge the gap between where producers are and where they intend to go. Yearly goals put producers on schedule to achieve their career objectives. Few people know what they want; still fewer decide when they want it.

A financial budget is a key element in determining producers' yearly goals. Before they can set intelligent production goals, they must first determine their financial needs. A yearly budget will show them the income they must produce—as a minimum.

As production goals are planned for the year, producers will find it helpful to establish two kinds of goals: minimum and superior.

Minimum goals are what must be accomplished this year; it's what the producers will do regardless. Acceptable minimum goals are goals to which the producers are committed and they are set realistically high. They require a complete commitment to their achievement as there is no room for compromise with minimum goals. A responsible commitment must be made to their achievement.

Superior goals are flavored with optimism; they are the numbers producers hope to achieve. Superior goals are over and above minimum goals. Superior goals are bonus goals.

You'll want to give careful thought when coaching and setting minimum and superior goals because they are small keys that unlock big futures in selling. Study Exhibit 1.5 "This Year's Production Goals."

Exhibit 1.5 / *THIS YEAR'S PRODUCTION GOALS*

PRODUCTION GOALS FOR 2XXX		
Key Result Areas	Acceptable **Minimum**	**Superior**
Paid Transactions	_____	_____
Life MDRT Credits	$_____	$_____
Disability Income	_____	_____
Annuity	_____	_____
Long-Term Care	_____	_____
Equity Sales	_____	_____
Other MDRT	_____	_____
Total MDRT Credits	$_____	$_____
MDRT Credits Per Transaction	_____	_____
Expense Allowance	_____	_____
P/C First Year Commissions	_____	_____
Renewal Income	_____	_____
Other Business Income	_____	_____
Total Revenues	$_____	$_____
New Clients	_____	_____

Exhibit 1.5 cont'd. / *THIS YEAR'S PRODUCTION GOALS*

SELF-DEVELOPMENT GOALS

Selling skills I will develop this year:_____

_____

_____

Knowledge I will acquire this year, i.e., LUTC, CLU, CFP, ChFC, CPCU, RHU, CSA, company, university and industry training courses: _____

_____

_____

_____

Habits I will strengthen will include the following: _____

_____

_____

I will sharpen my selling skills and increase my average size case to $_____.

My persistency will be _____%.

The most effective way for me to reach each of the above goals is:

_____

_____

Step 4 – Fix an Action Plan

An inventory has been taken of where the producers are currently. They have seen their dreams and decided where they would like to go. They have specified what they must do this year to advance toward accomplishing their goals. Now, they take the process one step further. It's here that they will guarantee their expectations. Ask them to thoughtfully answer this question:

What is it that I must do each week in order to achieve my goals for this year?

They have planned their work, now they must work their plan. When goals are met on a weekly basis, the year becomes successful. It's here, with each week's activity and results, that the victory is clinched.

Therefore, a weekly plan of action must be built that will ensure success. A Weekly Effort Formula becomes indispensable. Obviously, no pat formula can be developed that will be adaptable to every producer who comes into the business. The activity requirements necessary for success varies according to producers' previous experience, background, and market. Then, too, that requirement changes as the producers gain experience, knowledge, skills and confidence.

However, it does serve producers' best interest if their activity can be measured weekly against a clearly defined standard. A Weekly Effort Formula, when calculated, can be an enormously helpful self-management tool. In the Weekly Effort Formula charted in Exhibit 1.6, you'll see a Guideline on the left-hand side. A personalized Standard can then be developed on the right side. Building the Weekly Effort Formula and adhering to it religiously is the equivalent of having goal attainment insurance.

WHEN THE FORWARD MARCH BEGINS, IT'S THE INDIVIDUAL WITH THE PLAN WHO LEADS THE WAY.

The Kinders

Exhibit 1.6 / *WEEKLY EFFORT FORMULA*

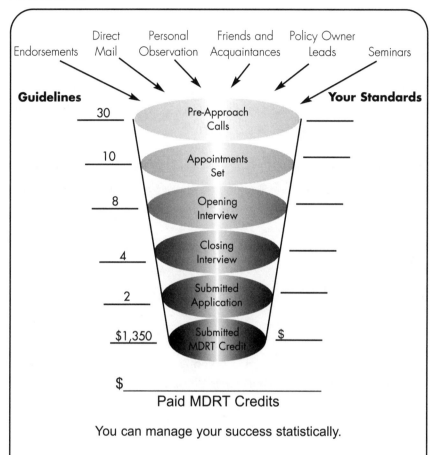

Endorsements   Direct Mail   Personal Observation   Friends and Acquaintances   Policy Owner Leads   Seminars

Guidelines   **Your Standards**

Guidelines	Stage	Your Standards
30	Pre-Approach Calls	___
10	Appointments Set	___
8	Opening Interview	___
4	Closing Interview	___
2	Submitted Application	___
$1,350	Submitted MDRT Credit	$ ___

$_____
Paid MDRT Credits

You can manage your success statistically.

DEFINITIONS

PRE-APPROACH CALLS - Contact call to arrange an appointment under favorable conditions.

APPOINTMENTS SET - Appointment has been agreed upon.

OPENING INTERVIEW - Probing, fact-finding interview to determine whether or not you have a prospect. A prospect is an individual who recognizes a need(s), reveals a "hot button," will make a money commitment, is insurable and will buy from you.

CLOSING INTERVIEW - Presentation of the recommendation where you ask the prospect to buy.

SUBMITTED APPLICATION - Application sent to the home office.

SUBMITTED MDRT CREDIT - Business submitted.

ENDORSEMENT - The name of a person who can be contacted on a favorable basis, using the influence of a third party.

MANAGEMENT'S MANY RESPONSIBILITIES

Let's look at the several responsibilities you, as the leader, must understand and fulfill.

√ **KNOW THE JOB.** Your job description is quite simple: *It's to make good.* That means to achieve production growth through producer development with profitable operations.

√ **DEVELOP A SUCCESS MODEL.** This identifies the key elements present in high performance organizations (Exhibit 1.7). *These are the issues you must think about, develop and implement.*

√ **MAKE GOOD ON ALL COMMITMENTS.** This one is so obvious it might seem unnecessary to include. Yet, if you need evidence to support its inclusion, listen closely to the comments of others you respect.

We like what Dr. Derek Bok, the president of Harvard, had to say: "Be very careful about what you promise—and break your back to fulfill all commitments you make. In that way, you build trust." We've always believed, "A commitment made is a debt unpaid."

√ **BE PERCEIVED AS BEING EXCITED ABOUT WHAT YOU ARE DOING.** Your associates will feed off of your enthusiasm. No trait is more noticeable in leaders than the excitement they demonstrate for their colleagues and the organization's future.

"Having a passion for what you do, a sense of mission that comes from the heart, gives you the energy, drive and enthusiasm that's contagious and essential for leading an organization," says Elizabeth Dole. Yes, enthusiasm is contagious. Why not have an epidemic?

Exhibit 1.7 /*SUCCESS MODEL*

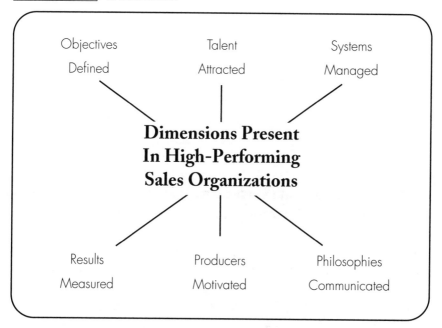

We are all blind until we see that in the human plan nothing is worth the making if it does not make the individual. In vain we build the organization, unless its builder also grows.

Edwin Markham

√ **Be an encourager.** Encouragement has been called the oxygen of the soul. Everyone has the need for an occasional booster shot. Those leaders who provide encouragement on a regular basis are admired and followed.

√ **Do the right things right.** Leaders in our business, who are enduringly successful, achieve superior results by focusing on the right things day in and day out.

"Leaders, to be effective, must have the personality type that allows them to be magnificently boring on a consistent basis." So says Stan Benfell, the talented insurance executive.

√ **DEVELOP COMMUNICATION SKILLS.** Nowhere is it more critical to be an effective communicator than in leading people or sales organizations. High on your self-development list should be the sharpening of your communication skills. This will pay you good dividends.

√ **MAINTAIN A HIGH ENERGY LEVEL.** Dr. Kenneth Cooper, the aerobic guru, says you can't store physical fitness. Being the leader at the top is demanding.

We suggest Vince Lombardi was right when he said, "Fatigue makes cowards of us all."

√ **ACT MORE LIKE A COACH THAN A BOSS.** The coach works at bringing out the best in others. As a coach, you're accessible. You cause associates to stretch for performance goals.

Most of all, recognize that feelings always precede facts. Why was Toscanini "the greatest coach" in his field? One New York Philharmonic Orchestra member said it was because Toscanini could feel a mistake before it happened. That's what makes a good coach—and leader.

EVERY MORNING IN AFRICA, A GAZELLE WAKES UP. IT KNOWS IT MUST RUN FASTER THAN THE FASTEST LION OR IT WILL BE KILLED. EVERY MORNING A LION WAKES UP. IT KNOWS IT MUST OUTRUN THE SLOWEST GAZELLE OR IT WILL STARVE TO DEATH. IT DOESN'T MATTER WHETHER YOU ARE A LION OR A GAZELLE; WHEN THE SUN COMES UP, YOU'D BETTER BE RUNNING.

√ **MAKE EVERY OCCASION A GREAT OCCASION.** Strive for excellence in everything you do. *Remember, there are two ways to do the right thing.* One way simply tackles the task with "main strength

and awkwardness." The other way does it with preparation and finesse, thereby compounding the dividends.

Associates quickly recognize a leader committed to excellence. That is the individual who sees it big—does it right—and gives it class!

THE IMPORTANT THING

"I find the important thing in this world is not where you stand," said Oliver Wendell Holmes, "but rather the direction in which you are headed. To reach a port you must sail, sometimes with the wind, sometimes against the wind . . . but always you must sail and not drift, nor lie at anchor."

Leading your organization in the right direction requires you to fix your eye upon your goals—visualize them with every ounce of your being—and set out toward their achievement.

> *EXPERIENCE IS WHAT YOU GET WHEN YOU DON'T*
> *GET WHAT YOU WANT.*
>
> *Dennis Clark*

Become a sponge for information and ideas that will help you plan better. You don't have to waste years making mistakes that others have made before you. You'll be surprised how quickly you and your associates will reach and surpass your goals. But don't be impatient. Know and have faith that what should happen will happen in time. As Emerson wrote: "Let each learn a prudence of high strain. Let each learn that everything in nature, even dust and feathers, goes by law and never by luck—and that what each sows, each reaps!"

That's it; that's all there is to it. Take stock of your present situation for it is nothing more or less than the result of the sowing. Then decide what must be sown—today and tomorrow and the next day. And in the sowing, realize with certainty, that having sown, the abundant harvest must come.

In this chapter you were assisted in completing a simple process for setting goals and fixing plans of action. We believe you will find this to be a practical approach for making you the consistent, effective planner your associates need for you to be.

VAL'S VIEWS ON PLANNING

Early in my business career, I discovered planning was the process of deciding desired results. Planning defines the time periods for making dreams become realities.

Someone gave me the book, *Think and Grow Rich*, by Napoleon Hill. This literary masterpiece literally changed my life. I learned the importance of planning a definite chief aim—a dream.

One of the many Napoleon Hill disciples was Earl Nightingale. Nightingale developed this philosophy that we sell to our associates.

DREAM NO LITTLE DREAMS, THEY PRODUCE LITTLE,
IF ANY PASSION OR ENERGY. DREAM THE BIG DREAM.
WHEN A BIG DREAM IS RECORDED IT WILL NEVER DIE —
UNTIL YOU CAN TOUCH IT WITH YOUR HAND,
AND SEE IT WITH YOUR EYE!

Make your agency building dream a big one and keep that dream alive until it becomes reality!

Chapter Thoughts and Ideas
I'm Using or Planning to implement

√   Results require planning.

√   Planning forces creative thinking.

√   Planning gains responsible commitments.

√   The Operational Plan must be emotionalized.

√   Planning comes before doing.

√   Planning brings about standards.

√   Planning communicates expectations.

√   Key Result Areas bring about focus.

Chapter 2 / COMMUNICATING

EFFECTIVE LEADERS STAY SOLD ON THEIR BELIEFS. THEY ARE UNSWERV-ING, UNCOMPROMISING, AND EVEN RELENTLESS IN COMMUNICATING THEIR BELIEFS. THEY KNOW STRONGLY HELD BELIEFS INTENSIFY THE DRIVE FOR ACHIEVEMENT.

Peter Drucker

Some years back we were engaged to speak to the Baltimore Orioles baseball team. "Mr. October," Reggie Jackson, was in his heyday. The colorful Earl Weaver was the manager of the Orioles. Weaver had a rule that no one could attempt to steal a base unless he gave the steal sign. That rule was upsetting to Jackson because he felt he knew the pitchers and catchers well enough to judge on his own when he could steal.

Broadcast Good News

In an early inning of a game one day, Reggie decided to steal, without the sign from Weaver. Jackson got a good jump off the pitcher and easily beat the throw to second base. As he shook the dirt from his uniform, he smiled with delight, feeling he had validated his judgment. Weaver later took Jackson aside. He passed along his plan and philosophy and explained why he hadn't given Reggie the steal sign.

The next batter was Lee May, an effective power hitter. Since first base was open, the Texas Rangers intentionally walked May. The batter in the lineup after May hadn't been strong against the Ranger pitcher, so Weaver had to send up a pinch-hitter for him. That left the Orioles without the bench strength they needed later to win the game.

Jackson saw the stolen base as involving only the relationship between pitcher and catcher. Weaver was calling signals with the entire game plan in mind. The leader makes moves based on the *big picture*—based upon the organization's philosophies and plans.

COLOR CODE

You communicate to an audience of associates, staff members, clients and friends of the organization. The aim of all communication is to inform, instruct or inspire. We recommend color coding all communication. Information can be put on yellow stock, instruction on green and inspiration on blue. If you three-hole punch each release it suggests to the readers that they may wish to file each sheet for future reference.

PERSONAL LETTERS AND NOTES

No investment in recognition yields better results than timely e-mails, faxes, or personal notes. Somewhere along the way, managers have forgotten the recognition power of the written word. If you err, do so on the side of sending too many recognition notes, rather than too few.

Jack Welch, the highly respected former CEO at General Electric, formed the habit of writing 25 congratulatory or thank you notes each morning before turning to his busy schedule. Something to think about.

Our longtime friend and client, Nick Horn, in San Ramon, California, has this to say about effective communication: "Write personal notes to everyone . . . from your top planner to your receptionist and mail room administrator. Catch them 'doing something right' and let them know you know what they did and appreciate it. If you can involve someone else—'Mary told me what you did, John'—it's even better." Nick strives to personally handwrite 100 or more notes each month.

Also, develop with each individual a list of the "balcony people" in their lives. Those are the people who will be interested in their progress. They are the few, but important, encouragers each one has. Selective information can be shared with this group—and it's effective.

Also, remember the additional impact that comes by using a P.S. or by adding a short, handwritten note.

IMPACT WORDS

We read once where Mark McCormack advanced a theory that an individual's written communications are probably more revealing than any other single item in the workplace.

We were so intrigued by his observation and conclusion that we decided to test it out on ourselves. We reviewed several years' worth of memos, letters, faxes, and e-mails and found the exercise revealing. Here are the words that regularly popped up:

Exhibit 2.1 / *IMPACT WORDS*

❑	Commitment	❑	Opportunity
❑	Excellence	❑	Professionalism
❑	Formality	❑	Timely
❑	Focus	❑	Monitoring
❑	Extraordinary	❑	Follow-up
❑	Proactive	❑	Networking
❑	Responsive	❑	Balance
	❑ Leader		

All of us can learn something by studying our writing habits. Words don't lie; they are revealing. If you haven't stepped back to examine the words you use day in and day out, it will be rewarding and revealing for you to do so.

Here's a thought for your mental chewing and digestion: "Seventy-five percent of our income depends upon our communication skills—talking and listening." That's worth thinking about.

> *THE BEST ADVICE I EVER CAME ACROSS ON THE SUBJECT OF CONCENTRATION IS: WHEREVER YOU ARE—BE THERE!*
>
> *Jim Rohn*

FLASH BULLETINS

Good news is going to surface and when it does, give it immediate visibility. The news might be a large sale, an award, a qualification for the Million Dollar Round Table (MDRT), an exam passed, or even a Little League home run.

Make it standard operating procedure to acknowledge all significant achievements—and do so quickly. It's a simple equation: The impact of any recognition is in inverse proportion to how long you delay releasing it.

"Bragging Board"

When you congratulate or thank an associate, make it a "poorly kept" secret. Place a copy of the note on the organization's information board.

This "Bragging Board" idea helps create a sense of pride in the outfit. It turns individual recognition into a team affair.

The Monday Morning Memo

This is a single page bulletin that reaches all associates early Monday morning. It highlights the good things that happened the previous week; the news may be business or non-business related.

A recent study found that what distinguished high-performing sales groups from those groups performing below their potential was the wide variety and frequency of celebratory events. Solicit the assistance of your staff in helping to maintain a culture of celebration.

WEEKLY MEETINGS ARE BECOMING INCREASINGLY MORE DIFFICULT TO PULL OFF WITH THE "MILLENNIUM AGENT." USE TECHNOLOGY TO YOUR ADVANTAGE, MAKING CERTAIN YOU KEEP THE PERSONAL TOUCH.

Brian B. Heapps, CLU
General Agent
Signator Financial Network

Exhibit 2.2 / *INSPIRING BULLETINS*

MAKE BULLETINS SPARKLE

Here are a few items that will make your bulletins more inspiring.

⇒ Sales figures (See Exhibit 2.3)

⇒ News of advertising releases

⇒ New sales ideas (See Exhibit 2.4)

⇒ Competitive information

⇒ Reprints of testimonials or case histories

⇒ Hints on sales techniques

⇒ Facts about the industry

⇒ New publications, audio tapes, video tapes, software, etc.

⇒ Company news, information, and product announcements

⇒ Publicity releases

⇒ Items about associates and their families

⇒ Changes in personnel

FIRST DAY PCA MONTHLY REPORT

PCA stands for Percentage Commitment Achieved. This type of report reinforces the annual commitment developed with the producers. Also, it can provide the platform for meaningful recognition.

Make the masthead of the report attractive. You may want to "burn in" a philosophy or two, i.e., "A Commitment Made is a Debt Unpaid."

Recognize your year-to-date leaders at the top of the report then follow with your top ten producers on the front page. Use the suggested format as shown on Exhibit 2.3. This "Honor Roll" lists from best to poorest on the PCA Score in the last column. All other producers are shown, with their numbers, on the back page or subsequent pages.

The important strategic move here is to produce and release the PCA Report on the first working day of each month.

Remember, this Monthly PCA Report will necessarily be "quick-and-dirty." It represents your administrative assistant's best, studied picture of the results for the month. The precise numbers will show up during the middle of the month in the monthly bulletin.

A GOOD BOSS LETS IT BE KNOWN TO EMPLOYEES THAT HE'S SAYING THE SAME NICE THINGS ABOUT THEM TO OTHERS IN PUBLIC AS HE'S TELLING THEM IN PRIVATE.

Mark McCormack

Exhibit 2.3 / *HONOR ROLL*

MONTHLY PCA REPORT

Month ending _____

Congratulations to our leader _____

_____

_____

We salute _____ on his/her impressive move
into _____ place.

Producer's Name	Month's MDRT Credits	Year-To-Date MDRT Credits	Responsible Commitment	PCA Score
1.				
2.				
3.				
4.				
5.				
6.				
7.				
8.				
9.				
10.				

"A Commitment Made Is a Debt Unpaid."

YOUR MONTHLY PUBLICATION

The second form of reporting takes place in your monthly publication, which should be sent out about the 10th of each month. This publication should include reports on paid cases and MDRT credits, special recognition for company honor clubs and, if appropriate, special pages devoted to your organization's standings for the year in production growth and manpower development. Also included should be a page devoted to the organization's progress regarding the major objectives for the year.

In addition, this monthly publication should include bits of information about your associates and their families. We feel that a wider range of recognition can and should be given here rather than in the PCA Report which comes out the first working day of each month.

SUCCESSFUL TEAMWORK REQUIRES DOING LOTS OF UNSPECTACULAR LITTLE THINGS, CONSTANT ATTENTION TO THE DETAILS, BUILDING ONE-ON-ONE RELATIONSHIPS, FOLLOWING UP ON COMMITMENTS AND AN OBSESSIVE CONCERN FOR COMMUNICATING INFORMATION.

Glenn Parker

NEW SALES IDEAS

A new sales idea, similar to Exhibit 2.4, is the centerfold of each bimonthly issue of *Round the Table* magazine published by the Million Dollar Round Table.

Exhibit 2.4 / *SAMPLE SALES IDEA*

POWER —
COMPOUND INTEREST AND TAX
DEFERRAL

If a dollar doubled every year,
what would the value be in 20 years,
if taxes were deferred until after the 20th year?

$754,974.72

Now take the same dollar doubled,
but which was subject to a 28% tax each year.
What would that dollar be worth in 20 years?

$51,353.37

*Talk to us today and discover how you can
fully utilize tax-deferral investments.*

MEETINGS

"Make every occasion a great occasion" is a favorite philosophy of ours. Sales meetings afford you that opportunity.

An agenda is always appropriate as a starting point. It sends a message to the audience: This meeting was important enough to justify advanced planning on my part.

Again, apply the test. Does the planned agenda assure us of informing, instructing and inspiring?

Set the stage for a successful experience. Use a square room, not a rectangular one. Make the room a bit crowded rather than too large. Have a prepared strategy for opening and closing. Do your homework. What and who can you recognize?

We're not much on refreshments. Snacks contain too many calories and can distract from the purpose of the meeting. The budget impact can be better invested in books, cassette tapes or discs that allow you to recognize high achievements.

- **ONE-ON-ONE BREAKFASTS OR LUNCHES.** This keeps personal communication lines open by facilitating listening and learning. It can be used to express appreciation for contributions being made.

- **AGENCY OPEN HOUSE OR AWARDS BANQUET.** Whatever the format, the purpose is the same—to bring the team together for a celebration of what was achieved throughout the year, and to recognize those who excelled. This is a time to share successes with family and associates.

- **SPONTANEOUS MEETINGS.** "Managing by walking around" is an effective way of communicating your interest in what is happening. It's a reminder to others that you are available and care about what's going on in your organization, and how you can be helpful.

YOU CAN LEARN AN AMAZING AMOUNT BY JUST WANDERING AROUND WITH YOUR "RECEIVER" ON AND YOUR CELL PHONE OFF. LOOK FOR THE ENERGY AND EXCITEMENT LEVELS. ONCE YOU FIND THAT ENERGY, ENTHUSIASM AND CREATIVITY ARE AT A HIGH LEVEL, YOU DON'T HAVE TO WORRY.

Robert Townsend

THE TELEPHONE

As technology continues to change, so does the value of the telephone. Using voice mail you are able to stay in touch with instant communication whether you are in the office or on the road.

Today's hectic and competitive business schedules leave little time to detail or document your daily activities, except at night or on the weekends. Imagine how easy and productive it would be if, after a business meeting, you could make a call from your cell phone. You then detail the discussions from your meeting while the information is fresh in your mind as well as in the other person's. Imagine having a letter, proposal or offer on your letterhead with your signature delivered to the receiving party before you arrive at your next appointment. Consider how impressed your associates, prospects and clients will be that you were able to immediately respond in writing.

We recommend you investigate the new telephonic "document-on-demand" resource, designed for the mobile business executive. The timesavings alone can be invaluable in using voice-to-text services.

A Word of Caution

The proliferation of voice mail and e-mail has made it easy to become trapped in business and to forego the human touch. Seldom a day goes by without our hearing someone complain about how they couldn't talk to a human being at such and such company. Here's a habit that creeps in on an office and consistently devalues the basic requirement for human interaction in business.

Anyone who has experienced the aggravation of automated telephone responses knows to avoid them like a plague. Resist the tendency to move to a "humanless office." It invites customers to take their business elsewhere.

THE DIFFERENCE MAKER

Early in our management careers, our mentor, Fred Holderman, told us that the key to success is not necessarily doing something spectacular or eye-catching, but doing the little things exceptionally well.

When we think of Olympic gold medal winners, it's tempting to pretend they are somehow "extra different." We tell ourselves they were born with incredible strength or unusual talent, or had coaching we could never get for ourselves. We look at Michael Jordan or Tiger Woods, or we compare ourselves to a Barbra Streisand or a Johnny Mathis as entertainers and say, "I could never do that."

While there is truth in acknowledging their incredible talent, there is also a lie in pretending that because we don't have their genetic gifts, we are somehow excused from the necessity of giving it our best. That is simply not true!

The great majority of highly successful leaders, in any area of life, including athletics or entertainers, are those who worked a bit harder, stayed a little longer, and did a fraction more.

The highest paid managers in our business earn many times more than the average income. Is that because they are 100 times smarter? Are they 50 times more ambitious? Do they work 20 times harder or do they have more hours in a day? Of course not!

The highest paid, most successful managers do the little things extremely well. They remember the details, acknowledge associates' achievements, keep promises, return phone calls, remember to say "Please," "Thank You" and "Congratulations!"

They go the extra mile in communicating good news. They catch their associates doing something exceptionally well. They recognize it, and it makes a difference.

Take care of the "little things" in communicating and the difference will be reflected on your production board.

WATCH WHAT DIRECTION THE FEET POINT WHEN THE MOUTH STOPS MOVING. YOU WANT A CONSISTENCY BETWEEN MOUTH AND MOVEMENT.

James Dignam

Exhibit 2.5 / *LITTLE THINGS*

THE MIGHT OF LITTLE THINGS

Substantial improvement in production results can be greatly influenced by taking care of the "little things." Many times you can improve your score immediately and dramatically if you think more about handling these important little things. They include:

- Pay attention to detail.
- Communicate your expectations.
- Make good on every commitment.
- Build relationships; be available, be consistent, respect confidentiality.
- Know the score, report the score and watch the score improve.
- Develop a "Bragging Board."
- Be an idea person.
- Instill "advisor" mentality.
- Develop a Key Office Person (KOP).
- Be systems-oriented; stay personally organized.
- Maintain a flow of quality prospective producers.
- Make production jump; help new producers get off to a fast start.
- Conduct weekly PEP Sessions (Performance, Evaluation and Planning); utilize a Weekly Progress Guide.
- Involve experienced producers.
- Make meetings mean money—inform, instruct and inspire.
- Expect associates to believe in self-development and personal growth.
- Encourage appropriate family involvement.
- Help producers become better known.
- Maintain physical fitness.
- Develop a mentor; achieve "mentor status."

Foster feelings of respect, confidence, and enthusiasm by the example you set in your personal and business life. Lead by example. Taking care of the "little things" paves the way for taking care of the monumental; it's the difference maker.

VAL'S VIEWS ON COMMUNICATING

A great deal of "static" occurs in management communication. This results in pointless statements and inconclusive remarks. Much of it is unnecessary and can be eliminated. It requires us to think through carefully what we want to say and how it's going to be received. This cannot be overemphasized.

It's important for us to gain understanding. We must spell out, in clear-cut language, our expectations.

Every communication, verbal or non-verbal, should be put to the test—How will this affect team morale?

We feel you excel in agency building when you have the right people properly coached and motivated. That requires effective communication.

CHAPTER THOUGHTS AND IDEAS
I'M USING OR PLANNING TO IMPLEMENT

√   Communicate plans and philosophies.

√   The written word has recognition power.

√   Send First Day PCA Monthly Report.

√   Make the monthly publication sparkle.

√   Produce sales ideas.

√   Publish flash bulletins.

√   Send Good News Bulletin.

√   Inform, instruct, and inspire.

Chapter 3/*RECURITING*

For years, Bud Wilkinson, the legendary Oklahoma football coach, and Duffy Daugherty, from Michigan State, conducted the popular Kodak Coaching Clinic. Coach Daugherty always opened the clinic with an intriguing question:

"In your leadership position, do you under-stand the significance of the number 10?"

> **Be a connoisseur of talent. You win with talent.**

He would go on to say that ten percent of the players who show up will perform in a superior way without any coaching. They don't need it—or want it. "Be smart enough to stay out of their way," he would add, "and let them perform!"

Next, he would sketch a big number 20 on an easel and ask another question:

"Do you know the importance of this number?

Duffy would then explain that twenty percent of those who show up can't or won't ever perform at an acceptable level. "Identify and cut loose this group quickly," Daugherty would add. As we've always said, fail your failures fast! They waste your time and become a negative influence on the program you are building.

Finally, colorful Coach Daugherty would print the number 70. "These are the players who have the right stuff. They can and will become winners, providing they get lots of hands-on coaching and motivation from you and your staff."

Coach Daugherty always concluded with this thought: "Never get the idea you can build championship teams consistently by recruiting only the 'ten percenters.' The success of your program hinges on your ability to attract the seventy percent crowd and bring them through as winners."

Many times the "seventy percent crowd" is not effectively developed. That happens because of our tendency to choose our managers from the ten percent group. Those "ten percenters" seldom make good developers of people. They do not understand the need for simplicity. Their sales strategies are not transferable. Moreover, they do not understand the need and the power of repetition in the training process.

THE MOMENTUM BUILDER

Remember, recruiting is the momentum builder in our business. You were positioned in a leadership role with the expectation that every year you would successfully complete the recruiting assignment. Many agency builders continue to look for the panacea. They hope to find a breakthrough strategy that will pave the way for them to consistently recruit the top "ten percenters."

The unfortunate mathematical truth is that only ten percent of the prospective producer population is going to be in the top ten percent.

Where does the discovery of this mathematical fact take you? We believe it moves you to the key thought—the secret of every effective recruiter we've ever known. We suggest you write it on the mirror, paste it on the wall, print it in your planner, record it front and center in your mind. Here it is:

Recruiting successfully requires the building of an environment that makes it possible for ordinary recruits to be attracted and then perform as if they were extraordinary "ten percenters."

THE FACT IS THE HIRING PROCESS ISN'T VERY CONDUCIVE TO COMPLETE CANDOR. PEOPLE WANT TO PUT THEIR BEST SELVES FORWARD.

Harvard Business Review

Let's burn in this key philosophy right at the start. Master agency builders disagree on many things. Yet, they are in complete agreement on one point: *Successful recruiting takes place where expectations are high and the environment is conducive to success.*

This is a simple fact, but one generally missed. Charles O'Reilly, III, develops that theory quite effectively in his fine piece of writing, *Hidden Value.*

LEARN ABOUT "THE KEEPERS"

One visit to a Million Dollar Round Table meeting will convince you that successful producers come in all shapes and sizes. They vary widely in backgrounds, education, age, marital status, and experience. But the "keepers," those who persevered and stayed, had these things going for them:

- **COMMITTED MANAGEMENT.**

  These people had a manager who was 100% responsible for their early sales results.

- **OPTIMISTIC ATTITUDE RELATIVE TO THE SUCCESS POTENTIAL.**

  They had the opportunity to witness daily evidence of the kind of success they wanted to achieve.

- **MARKETING STRENGTHS.**

  These producers brought with them contacts and social mobility skills.

- **CLEAR-CUT METHODOLOGY FOR SELLING AND MARKETING.**

  They learned quickly how to put in a good day's work, and make sales in sufficient numbers.

- **STAYING POWER.**

  Their previous history revealed a "take charge pattern" for responding to situations and making things work out favorably.

Relative Development Potential Grid

Let's ask you to move away from the text just long enough to complete an interesting exercise. Take some time to identify those producers who have completed five years in the business. You judge them to be winners. They have completed the so-called "apprenticeship years" and are producing successfully.

Now, analyze how they grade on the grid shown in Exhibit 3.1. Have they been optimistic about the possibilities in this business? Do they have marketing strengths? Did they adopt early on a strategy for selling? Did they have a manager or mentor who was committed to registering them as an early success? How about staying power? Was that apparent as you studied their history? This grid might also prove valuable as a selection tool.

Studies reveal this interesting fact. Producers who succeed in our kind of business come predominantly from two sources:

1. Managers' contacts; and

2. Successful producers' introductions.

Dr. Jim Goodnight, SAS Institute's Chairman and CEO, believes in "hiring adults, treating them as adults and then applauding them when they perform like adults." We believe the *right culture*, even more than the *right people*, makes this possible.

As a leader you have the opportunity to provide a creative, resource-rich environment for your organization.

Michael Vance

Exhibit 3.1 / *POTENTIAL GRID*

RELATIVE DEVELOPMENT POTENTIAL GRID

(Assess a Candidate on a Point Schedule of 1=low, 5=high)

Career Professional	Committed Management	Optimistic Attitude	Selling Methodology	Marketing Strength	Staying Power

THREE CONSTANTS

We assume you are fully committed to the development of a high-quality sales force—a Master Agency. This being true, it becomes clear that three concerns must be constant in your recruiting plan:

1. Attraction of producers;

2. Retention of producers; and

3. Productivity of producers.

Any agency builder who attains satisfactory results in those three key areas will enjoy:

• Consistent production gains in satisfying amounts.

• Superior client service capabilities.

• Pride in performance.

• An enviable reputation in the marketplace.

The first of the three concerns, attraction of producers, obviously is vital, and we'll talk considerably more about that throughout the remainder of the chapter.

The next two concerns, retention and productivity of producers, must be considered together. To attain success in one or the other is not sufficient. "Contrived success" could be achieved in either area without total or real benefits to the producer, your organization, your company, or the buying public. There is nothing short-term or temporary about the challenge connected with those two concerns. They are constant, and they will be eternal. Both should cause you to be more concerned with how you are doing as compared to how you are looking.

STRESS QUALITY RECRUITING

Inflation and budget requirements are now reaching the levels where "necessity" is replacing "desirability" as your motivation to achieve sound growth. The means of achieving such growth is the organization's capacity to give clients good financial counsel, prompt, courteous service, and value for dollars invested. The best guarantee of that capacity is the organization's retention of large numbers of productive producers.

The developmental needs of your organization call for a quality recruiting process to be implemented; it's a necessity.

SET HIGH STANDARDS

Recruiting quality producers, as we have seen, is a prime essential in building a successful team. Your company looks to you to attract producers who can sell effectively in high income markets. Induction of a sufficient quantity of high potential producers inevitably results in substantial and steady growth in premium production.

To be a successful recruiter, you must adopt a philosophy of high standards. If you set your standards high enough and early enough, your recruiting activity will grow progressively easier—and your results will become progressively better.

A "success syndrome" is the central point of a philosophy of high standards. The presence of successful, high quality associates in your organization attracts more of the same. Ideally, as prospective associates enter your offices, they should find themselves surrounded by an atmosphere of success. They should see evidence of positive qualities and dynamics.

Prospective associates should become aware of high quality men and women, high standards of production, high standards of office neatness and arrangement, high standards of income, and high standards of business management. They should be made to feel it, taste it and sense it. As a result, they will have a natural inclination to become an integral part of the *quality* organization you are building.

There is no question about it; it's always easier to accomplish the recruiting job successfully in an organization on the move, in an operation where things obviously are happening, and in one that has an atmosphere of success.

PROJECT PROFESSIONAL PRESENCE

Important as appearance is, we are talking about far more than that. We're talking about becoming a person who has "attraction power." The ability to attract comes to those recruiters who have these five qualities:

1. Communication skills;

2. Charisma;

3. Self-confidence;

4. Optimism; and

5. Good manners.

Presence is the total picture of you, which is painted on the minds and emotions of others by everything you say, do, and appear to be. Strive to be the kind of person you want others to be, and that others want to emulate. If you do, you'll have taken a giant step toward being the effective recruiter you want to be.

TO ATTRACT ATTRACTIVE PEOPLE, YOU MUST BE ATTRACTIVE. TO ATTRACT POWERFUL PEOPLE, YOU MUST BE POWERFUL. TO ATTRACT COMMITTED PEOPLE, YOU MUST BE COMMITTED. INSTEAD OF GOING TO WORK ON THEM, YOU GO TO WORK ON YOURSELF. IF YOU BECOME ATTRACTIVE, YOU CAN ATTRACT.

DECIDE ON A PROFILE

Knowing the kind of people you are looking for is as important in recruiting as it is in prospecting. You should decide upon the profile of the producer who will fit and grow best in your culture. Experience, age, markets, contacts, income requirements, background and a number of other factors should be considered. In other words, you should start your recruiting activities by building the profile of the producer you want to attract; the description of the person best suited to your situation.

Rarely will you find someone who fits your description precisely. We have discovered there is no prototype for the perfect producer. Successful individuals come in all shapes and sizes, from all kinds of backgrounds with varying degrees of education, and with assorted business experiences. Still, we know successful producers generally have certain traits and abilities in common. You want to remind yourself of those qualities so you can continually recruit and attract the person with the greatest chance for success.

Keep repeating your response to this question: *Who succeeds around here?* Make sure the "culture fit" is a good one.

KEY CONCEPTS

Consistently inducting and developing quality individuals is vital to the successful building of a sales force. Prospecting for the right kind of candidates is one of your continuous and most essential functions. Developing sound concepts can be most helpful to you in performing that function.

Here are three concepts for starters, including what to do about them.

1. The need for quality producers never diminishes.

Build a reservoir of high-potential candidates from which you can draw when you are ready to bring new people into your organization.

2. There is a limited supply of high-potential candidates who are currently highly disturbed with their present jobs.

   Keep in touch with those you'd like to have in your organization. Things often happen in people's jobs, their lives, or their family situations that can cause them to become "live prospects" for you, sometimes almost overnight.

3. Most successful producers are highly competitive people and frequently come into our business from "contest-living" jobs.

   Look for candidates among commissioned salespeople, coaches, small business owners, etc.

UNDERSTAND THE SALES FORCE MODEL

Again, we remind you that the only means of achieving consistent, profitable production gains is through the development of producers. Your agency building program will succeed to the extent you increase the numbers of producers who have the contacts, selling skills and self-discipline necessary to sell substantial amounts of insurance on a consistent basis.

Extensive industry studies of past results show considerable turnover during the first year or so that producers are in the business, but substantial improvement and leveling of retention after three full calendar years as they become more experienced. Obviously, the greater the number of "experienced producers" you have, those in the business three or more full calendar years, the greater and more consistent will be your production. (In a later section, we will address adding to the Experienced Sales Force through the acquisition of experienced producers from another company. Here, we are talking about developing our own, and that requires three years plus the appointment year.)

With this in mind, let's examine and discuss the Sales Force Model and its various components. (This concept was first introduced by Coy Eklund, the then Equitable CEO, in a fine piece of writing entitled *Agency Organizing: A Case Example*, and published by The American College.)

THE FOUR DEVELOPMENT CLASSES

In this model, new developing producers are grouped into separate calendar year categories that we call the Four Developmental Classes.

Class A is made up of producers who are in their *Appointment Year* which is, by definition, always a fractional year. Class B producers are said to be in their *Base Year*, because it is their first full calendar year. Producers in Class C are in their *Commitment Year*, the year in which there is a considerable strengthening of the relationship between the producer and the company. Finally, Class D producers are in the *Delivery Year*. This is the graduating year, at the end of which producers are delivered to the *Experienced Sales Force*.

The Experienced Sales Force

For purposes of the Sales Force Model, all producers in the organization who have completed three or more full calendar years comprise the Experienced Sales Force. They are the prime movers of the sales force.

The Segmented Sales Force

Now, let's combine the sections so we can view a segmented version of the Sales Force Model. Exhibit 3.2 illustrates such a model that holds the significant segments of the Total Sales Force in fixed positions for an entire calendar year. In this way, desired measurements can be made annually, such as retention ratios for each of the four development classes, and the productivity of each of the six segments.

Exhibit 3.2 / *TOTAL SALES FORCE*

TOTAL SALES FORCE

PLAN RECRUITING ACTIVITY

Just as it takes so many calls and so many interviews, on the average, for a salesperson to obtain a sale, it likewise requires so much recruiting activity, on the average, for a manager to obtain one new quality appointment. Therefore, in planning your recruiting activity, it's important that you understand and build a recruiting activity success formula.

Our statistics show that in order to contract one person, most recruiters need at least 30 initial contacts. That number gives them five individuals who will pass the selection test which, in turn, gives them one producer they will appoint, based on the averages, of course. (See Exhibit 3.4.)

Exhibit 3.3 / *RECRUITING SUCCESS*

Understanding these ratios enables you to strategically plan and achieve the necessary activity to reach your recruiting goal each year.

Exhibit 3.4 / *THE STARTING POINT*

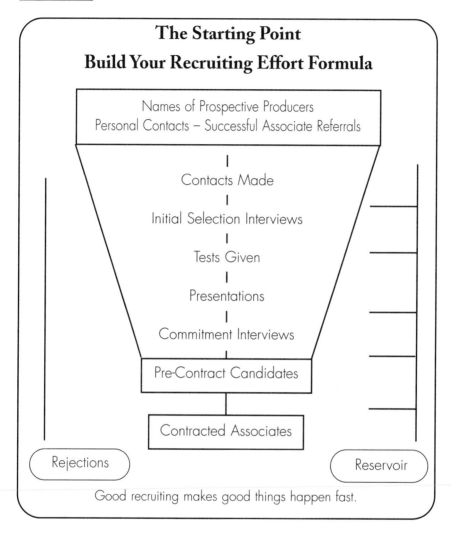

The Starting Point
Build Your Recruiting Effort Formula

Names of Prospective Producers
Personal Contacts – Successful Associate Referrals

Contacts Made

Initial Selection Interviews

Tests Given

Presentations

Commitment Interviews

Pre-Contract Candidates

Contracted Associates

Rejections

Reservoir

Good recruiting makes good things happen fast.

SEARCHING FOR TALENT

Certainly, any study of producer expansion would lead to the conclusion that finding the individual with the right qualifications is one of the most vital factors in favorable retention.

We strongly advise "pinpoint prospecting," that is, searching for individuals with the specific desired qualities, then hiring them "on purpose." We also advise avoiding those prospects who are always available to all recruiters. Experience teaches that hiring available "pop-ups" usually winds up being costly. They generally become "pop-outs" almost as quickly and easily as they popped up.

The search for high potential prospective producers must be continuous and systematic, just as the search for high potential prospective buyers in selling. Yes, successful recruiters seek quality candidates among several sources on a regular, continuous basis. Let's consider some of the more productive of those sources.

YOU WIN WITH TALENT!

Woody Hayes

Personal Observation

The most effective recruiters generally recruit through personal observation and selling activity. This method is uniquely personal because it permits recruiters to apply their own standards and to exercise their own judgment.

You should always be on the alert for prospective producers in your daily activities. Instinctively appraise, as prospective associates, those you see, meet, or sell. Stay in circulation. Determine what is happening in your area, where the "right kind" shows up.

The most important word in recruiting through personal observation is exposure. Make contacts with many different people day in and day out, and keep your eyes open for quality, prospective producers as you do.

Present Sales Force

No others know more about the kind of people you want and the kind of opportunity you have to offer than do the present members of your organization. Moreover, they have selfish interests in wanting their associates to be the kind of people who will reflect positively on their organization. Successful producers have an ability to pick promising candidates of the very kind you want to attract.

Think for a moment about your new people who are excited and favorably impressed with their new profession. When they are talking with friends, who generally are the kind of people you are trying to attract, their enthusiasm and excitement for the business can be contagious. Communicate to new associates your expectations that they introduce you to prospective producers. Never fail to demonstrate appropriate and sincere appreciation to associates who recommend prospective producers.

Policy Owners

Policy owners, especially those you classify as clients, generally are a readily accessible source of candidates and referrals to candidates. It's reasonable to assume that those who have relied upon you to handle their financial matters are happy with both you and your work. Since you have created a favorable impression as a successful advisor, they can picture themselves, or others they might recommend, as having the same success. It's mostly a matter of helping them help you by making inquiries and asking leading questions designed to determine their own interest, or to produce an introduction to others.

Seminars

Attracting enough of the right kind, as we've indicated, is a formidable assignment. There is no reason to believe it is likely to become easier. It takes resourcefulness and focus. Successful agency heads look upon recruiting as a continual, rather than a sporadic, process. They are constantly on the alert for high potential candidates and they use their imagination to uncover them.

Seminar recruiting, utilizing computer generated presentations, is a resourceful, imaginative strategy. It makes possible a prospective producer's obtaining, as part of a group, information about your opportunity. As part of a group, the individual feels comfortable and quickly develops an open-mindedness to investigating the possibility of a job change.

This method of recruiting can produce uncommon results for you. The procedure flows something like this.

First, select the seminar site. Your conference room is best, providing it meets the desired specifications for a session of this kind.

Next, try to attract at least 20 people. For the most part, the individuals you invite should come from two sources: personal observation and referrals. After making the initial contact and gaining acceptance of your invitation to "take a look," confirm each appointment with a follow-up letter.

Finally, prepare and follow a seminar agenda along the following lines:

- Why We Are Here

- Why People Change Careers

- Financial Services

- Industry Growth

- Company Leadership

- Organization Performance and Plans

- Products We Sell

- Markets We Penetrate

- Career Path Possibilities

- Rewards We Earn

- Individual Success Stories

- Education and Training

- Support and Recognition

- Professional Status (CLU, MDRT, NQA, ChFC, CFP)

- Organization Highlights

- Testing and Interviewing

- Questions from the Floor

- Action Steps (Have those attending complete a simple card or form, something to indicate their interest, as well as when and how you can get in touch with them.)

Make the seminar experience both informative and interesting. Stay sensitive to the kind of support items that are timely and relative. Current feature stories on the opportunities in selling, articles published by you and your producers, honor rolls showing achievements, timely commentaries, any industry reports on your company, and the company's annual report are examples of third-party information items which generally are convincing. Thoughts like those developed in Exhibits 3.6 and 3.7 also might prove helpful as handouts.

College Campuses

Many high potential, quality young people are being recruited directly from the college campus. A number of today's graduates seem to be interested in more meaningful careers than most other businesses offer.

The financial services industry has a strong appeal to the younger crowd. Obviously, some caution should be used when recruiting younger people. The individual you want directly from the college campus should have demonstrated definite leadership qualities and have a history of success. Coaches, professors and student leaders can be helpful in identifying the most promising candidates on campus.

A visit with a young person's parents generally is desirable. Sometimes they are called upon to assist their son or daughter in making the career decision. You can support the parents by helping them understand the opportunities in the financial services arena. Parents can also be valuable centers of influence and can, in various other ways, greatly aid your young associate in becoming established in the business.

Selling as a Searching Strategy

We feel that an exceptionally effective way for you, as an experienced salesperson, to look over prospects is by contacting them for the purpose of selling them financial products. In that way, you will find it fairly simple to uncover such important information regarding their:

- attitudes toward the products or services you recommend;

- relationships with their families;

- ability to manage money; and

- responsiveness to you.

By this method, developing the skill to evaluate selling potential accurately, and to measure compatibility, seems to come easier. Also, you tend to attract, rather than recruit, when you use this searching strategy.

As you attempt to sell prospective producers, you are reviewing them and screening them as a normal part of the selling job. In addition, however, you'll discover they will reveal helpful screening information in a selling interview that might never surface if you made the approach solely for the purpose of interesting them in a job opportunity.

Uncover the "Thread of Discontent"

During the searching process, as you consider talented individuals, it is imperative that you look for or develop a "thread of discontent" with their present situation. It's that thread of discontent that permits or motivates prospective producers to change careers. Your initial contacts must either reveal a thread of discontent that is readily apparent or develop one that lies more deeply hidden but one that is, nevertheless, there. If such a thread of discontent is not strong enough within candidates, your chances of recruiting them, at least for the moment, are not good.

Locating a thread of discontent will not always be easy with the kind of candidate you want. We've already stated, high potential prospective producers are often experiencing a relatively high degree of satisfaction and success in their present employment and ways of life. Therefore, if a candidate does not openly show signs of discontent, suggest possible concerns, probe areas of potential frustration, and ask about possible disappointments in a future job.

Remember: No discontent—no motivation to make a change!

IT'S THE THREAD OF DISCONTENT THAT MOTIVATES OR PERMITS PRODUCERS TO MAKE A CHANGE. YOUR KIND OF CANDIDATE MIGHT NOT BE CANDIDLY DISGRUNTLED SO PROBE FOR ANY FUTURE POTENTIAL DISSATISFACTION.

Maintain a Large Reservoir

Up front, we predict that the stars you bring into the business will have been nourished and developed in your reservoir. You'll find it a wise investment of your time to set up and maintain an active tickler file for prospective producers, much like the one you use to keep track of prospective clients.

Most of the high potential individuals you contact about a career opportunity will not be interested at the time of the initial contact. They simply will not currently have, or be motivated strongly enough by, the thread of discontent we discussed earlier. Over a period of time, circumstances do change and situations develop that arouse discontent and an interest in the prospective producer to consider a change of occupation. This is one of the principal reasons it's so important to keep good records of the high potential people with whom you talk.

We refer to this collection of high potential prospective producers as your "reservoir." You'll want to build your reservoir to 25 or more quality people as quickly as possible.

You will also need a system for following up and staying in touch with those individuals who are in your reservoir. They may not be interested now, but they may develop strong reasons to become interested at some time in the future. "Spoon feed" them on the advantages of the business; sell them the opportunity; sell them on you. Building a reservoir will be helpful to you in developing a quality organization. In our judgment, it separates the superior recruiters from those who are, at best, marginal.

Build a viable reservoir and enjoy the good recruiting luck and high quality people it helps attract to your organization over the years.

Exhibit 3.5 / *RESERVOIR CARD*

RESERVOIR CARD FOR_____ #

RECRUITER_____

PROSPECTIVE PRODUCER
RESERVOIR CARD

RECORD OF CONTACTS

Initial Contact Date_____No._____

Date	Purpose	Result

Name	Birth Date
Home Address	Telephone
Business Address	Telephone
Education	Marital Status	Spouse Name/Age
Children: Names/Ages		
Occupation		
Income	Home: Own, Rent	Health
Probable Thread of Discontent		
Debt Load; Mortgage	Other	
Family Background		
Sales Experience	Unique Talent	
Life Insurance Ownership		
Known Successes		
Other Observations		

References
_____
_____

Test Results   _____
KBA Selection Score (100 pt. guide) _____
Test Date   _____

Confidential

Copyright 1982 Kinder Bros. & Associates

Exhibit 3.5 cont'd / *RESERVOIR CARD*

THE KINDERS' PATTERNED SELECTION INTERVIEW

This battery of questions will assist you in the evaluation of prospective producers. These probing questions should be asked of the applicant and his or her responses recorded in the spaces provided. Each response should be carefully evaluated to determine whether or not this candidate should be retained in your reservoir. Review this information carefully before each monthly contact.

QUESTION 1. Are you getting along in your job as well as you would like to be? (Thread of Discontent)

_____

QUESTION 2. When, in your opinion, is a person successful? (Philosophy)

_____

QUESTION 3. What do you enjoy most about your present job? (Achievement, Drive)

_____

QUESTION 4. What type of hobbies do you enjoy the most? (Energy/Self-Improvement)_____

_____

QUESTION 5. What is the major strength you have that would help you to succeed in selling? (Self-Image)

_____

QUESTION 6. Based upon today's values, five years from now, how much money would you expect to be earning? (Ambition)_____

_____

QUESTION 7. What motivates you? (Motivation)_____

_____

QUESTION 8. What adjectives would your closest associates use to describe you? (Self-Image)_____

QUESTION 9. What is it about a sales position that might be attractive to you? (Sales Aptitude)

_____

QUESTION 10. What would you say is your major weakness? (Self-Analysis)

_____

QUESTION 11. What is the most important character trait you picked up from your parents? (Family Influence)

_____

QUESTION 12. How much difficulty would you experience learning to work alone? (Self-Discipline)

_____

OBSERVATIONS TO MAKE DURING THE INTERVIEW	
_____	Character
_____	Alertness
_____	Intelligence
_____	Energy
_____	Competitiveness
_____	Self-Confidence/Self-Image
_____	Appearance
_____	Stability
_____	Empathy
_____	Communication Skills
_____	Interpersonal Skills

Look for Key Producers

We have watched organization after organization climb the company honor roll because its agency head became sold on the impact of hiring a key producer, then attracted and recruited one. What a difference it makes in an organization!

A "key producer" has a definite following—attraction power and lots of it. This person is an individual who finds it easy to rally people to a cause. This is an individual who builds relationships and loyalties—and many of them.

Key producers generally are easy to spot, but often difficult to recruit in a hurry. However, when recruited, they immediately help attract other high potential people, those who will follow them.

The presence of a key producer will enhance the reputation of your operation and attract others to your organization. As a result, recruiting the key producer will help you shorten the time in building a strong, successful organization.

The results are almost always rewarding and lasting. Resolve to attract a key producer.

Exhibit 3.6 / *INTEREST-AROUSING STRATEGY*

AN INTEREST-AROUSING STRATEGY

"Chris, let me ask you a question. Based on your abilities, energy, and ambition, do you see yourself in a six-figure income in five years? In ten years?" (The desirable candidates you talk with will answer in the affirmative. Then you move forward.)

Question 1. "Think about this. What is the population of the United States?" (Here you will get into a discussion of the fact that it's somewhat in excess of 255 million.)

Question 2. "Chris, of this population, how many are actively employed in the work force?" (This discussion will lead you to the conclusion that there are probably 150 million people between the ages of 16 and 70 who are or would like to be actively employed.)

Question 3. "Of those people actively at work in the United States, how many of them are making $100,000 a year?" (Naturally, this will lead to a discussion that a very small percent, less than 2%, are in this category.)

Question 4. "Chris, would you like to be in that elite group?" (Most candidates you talk with will answer in the affirmative. Then, move forward as follows.)

"Chris, we know there are only five areas you can pursue that will bring you into this affluent earnings group.

"First, you could become a topflight athlete or entertainer. That is not a reasonable goal for most of us to pursue, wouldn't you agree?

"You could become a trained professional—doctor, lawyer, CPA, engineer, etc. Do you have this type of education, or are you in a position to return to school and get it?" (The answer is generally, "No.")

"You could become a sole proprietor; you could go into business for yourself. However, of all the businesses that start up every year in the United States, at the end of two full years a good percentage of them are no longer around. The reasons are lack of capital and lack of management experience! Chris, do you have the capital or the experience to set up a business for yourself to become a sole proprietor?" (Generally, the answer here is also, "No.")

"You could climb the business hierarchy. You could go to work for a major company and strive to get to the top. That requires patience, some geographical moves, a little luck, some politics, and loss of a certain amount of your independence. Would this path be of interest to you?" (Here again, the answer is generally, "No.")

"This moves us, then, to the final career area where you could earn a substantial income. It is in creative sales—stocks and bonds, real estate, computers or the financial services industry. It's this category that I'd like to explore with you over the next few weeks. When would be a convenient time for you?"

Fast Start Potential

Tough-minded managers believe there are only three reasons why individuals fail in today's marketplace. They were selected poorly, they were managed poorly or they did not bring "to the table" a fast start potential.

Once again, history shows us the importance of registering new producers as successes early in the game. A producer's production in the first ninety days is a strong indicator of career success. During your searching, be sensitive to your need for the fast start potential.

EVALUATING POTENTIAL

By way of review, keep in mind the very nature of this selling job; it has some unique characteristics. It is not an ordinary means of making a living; it's an entrepreneurial kind of employment. To be successful, producers must have integrity, initiative, and industry, coupled with an extreme degree of self-management ability. They need self-confidence, self-reliance, and self-discipline in abundance. Above all, they must have the self-generated brand of determination that will carry them through to career success even though they dwell in a negative atmosphere much of the time. You'll want these type qualities in individuals you ask to join your organization.

After analyzing the results and records of many, we are convinced the typical producer yields little in the way of encouraging results in five out of six working hours. In the beginning, four out of five prospects who are seen will tend to deflate egos. Courage and commitment certainly are two cardinal virtues you'll want to observe in anyone you contract.

Know What You Don't Want

Conversely, experience with individuals who didn't make the grade convince us that, unless you can locate other positive, offsetting factors, you should take a cautious recruiting position when you have the following situations:

√ **LACK OF A SUCCESS PATTERN.** An unwillingness to pay the price necessary to achieve success.

√ **A STRANGER.** The lack of a natural market and adequate contacts.

√ **EXTREME YOUTH.** No history of leadership.

√ **WEAK OCCUPATIONAL BACKGROUND.** Job experience is limited to a changeless climate that was neither demanding nor competitive.

√ **LACKS MONEY MOTIVATION.** The individual is accustomed to a much higher range with corresponding extra high budget requirements, or has adjusted to an unusually low standard of living.

√ **DOMESTIC DIFFICULTIES.** Current marital or family problems.

√ **HEALTH PROBLEMS.** The person has been ill a month or longer in recent years.

√ **INDEBTEDNESS.** The carrying of heavy financial burdens.

√ **POOR LIVING HABITS.** A "reformed" drinker, gambler, or spender.

√ **LACK OF A HIGH ENERGY LEVEL.** Experiences definite weight or metabolism problems.

The Key Evaluation

In your evaluation process, there is a great need for consistency during your consideration of prospective individuals you want to attract who appear to have the profile characteristics of the organization. If there is a "danger factor" involved, determine the degree to which it exists. You can then decide if there are outstanding, positive factors that will minimize or even completely offset the weaknesses. Contract only those candidates you feel satisfy your predetermined standards and have the potential to be the kind of performers you want on your team.

Compatibility of the manager's and the associate's personalities is also extremely important to the individual's success. If you genuinely feel a person will succeed and you are enthusiastic about his or her joining your organization, the person's chances for success are greatly enhanced. This is the key evaluation only you can make. A thorough fact-finding interview with an individual generally will reveal clearly whether or not you like the individual.

Woody Hayes, the legendary Ohio State football coach, said something to the effect that the kind of person you select to play on your football team has a great deal to do with your ultimate success or failure as the team's coach. We agree with Coach Hayes. We also agree with our former "coach," Fred Holderman, who used to say it in another way: "Let's hire individuals we can stay excited about—the kind who will later attract others. We can make this kind of individual successful. They will help us build a great sales team."

YOU CAN MAKE BAD WINE WITH GOOD GRAPES, BUT YOU CAN'T MAKE GOOD WINE WITH BAD GRAPES.

Pat Smith
Domaine Chandon

Sell the Career to Everyone

Whether or not you ultimately decide to recruit a candidate, you should make it clear that a career as a professional in today's financial services arena is an attractive, exciting, and unusual opportunity for personal and financial success. Your description of the business should include some of the key points about the many products you sell as well as information about the industry, your organization, and yourself.

There are at least two important factors for selling the career to all candidates. You'll want those who don't join you to be favorably impressed by the opportunity you offer because they can be helpful to you in locating or recruiting other candidates.

On the other hand, with respect to those who do join you, you will likely attract higher quality people if you make them see that the career offers them a great opportunity for success and a challenge to be leaders among other successful professionals. There are many individuals who could be good prospects for your team but who have not considered the business because they are unfamiliar with the job and its rewards. During initial interviews, you should whet their appetites by describing what a successful professional does—the income, the job satisfaction, and the many services rendered to clients.

Expansion Mood

As you set the stage for effective evaluation, be certain to put a heavy emphasis on the fact that you are building a dynamic organization. Give yourself a reputation to live up to. Project this thought throughout:

WE ARE IN THE EXPANSION MOOD. WE EXPECT TO INVITE INTO OUR
ORGANIZATION AS MANY AS (NUMBER) NEW ASSOCIATES THIS YEAR.
WE FEEL THE (YOUR COMPANY) OPPORTUNITY IS UNUSUAL FOR
SOMEONE OF YOUR BACKGROUND AND ABILITIES.
THIS IS WHAT BRINGS US TOGETHER TODAY; EXPLORING THE
OPPORTUNITY AND EVALUATING YOUR POTENTIAL WITH US.

Interview Guidelines

In order for the evaluating sessions to be as productive as possible, they should be arranged and staged properly. There are certain general procedures you will be well-advised to follow.

√ Inform your assistant there are to be no interruptions.

√ Spend only brief amounts of time on the pleasantries of the day. Make candidates feel relaxed but don't overdo it. These are business sessions.

√ Build and maintain your candidates' trust. The only ideal relationship for successful interviewing is a feeling of mutual trust.

√ Develop your interview techniques to obtain definite and accurate information with respect to the various points you are covering.

√ Be a good listener. Do not dominate the conversation. Let candidates talk and you'll learn a great deal about their strengths and weaknesses. Prospective associates should do 70% of the talking. A good interviewer is a good listener. (See Exhibit 3.7.)

√ Ask one question at a time, and give candidates enough time to think about the question before answering.

√ Let your prospects falter and flounder—but let them finish! By keeping quiet as much as possible and permitting prospects to complete their stories, you can obtain valuable information.

√ Phrase the questions so you do not indicate the desired answer. Avoid the leading question in selection interviewing. You are trying to acquire an unbiased look at each candidate. Leading questions tend to give you impressions of candidates as you would like them to be, rather than as they really are.

√ Assume a neutral position. Don't pass judgment, don't take sides, and don't argue. Avoid counseling, coaching, or criticizing candidates. You want a free flow of information.

√ Leave the selling to the candidates. Don't let your eagerness for a new appointment lead you into the trap of looking for positives and skipping over the negatives. Remember, you are selecting people for a job where the basic task is selling. Don't be too quick to buy. Put your emphasis on uncovering as much important information as you can. Prospective individuals with good sales qualities will see to it that you discover those qualities.

√ Watch your tone of voice and the emphasis you give to various questions. It is obvious that a sarcastic tone of voice and delivery, for example, can impart a completely different meaning than the words alone would convey.

During the questioning process, find ways to give prospective producers the opportunity to sell you on their sales and self-management potential.

Exhibit 3.7 / *GOOD LISTENING*

GOOD LISTENING COMMANDMENTS

➲ **Stop talking!**
You can't listen if you are talking.

➲ **Put the talker at ease.**
Help him or her feel free to talk.

➲ **Show the individual you want to listen.**
Look and act interested. Don't read your mail while the person talks. Listen to understand rather than to respond.

➲ **Remove distractions.**
Don't doodle, tap or shuffle papers.

➲ **Empathize.**
Try to put yourself in the prospect's place.

➲ **Be patient.**
Allow plenty of time. Don't interrupt or complete sentences.

➲ **Do not argue or criticize.**
This puts an individual on the defensive. He may "clam up" or get angry.

➲ **Ask questions.**
It develops points further.

➲ **Stay poised.**
A disgruntled person gets the wrong meaning from words.

➲ **Stop talking!**
This is the first and last rule because all the rest depend on it!

Keith Davis, *The Dynamics of Organizational Behavior*

Exhibit 3.8 / *STRENGTHS*

HOW OTHERS WOULD VIEW MY STRENGTHS

This can be a revealing exercise. Ask your candidate to respond to this scenario: What would the people who know you best put on the list of strengths they feel you would bring to a selling job?

1. I'm _____	21. I'm _____
2. I'm _____	22. I'm _____
3. I'm _____	23. I'm _____
4. I'm _____	24. I'm _____
5. I'm _____	25. I'm _____
6. I'm _____	26. I'm _____
7. I'm _____	27. I'm _____
8. I'm _____	28. I'm _____
9. I'm _____	29. I'm _____
10. I'm _____	30. I'm _____
11. I'm _____	31. I'm _____
12. I'm _____	32. I'm _____
13. I'm _____	33. I'm _____
14. I'm _____	34. I'm _____
15. I'm _____	35. I'm _____
16. I'm _____	36. I'm _____
17. I'm _____	37. I'm _____
18. I'm _____	38. I'm _____
19. I'm _____	39. I'm _____
20. I'm _____	40. I'm _____

Exhibit 3.8 cont'd / *STRENGTHS*

HOW OTHERS WOULD VIEW MY STRENGTHS

How candidates perceive themselves reveal evaluation insights you will develop in no other way. You should expect to find at least 15 of the 20 characteristics listed on their lists from the left column (1-20).

1. I'm goal-striving	21. I'm enthusiastic
2. I'm honest	22. I'm creative
3. I'm optimistic	23. I'm persuasive
4. I'm energetic	24. I'm assertive
5. I'm industrious	25. I'm resourceful
6. I'm competitive	26. I'm organized
7. I'm mentally alert	27. I'm well educated
8. I'm confident	28. I'm personable
9. I'm proactive	29. I'm decisive
10. I'm persistent	30. I'm ambitious
11. I'm healthy	31. I'm conscientious
12. I'm religious	32. I'm courageous
13. I'm money-motivated	33. I'm a good communicator
14. I'm loyal	34. I'm appearance conscious
15. I'm balanced	35. I'm a good listener
16. I'm coachable	36. I'm time conscious
17. I'm close to family	37. I'm "street smart"
18. I'm responsible	38. I'm consistent
19. I'm well-known	39. I'm a student
20. I'm a good money manager	40. I'm a team player

What to Evaluate

If you were to define the kind of successful, established salespeople you want to have in your organization, you would include a number of important qualifications. Which of those qualifications are, and which are not, important for prospects to have? The practical means of making such a distinction is to determine the degree to which each of the important qualifications can be developed by effective management.

If a particular qualification can be developed, it's not too important that prospective associates possess it when a contract is offered. However, if it can't be developed because it's part of the basic make-up of good salespeople, you must evaluate it in candidates and require it of those you attempt to recruit.

Product knowledge, a selling procedure, an understanding of marketing, and a healthy self-image, for example, are all vital qualifications of successful, established performers. Yet, they are not essential for candidates to possess; they can all be developed on the job. Your evaluation should focus primarily on those characteristics that are important for prospective salespeople to possess—the characteristics that are much more difficult or impossible to develop after people are already aboard. Examples of these vital characteristics are integrity, mental alertness, passion for achievement, a high energy level, money motivation, and staying power.

Once you've determined the vital characteristics you want it's important you know what questions to ask and how to interpret answers so you can make responsible judgments.

If you're prospecting among the "right kind" —higher potential candidates—you'll find recruiting is generally not a quick sale proposition. You must explore each candidate's qualifications carefully. If you like what you find, match that candidate's ambitions to the sales career opportunity.

For help in asking the right questions and evaluating the essential qualifications, we recommend two tools: the Patterned Evaluation Interview and the evaluation test or tests provided by your company.

ALWAYS BE LOOKING FOR THE SIX VITALS: INTEGRITY, MENTAL ALERTNESS, PASSION FOR ACHIEVEMENT, A HIGH ENERGY LEVEL, MONEY MOTIVATION, AND STAYING POWER.

Patterned Evaluation Interview

In your evaluation interview, keep in mind that the probing you do must always be pointed toward helping both the prospective associate and you focus on the "thread of discontent." Quite obviously, you will be gathering important information and insights during the initial interviews and these are helpful. However, locating the thread of discontent and making that dissatisfaction a motivating factor for the candidate's considering a career change are far more important to you as a recruiter.

The Pros and Cons of the Patterned Interview

Patterned Interviews follow a carefully selected set of questions that are designed to improve interviewing efficiency and eliminate irrelevant questions. Refer again to the questions shown on the Reservoir Card (Exhibit 3.5). You will have questions of your own that you will want to add to this selection. It's a probing type of interview in which you are reminded of specific areas that should be uncovered during the interview process.

The major disadvantage of the Patterned Interview is that, although it ensures thoroughness, it will cut down on the spontaneity of the interview. It often reduces the possibility of following, or listening to, important matters mentioned by the person being interviewed. You might actually become more focused on the questions than on the answers.

The remedy, of course, is to keep your principal objectives always in mind. You are attempting to determine the answer to three basic questions.

1. *What is the thread of discontent and how does the sales opportunity offer solve that problem for this individual?*

2. *Will this individual produce a consistent effort?*

3. *How strong will our relationship with this individual be over the long haul?*

When used properly, a Patterned Interview can be a most valid and effective evaluation tool.

Legal Considerations

In recent years, as you know, there has been an increasing amount of legislation (both state and federal) regarding the selection process. The majority of the laws are aimed at tools used in the evaluation process—tools such as application blanks, interview forms, and tests.

The implications of these laws are far-reaching, particularly as they apply to the recruiting and selection process. You must be up-to-date not only on all new legislation in this field, but on interpretations resulting from cases being resolved in the courts. Under the circumstances, you must have ready access to current literature on this topic as well as to legal counsel. (For further details, write to: Equal Employment Opportunity Commission, Personal Testing and Equal Employment Opportunity, Washington, D.C., or call 1-800-669-4000.)

Exhibit 3.9 / *SUCCESS PREDICTABILITY PROFILE*

SUCCESS PREDICTABILITY PROFILE
LOOKING AT THE CANDIDATE'S HISTORICAL PATTERNS

You'll find this evaluation discipline to be a helpful tool in making sound judgments on candidates. Its focus is strictly on history. We believe what the individual has done in the past is still the single best indicator of what he or she will do in the future.

Your success in building a high performing sales organization depends upon the kind of people you attract and keep. Be and stay consistent in attracting high potential, prospective producers. Individuals who have already demonstrated a behavior pattern that produces a "success package" of positive attitudes, passion for achievement, energy and stability are the individuals you can develop into independent, responsible producers.

Points Allotted	Criteria	Points Scored
20 or 0	Experienced Associate Endorsement.	_____
15 - 0	Has demonstrated passion for achievement.	_____
15 - 0	Has fast start potential and market strength.	_____
15 - 0	Has an optimistic attitude.	_____
10 or 0	Has been a successful commissioned sales representative, coach, sole proprietor, farmer or accountant.	_____
10 or 0	Current monthly income in $3,000 to $5,000 range.	_____
10 or 0	Has a college degree.	_____
	Ownership of *permanent* life insurance:	
5	$100,000	
7	$100,000 — $250,000	
10	$250,000 and over	
5 or 0	Has held office in an organization (during last 18 months).	_____
10 - 0	Is financially stable (examine net worth statement).	_____
5 or 0	Has engaged in self-improvement (during last 12 months).	_____
	Has Dependents:	
5	One	
10	Two or more	

TOTAL POINTS [   ]

Points	Potential
100 and above	Superior
80 - 99	Acceptable
65 - 79	Doubtful
Under 65	Unqualified

Exhibit 3.9 cont'd / *SUCCESS PREDICTABILITY PROFILE*

SUCCESS PREDICTABILITY PROFILE
RECRUITER'S REPORT

1. How has this person demonstrated a high need to achieve?

   _____

   _____

2. What evidence did you develop to support the fact that this candidate brings to us a strong market and good contacts?

   _____

   _____

3. Why do you consider this person to be energetic?

   _____

   _____

4. Will this person perform and mesh in our culture? ___ Yes___ No

   _____

   _____

5. What evidence did you develop to support financial stability?

   _____

   _____

6. In what ways do you feel family members will be supportive?

   _____

   _____

7. Describe what attracts you to this individual.

   _____

   _____

Date	Recruiter	Location

Stimulate Candidates' Interest

If you have followed the suggested evaluation procedure to this point, you have been asking the candidates pertinent questions and making important observations throughout your evaluation interview. Assuming you are in a positive posture relative to those individuals, we recommend you now take a forward step toward motivating them to investigate the opportunity with your organization more fully. The strategy for doing so is to sell the candidates further on you, your sales team, the industry, and the advantages of a sales career in the financial services industry.

They have been telling you about themselves. A logical next step is to tell them about you, the people you've developed, your organization and company leaders. You should do that rather briefly at this point because you will want to do it in greater depth during the "attracting stage" that we'll discuss next. Briefly describe the career. Romance its specific advantages and opportunities as they relate to the respective individuals.

Of course, you may have determined that the person being interviewed is not a candidate for you at this time. If this is the case, take the necessary precaution to conclude the discussion on a very favorable basis. Make the individual an "ambassador of goodwill" for you and your organization. It might be that you will want to file a card on this person for your reservoir so you can keep in touch and continue to "spoon feed" him the opportunity over a period of time.

Remember: The better you know and like the people, and the better they understand what is expected of them, the better your chances of reducing costly turnovers if you recruit them.

Aptitude and Trait Testing

It's virtually impossible to build a successful organization if the individuals attracted are of limited potential. For that reason, some method of pre-determining candidates' aptitudes, traits, behavioral patterns and likelihood of success before contracting them is important to you as well as to the candidates.

Most companies provide evaluation tools to help their managers obtain valid information of this kind. Tests and evaluations afford the kinds of "appraisal feedback" that help managers pick high potential candidates and then train them most effectively.

We strongly recommend your full use of the evaluation tools and assistance your company provides in this area with every candidate. This is the point in the evaluation process where you should schedule an hour or so with your candidate for that specific purpose.

Between Interviews

To maintain interest and reinforce your professional approach between interviews, send a letter to the candidate immediately following each interview. Such a letter should be personal and include confirmation of the next interview. Appropriate brochures or other support material should be included with the letter.

At the completion of each interview, take time to jot down your reactions to that particular interview. What have you learned? What are the individual's strengths? Remember, if you contract this candidate, you will be attempting to build upon those strengths while making the person's weaknesses irrelevant. What additional information should you probe for in the next interview? What can you do to move the decision process along?

ATTRACTING YOUR KIND

In subsequent interviews, keep in mind that the more exposure you have to an individual, the better you will understand the individual and the better that individual will understand you. You also improve the odds of your accurately determining the interconnection among the prospective producers and yourself. This is an important reason why you should have as many recruiting interviews as possible. It's also the reason why you undoubtedly will have far better retention ratios as a result of contracting people whom you have known over a period of time and have, preferably, sold and serviced as clients.

Each recruiting interview should have a predetermined objective you are trying to achieve. Early in the interview process, as we discussed before, you are trying to determine many things about the candidate. The most important, of course, is this person's "thread of discontent." When the thread of discontent is uncovered, continue to talk about it in subsequent interviews to make sure that it remains a key consideration in the individual's thinking. You should continue to show how the problem can be handled through a sales career opportunity with you.

It is during these subsequent attracting interviews that you determine the kind of individual with whom you are dealing. We believe that, throughout these interviews, you should always be attempting to answer the three, significant questions:

1. *First, what is this individual's thread of discontent?*

   How will your career opportunity solve that problem?

2. *Second, will this individual produce a consistent effort?*

   People in our business do not succeed, necessarily, because they have more ability. They excel because they have the desire, discipline and energy to work hard from the day they enter the business.

3. *Finally, do I like this individual?*

   Will we have a good relationship? Do we mesh well? Do I see and feel a strong, fast start potential?

Keep in mind that, generally, what the candidate has done in the past is the best indication of how he most likely will perform when contracted.

Those are the major factors that must heavily influence your decision as to whether you truly want an individual in your organization and whether you should move forward in your attempt to contract that candidate.

Make the Decision

Obviously, the most important element in making the decision as to whether to attempt to contract a prospective associate is the judgment and common sense of the manager making the decision.

THERE ARE TWO KINDS OF INDIVIDUALS WHO NEVER AMOUNT TO MUCH—THOSE WHO CANNOT DO WHAT THEY ARE TOLD, AND THOSE WHO CAN DO NOTHING ELSE.

Cyrus H. K. Curtis

The gut feeling you have after interviewing and spending time with a candidate will largely determine your decision as to whether ihat individual would be successful as a member of your organization. That feeling is all-important for you must be ready to "live" with the prospective associate and do everything in your power to make that person successful if your decision is to contract the candidate.

For that reason, we recommend you carefully complete the Final Evaluation Checklist shown in Exhibit 3.10. We have developed this decision discipline over the past several years. We feel it will do much to strengthen your decision by causing you to examine the history of the candidate one more time.

Be reminded, again, that you are evaluating the six vitals: integrity, mental alertness, passion for achievement, a high level of energy, money motivation, and staying power.

Exhibit 3.10/*FINAL EVALUATION CHECKLIST*

FINAL EVALUATION CHECKLIST

CANDIDATE:			GO	?	NO-GO
*1.	Shows evidence of high integrity	EVIDENCE:			
*2.	Displays mental alertness	EVIDENCE:			
*3.	Possesses achievement drive	EVIDENCE:			
*4.	Has high level of energy	EVIDENCE:			
*5.	Is money motivated	EVIDENCE:			
*6.	Has displayed staying power	EVIDENCE:			
7.	Sales type and is coachable	EVIDENCE:			
8.	Is favorably and well-known (Markets)	EVIDENCE:			
9.	Lives within his/her income	EVIDENCE:			
10.	Has had a college level education	EVIDENCE:			
11.	Has an income range between $36,000 and $60,000 a year	AMOUNT:			
12.	Entrepreneurial	EVIDENCE:			

*These represent the vital factors. **DECISION:**
A questionable or no-go evaluation in
any one of these areas is a strong
reason for rejecting the candidate.

Support the Decision

After you have made a tentative decision to contract a candidate, it generally is wise to seek some outside support for that choice before you finalize it and actually make a job offer.

The references the candidate gives you might be helpful in several ways. The quality of the people given enables you to make a quick appraisal of the prospective producer's natural market. Poor references with respect to occupation or income, for example, might be a danger signal indicating that the candidate's higher income market potential is limited.

The value of contacting references is questionable for almost all candidates offer people who will say complimentary things about them. Consider contacting those people, however. You might learn more by what they don't say than by what they do say. Or they may inadvertently touch on relevant facts the candidate did not mention. Again, we see the value of your knowing the candidate over a period of time and making your own observations during that period.

Previous employers and business associates usually are excellent potential sources of reliable information about the candidate's personal habits, strengths and weaknesses. The best method of securing this kind of information is through a personal visit. If that is impractical, the next best method is to use the telephone. Obviously, such two-way communication can be invaluable in finding out how these people feel about the candidate—from their pauses and tone of voice to what they actually say.

Gathering supporting information for your tentative decision is time-consuming. Still, it can also be cost-saving. It might help you avoid making a costly mistake in your selection. We feel it is a "must exercise," especially in those instances where you have not had time enough to make a meaningful investigation and evaluation of the candidate firsthand.

Sharpen Your Script

Now you move to the climax. This is where you must be at your best. Sharpen your scripts for the attracting presentation. Your aim is to attract "the right kind" of producer to your sales team. When we say "the right kind" we, of course, are talking about the individual you won't permit to fail. The person you have known and grown to respect—you won't let fail. The referral from a top performer in the organization—you can't let fail.

Do you see why your success comes from personal contacts and the referrals of your top associates? You're determined they can't fail; they must make good!

In prior interviews, your primary objective was to learn all you could about the candidate in order to decide whether to reject or attempt to bring the individual into your organization. Frankly, you've been a little guarded as to how much you said about the opportunity you had to offer, telling just enough to maintain interest.

Now, you've learned what you wanted to know and you've made a decision to move forward with an attempt to recruit the candidate if he or she shows the right spirit and interest in the job. During the presentation interview, you want to tell the candidate all about the opportunity, everything he should know and wants to know about it in order to make his decision.

Opportunities Are Unlimited

We believe selling financial services and products offers unlimited opportunities for the right individuals. Purchases are more substantial than ever before. The industry is riding high on the crest of a still rising tide as new markets are being developed. New or improved products are constantly being introduced that are rapidly finding public acceptance. Producers and advisors are becoming more professional as a result of improved selection, education and training, plus the addition of sophisticated computerized sales support.

As evidence of the growth and public acceptance of life insurance, the number of million dollar producers goes up each year. Earnings figures will vary, generally depending upon the producer's age and the kind of business sold. Nevertheless, including first year commissions and renewals, the million dollar producer typically earns in the neighborhood of $180,000 a year and up. For the professional who pays the price in terms of time, effort and study, it's a great business in which to make money.

Insurance sales have increased tremendously in the past ten years, and that increase in volume is being sold by a smaller percentage increase of producers. Evidently, those who are succeeding in our business are doing a better job and earning substantially more income. Truly, for the right people you can offer an "Opportunity Unlimited!" You have a good deal to talk about in your attracting interviews.

A POWERFUL INCENTIVE FOR PRODUCERS TO STAY AND PERSEVERE IN THE FINANCIAL SERVICES BUSINESS IS THE POTENTIAL TO EARN A VERY GOOD LIVING.

Russ Alan Prince

Combat Retention Problems

Despite its impressive growth record, our industry continues to fret over and suffer because of the difficulty involved in attracting enough quality people and retaining them. It's true of our entire industry; retention ratios haven't improved noticeably in the past 50 years. Not long ago, an article in a respected daily national newspaper stated: "High turnover plagues life insurance companies. Of nearly 23,000 new, full-time producers hired each year, 15,000 are gone by year-end. One reason: Inadequate training."

Strengthen Attitudes

Undoubtedly, that indictment is at least partially true. Based, though, on our experience, we don't believe "inadequate training" alone accounts for the condition. We believe another prime reason for the high dropout rate is that almost every new person carries into the business a "mental parachute."

After the enthusiastic message of a wooing manager wears off and the producer faces the moment of truth in front of an uncooperative prospect, he quickly begins to lose self-esteem. Soon the producer begins to believe the public's caricature of the persuasive, successful salesperson—the high pressure, aggressive, joiner type. As your new associate begins to believe this assessment, his self-image suffers, enthusiasm dwindles, and then he gives our business the timid, tentative try without paying the price of success. The result: the producer soon "pulls the rip cord" and "parachutes out of the business."

Far too many individuals entering our business have mistaken beliefs about the job and its requirements for success. Perhaps some of that is the fault of the home office management people in that they stress the need for new recruits while understressing the need for those recruits to have a more complete understanding of what the producer's job involves. Providing that understanding before contracting strengthens attitudes and commitments for later when producers must face the facts of the business all alone.

Tell It – Don't Sell It

We firmly believe retention is significantly improved when prospective producers are clearly made aware of the tough road they will be traveling during the early years. A frank picture of the difficulties of selling what we sell will scare off some candidates who might otherwise be contracted. By the same token, it tends to attract the right kind of individuals to whom the more usual practice of "selling the job" often fails to move. This is why we recommend that, in building your interviewing techniques, you employ the important underlying strategy of "telling it, rather than selling it."

First, remind candidates of the very nature of the job. It's not an ordinary means of making a living. The profession's unique characteristics require self-confidence and self-reliance in extreme abundance. Producers have a self-generated brand of "call courage" that will carry them through the sale even though they operate in a negative atmosphere most of the time. They need to understand that, at the start, most hours will produce little in the way of encouraging results. Most people they call on will tend to deflate their egos. Tough-mindedness and stick-to-it-iveness are among the many qualities they must possess in order to succeed and remain in the business.

Second, be completely candid with the candidates in all of your discussions and illustrations. If they join your team, you want them to come in mentally ready to accomplish the selling job which they understand and appreciate.

MAKE PROSPECTIVE PRODUCERS AWARE OF THE
TOUGH ROAD THEY WILL TRAVEL IN THE EARLY SELLING YEARS.
WE BELIEVE THIS INCREASES RETENTION.

Jack and Garry Kinder

Present the Opportunity

The attracting interview is the major thrust of your sales strategy in the recruiting process. It follows when you have determined that you are seriously interested in the candidate—who is also interested in you and the opportunity you are offering to the extent of returning for more specific information.

The attracting interview should be held in your office. It should be scheduled at a time during a workday when business is being conducted as usual. This is when you'll best be able to see how strongly a candidate desires to join your team.

Do not make the opportunity too easy for a candidate to accept. Make each interview a little more difficult than the previous one. That will either strengthen the candidate's desire to join your organization or will tend to cause the individual to "select-out" voluntarily.

You should have everything you say and do in this interview well-organized so you can cover all aspects of the business. Here are the points to follow.

- Review prior interviews and evaluations up to the present.

- Respond to the five key questions shown on the following pages.

- Reveal the problem areas of the job.

- Invite and respect the opinions of your associates, relative to the candidate's potential.

Review Progress To-Date

It is important to begin the presentation interview with a review of what occurred in (or as a result of) previous meetings. If possible, take the candidate back to the same emotional level at which the prior meeting ended.

If any problems have developed since the last meeting, such as difficulty in contacting references, this is the appropriate time to clear up such matters.

Respond to Key Questions

Prospective associates have many questions on their minds that must be answered to their satisfaction during the attraction process. However, there are five primary questions that all candidates ask. They may not openly express those questions, but you can be sure they are there just the same.

These five questions must be answered thoroughly and repeatedly throughout your presentations. Let's start our presentation interview discussion by briefly examining each one.

1. WHAT WILL I BE DOING?

You must explain to candidates exactly what they will be doing. Specifically, what they will be selling, to whom they will be selling, how they will develop higher income clients, what their daily activities will consist of, and how much time and effort will be involved.

2. HOW DO I LEARN TO SELL?

To answer this question, you should cover the specifics of the education and training programs. You need to show them you have proven marketing and selling strategies along with how those strategies work. Explain that through joint work you will first show them how to do the job, then you will let them do it while you watch. Afterward, you'll critique what they have done in order to help them do it better the next time. Candidates want to know how they will get started and be both productive and successful.

3. WHAT ARE THE REWARDS?

Explanations of commissions, renewals, service fees, and the full range of company benefits are in order here, too. Psyche-rewards and job fulfillment possibilities are also of special importance to modern day candidates. Be sure to tell them about such programs in your operation.

4. HOW DO YOU EVALUATE MY POTENTIAL FOR SELLING SUCCESS?

This is likely the most critical question you must answer. How do you evaluate their potential? What can they expect? What will you deliver? How good will they become with you?

5. HOW AND WHEN WILL I GET STARTED?

Everyone you talk with has budget requirements and expectations. Walk them through your clear-cut induction strategies and checklists. This is a confidence builder.

As you construct your presentation, stay mindful of the importance of dealing with these key questions. It is essential that you develop helpful material to draw from in the next several discussions.

Reveal Problem Areas

Every career has certain problems to overcome, and yours is no exception. The problems that the candidate will face, if he or she comes into the business, should be brought into the open at this point. Up to now, most of your discussions have been concerned with the positives. When the tough parts of the business are made known and examined now, they won't shock the candidate. The candidate will respect your straight talk. When it becomes necessary to face those problems later on, the producer likely will react more maturely because he is already aware of the problems and is expecting them.

Also, this kind of discussion further tests the prospect's courage and level of interest in the sales job. His reactions provide a good indication of whether or not he is ready to make a full commitment.

Here are some of the problem areas you will want to cover.

THE TURNOVER PROBLEM

The candidate probably has heard (or if not, soon will hear) of the turnover problem in our business. Bring it out into the open and discuss it right now.

First, review and help the individual understand "The Experienced Sales Force" concept developed earlier in this chapter. Compare our business with the medical profession. Explain that there are many dropouts during the trainee or internship period in both fields. Also explain, however, that the manpower loss rate is extremely low in your organization once individuals complete the trainee, apprenticeship period and become members of your experienced sales force. (Losses in this experienced group from all causes, including deaths, retirements and terminations, are less than 5% per year in almost every company we have examined.)

CALL RELUCTANCE

Another problem that you should bring up and discuss now with a candidate is call reluctance. That is a common phenomenon which virtually everyone faces. Helping them whip the problem is one of your primary jobs.

Relating at this time exactly what must be done to overcome call reluctance, and what support you provide through joint field work, will do much to avoid serious problems and termination when call reluctance is experienced later.

LOSS OF PERSPECTIVE

There really are only a few important things an individual must do in order to be successful in our business. Failure to stay focused on those few high priority jobs is one of the biggest causes of poor performance and dropouts.

In that regard, it's particularly important for you, as an agency builder, to understand that you really start "training" the individual from the first minute of your first meeting. From that point of view, the two functions of recruiting and training are inseparable. Start making certain from the beginning that the candidate feels the absolute importance of bringing self-discipline to your kind of work. Emphasize the need to maintain perspective and stay focused on the key elements of the job at all times.

COMMISSION INCOME

Many candidates have not previously experienced the commission form of compensation. They have questions about how it works, and some doubts as to whether they can manage and adjust to it emotionally. If they enter the business with those questions and doubts unsatisfied, they could become disenchanted with the job before they've had a chance to build up and reap its true rewards. It's vital that you explain the compensation system to them carefully, making sure to answer their questions frankly and completely.

Respect the Opinions of Associates

You'll want the candidate to see your facilities and learn about your support capabilities. Also, you should introduce other members of the organization to the candidate and encourage your associates' feedback.

Attempt to arrange those visits so certain associates are available to talk with the candidate in their offices. Discuss reactions to the candidate with your associates and respect their findings and feelings. Their endorsements will prove helpful if the candidate joins your organization.

Don't Shortcut

When the candidate is in the traffic pattern—that is, actively looking to make a quick job change and is available immediately—or when your recruiting need is pressing, you may understandably be tempted to speed things up a bit. Bear in mind that if you speed up the process by eliminating one or more steps in the recruiting process, you're gambling.

We strongly encourage you not to skip anything; maybe you should even slow it down a bit in "rush" situations. The stakes are too high in today's marketplace!

Exhibit 3.11 / *VOCATIONAL QUIZ*

VOCATIONAL QUIZ

What business, other that the financial services industry, offers you the opportunity to:

- go into a business of your own with $1,000 of capital?

- have only your clients as your boss?

- be paid exactly in proportion to your ability and results?

- have unlimited potential as to the amount of money you can earn?

- be allowed to tailor-make your own working hours?

- pick the people on whom you want to call?

- work without fear of having your quota raised or your territory or commission scale diminished?

- work without having your success pattern depend upon your ability to "butter up" the owner or the people at company headquarters?

- be in a position where there is no jealousy or bitter rivalry between yourself and your producers; where your success cannot in any way impair your producers' progress, or vice versa?

- be in a business that becomes easier and less demanding as you grow older, compared to the mounting pressures encountered in most businesses?

**LOOK NO FURTHER—
THERE IS NONE OTHER THAN THE
FINANCIAL SERVICES INDUSTRY!**

Exhibit 3.12/ *RECRUITING REMINDERS*

TEN RECRUITING REMINDERS

1. **Make a responsible commitment for reaching the recruiting goal.**

   Action I will take: _____

   _____

2. **Build a strategic recruiting plan.**

   Action I will take: _____

   _____

3. **Be contact conscious.**

   Action I will take: _____

   _____

4. **Recruit to specific target markets.**

   Action I will take: _____

   _____

5. **Stay proactive**

   Action I will take: _____

   _____

Exhibit 3.12 cont'd / *RECRUITING REMINDERS*

TEN RECRUITING REMINDERS
(Continued)

6. **Develop a systematic flow of successful endorsements from associates.**

   Action I will take: _____

   _____

7. **Design a well-structured, well-rehearsed, motivating presentation.**

   Action I will take: _____

   _____

8. **Maintain an active reservoir of future possibilities.**

   Action I will take: _____

   _____

9. **Take the time to cultivate and attract a Key Performer.**

   Action I will take: _____

   _____

10. **Professionally package and promote support materials.**

    Action I will take: _____

    _____

RECRUITING EXPERIENCED PRODUCERS

Today, there are forces at work that occasionally make the recruiting of experienced producers possible, and even desirable. The experienced producer is much easier to evaluate. Generally, there is a production pattern that is easy to identify and appraise. Probe for the important facts and listen to the dictates of your own conscience.

Begin this process by building the profile of the experienced producer you'd like to attract. The following list shows the key characteristics of the ideal candidate.

- An individual you like and respect.

- A person who is a "good fit" with your culture.

- Five plus years of successful experience.

- Consistent MDRT level production.

- Persistency above 90%.

- High ethical and business standards.

- Has an area of expertise.

Search for the Thread of Discontent

- Looking for a long-term relationship.

- Has outgrown the current carrier's ability to support his/her practice.

- Has a close, existing relationship with you or someone in the organization.

- Current company is undergoing significant change.

- Concerned about the company's long-term survival.

- Single-line producer who wants to expand into other product lines.

- Deteriorating relationship with the current company or manager.

Exhibit 3.13 / *PRODUCTION HISTORY*

EVALUATING PRODUCTION HISTORY

It's important to evaluate where the revenues are being generated. How does this pattern match your culture and company philosophy?

Net Annualized First Year Commissions

Product	Company	Current FYC Plan	Previous 3 Year's Actual Year 1	Year 2	Year 3
Traditional Life					
Universal Life					
Variable Life					
Term Life					
Total Life					
Fixed Annuities					
Variable Annuities					
Total Annuities					
Mutual Funds					
Long-Term Care					
P&C					
Other (specify)					
Total All Products					

Exhibit 3.14/ *PRODUCER ISSUES*

EXPERIENCED PRODUCER ISSUES

Key Producer/Producers _____

Staff Members _____

Business Goals _____

Primary Company _____

**Broker/Dealer
Relationship** _____

**Current Compensation
(Renewals/Trailers)** _____

Market Focus _____

Reason for Change _____

Reason to Join Us _____

Reason to Stay _____

**Who else are they
talking to?** _____

**What do they need,
want or expect?** _____

**Other Relevant
Information** _____

Exhibit 3.15 / *ASSETS UNDER MANAGEMENT*

ASSETS UNDER MANAGEMENT

Product	Company	Compensation	Previous 3 Year's Actual		
			Year 1	Year 2	Year 3
Fixed Annuities					
Variable Annuities					
Total Annuities					
Mutual Funds					
Other (specify)					
Total All Products					

Producer Attraction Issues

What's in it for me?

That's the key question the experienced producer wants answered. Here are a few possible issues you'll want to develop with experienced candidates.

- Dynamic local organization

- Company brand name recognition

- Competitive underwriting

- Broad, competitive product portfolio

- Benefit package

- Advanced technology

- Marketing support

- Out brokerage facility

- Mentoring

- Orphan leads

- Signing bonus

Book of Champions

One time we asked the late Ted Hoyer, from the well-known John Hancock family in Columbus, Ohio, what was his strongest recruiting strategy. Year after year, Hoyer attracted large numbers of high potential recruits and built Hancock's leading agency in the process.

Mr. Hoyer shared with us this interesting story. He learned that the immortal Michigan football coach, Fielding Yost, had developed over the years a *Book of Champions*. Coach Yost said this strategy permitted him to "win over" the parents of blue chip performers wherever they were living.

Yost's *Book of Champions* had two pages for each of his stars. The first page displayed pictures, statistics and recognition earned during the athlete's playing days. The second page showed pictures and information on the "finished product"—the Michigan graduate as a successful member of society. The *Book of Champions* message to the parents was subtle, but powerful: Encourage your fine young, athletic son to play for the Wolverines and we'll return to you in four years a well-educated individual who will perform equally as well after his football days are over.

Mr. Hoyer said that when he learned Coach Yost's secret, he and his managers immediately designed and developed their agency *Book of Champions.*

Show the Picture

When we learned about the Hoyer Recruiting Strategy, we put our "book" on slides. It provided our management team a powerful, standardized recruiting story to tell. We felt it gave us a competitive edge.

Today, developing an attractive PowerPoint™ presentation will do the same for you and your management team. You will increase the effectiveness of this kind of presentation by having some pictures made of your associates as well as of your organization plans, programs and activities.

Dick Cleary, the creative general agent in Boca Raton, Florida, is a master at taking advantage of the electronic age—he uses the Internet to help him recruit. He's developed one of the best computer presentations for recruiting we've seen. Dick has produced customized software for his associates that enhances their professionalism and advances their sales.

These kind of presentations help you and other recruiters in your organization stay on track. Consistently, it will assure you of covering the key points you don't want to overlook in your presentation.

DEVELOP YOUR "SUNDAY PUNCH"

As you gain experience, you'll naturally strengthen the things you say to candidates. Early in your career as a recruiter, you'll discover the most convincing and persuasive sales talk you deliver is the one based upon your own personal experience in the business. The story of what you have been able to accomplish, and what has been achieved by others whom you have attracted, is a presentation aid that we have commonly referred to as the important "Sunday Punch."

Think through and develop a script of your own using the outline shown in Exhibit 3.16.

Exhibit 3.16 / *SUNDAY PUNCH*

YOUR "SUNDAY PUNCH" OUTLINE

Your Own Background

My background has been . . .
I went to school . . .
My previous business was . . .
I chose to leave that business because . . .
I chose a career in the financial services industry because . . .
I chose this company because . . .
Let me tell you what I have accomplished . . .

Your Success Stories

The associates I have recruited have achieved . . .
In the future I intend to accomplish . . .

Your Organization

Let me assure you, I am proud to be associated with this organization.
This organization is outstanding because . . .
The reputation of our organization in the business community is outstanding.
    Let me review a few of our many achievements . . .

The Career

You are probably asking yourself, "What are the expectations for a new
    person joining this team, just starting out in a new career.
The income potential of sales is . . .
    (Note: The conservative approach is best. Build credibility by not
    overstating the early years' income potential.)
A selling career offers possibilities for personal growth unmatched in
    most jobs because . . .
Our associates are professionals and that means . . .
It would be hard to find a career, outside of medicine or the ministry,
    I suppose, where individuals provide as meaningful a service to others
    they serve. I say that because . . .
We all like to be recognized for our accomplishments, and our business . . .
The training our associates receive is among the best in the business.
    Let me tell you a little about it . . .
Successful producers have an opportunity to move into management.
    Almost all managers in our company are selected from among
    our associates. What this means is...

The Spouse Interview

Obviously, an interview with a spouse will not be appropriate in all situations. In the case of certain young, single candidates, you'll find it important and helpful to interview the parents of prospective associates. When it's suitable, however, you most certainly should have an interview with the spouse of each candidate you're interested in recruiting. Your principal objectives in this interview are to:

- Give the spouse a positive understanding of the career opportunity.

- Uncover any serious problems in the family situation that indicate the candidate will not receive the needed support.

- Lay the foundation for developing the spouse's trust and confidence in you as a leader.

Unlike most careers where a person's business life is fairly well structured, our business requires a great amount of self-discipline and control, as was pointed out previously. Since selling is so demanding, you need to make sure the demands are understood by everyone involved including, of course, the candidate's spouse.

When you are interviewing a candidate's spouse, there are several key points.

- Be sure you show interest in the spouse as a person. Inquire about the children, family activities, and personal ambitions for the family. That can be done without making the spouse uncomfortable or invading anyone's privacy.

- You want the spouse to believe in you. You are talking with a person about the most important things in life—family and security. Spouses, husbands or wives, will oppose you if they don't trust you—and they will win.

- It is important that you determine the makeup of the spouse. Encourage him or her to speak freely; you need to know if the spouse will be a help or a hindrance to the candidate's career. You won't be told in so many words, but by watching and listening you generally will be able to detect valuable clues.

- The spouse's attitudes toward insurance and insurance people, particularly toward the idea of his or her spouse as a salesperson, are very important. If the present attitude is negative in any of those areas, it's your job to sell the positive aspects.

- Of course, it's also important that you review the negative aspects of the career with the spouse: an apprenticeship to be served, working nights, little free time, difficulty getting started, commission income, etc. Bringing these facets of the business out into the open and discussing them up front will build continued confidence in you that is critical to your ongoing relationship. They will respect your honesty. If they believe that the sales career is the right opportunity, they will start making adjustments to their new way of life.

- Be sure to tell the spouse what success in the career will mean in terms of happiness as well as income. Focus on the solution you have to the candidate's discontent with the current job situation.

PRODUCERS ARE ADDITIONALLY MOTIVATED WHEN
THEIR FAMILIES ARE MADE TO FEEL THAT THEIR WORK IS IMPORTANT,
AND CAN TAKE PRIDE IN IT.

Bob Levoy

Finalize Arrangements

It's essential to plan your final attracting interview in advance so you have time to decide upon the important items you wish to cover and the contracting requirements you must schedule and complete. Depending upon the circumstances, your objectives will include:

- making the commitment final;

- reviewing subsidy arrangements, and how and when commission earnings are paid;

- reviewing licensing requirements;

- establishing the official starting date, and agreeing upon any pre-appointment training and assignments that need to be accomplished prior to the starting date;

- arranging for the completion of the necessary contract papers; and

- reviewing the career path.

This interview should end on a high note, with a mutual agreement that this decision is right for all concerned. Both parties must be committed to a maximum effort. Both must expect the new recruit to enjoy outstanding selling success in the years ahead.

We believe in the "professional partnership" approach to finalizing, advocated and taught to us years ago by the great Baltimore general agent, Irving Abramowitz. As Irving moved to the finalizing stage he indicated to his candidate that it is a "partnership type of relationship" that is being established. He spelled out what was expected of the associate. Abramowitz also indicated how he and the members of his organization were in position to assist in the professional growth of the people they invite into the "partnership." Irving said, "You can make it here with us faster and much better . . . and here are some of the reasons why." That's powerful and useable.

Invite your candidates to join you on a "partnership basis." Give them a confident, winning feeling right from the very start.

Record Recruiting Activities

You should keep current records in regard to your recruiting activities. Federal regulations make it mandatory that you maintain accurate records of all recruiting interviews and job offers. Those records must include the names, minority group designations and sex of those interviewed as well as those offered jobs. For any individual to whom no job offer is made, records must be maintained for at least one year. In addition to the above information, your records must show the reason why no job offer was made.

The way to be sure of profiting by your exposure and experience, while effecting improvements in your recruiting results as you move along, is to:

- keep an active tickler file as previously discussed (build the reservoir); and

- maintain complete selection records that will reveal your recruiting patterns.

It's only by keeping records of your recruiting activities, the prospects with whom you want to keep in touch, and your past selections, then consistently studying those records, that you can hope to improve your future recruitment choices.

Your success as an agency head depends heavily upon your ability to recognize the few primary factors in the job that will most rapidly propel you to success. One of those key factors, we have observed, is the attraction of high potential recruits who stick and build a permanent career with your organization.

There is not much question that it is getting tougher all the time to attract good people. Nonetheless, the job of developing more effective producers with fewer dropouts in the future lies squarely on your shoulders.

Research clearly shows a need for better recruitment and selection results. Moreover, we believe there are many managers who need a "retread course" in how to present the career opportunity. It is difficult to be a successful recruiter unless you have a convincing, balanced, career presentation that informs, enlightens and persuades.

With that in mind, let's summarize the major thoughts we have discussed in some detail with respect to recruiting.

A Key Responsibility

Stripped to its core, your job is essentially one of attaining production objectives through other people. To accomplish that, you perform a number of continuing managerial activities aimed at improving the performance of the individual members of your organization. This process starts with searching and selecting qualified people who can be trained and motivated to become highly productive.

Over the long-term, successful searching and selecting will be reflected in how well the members of your organization perform in their jobs, grow in knowledge, and achieve their individual success. In short, your future is all wrapped up in the recruits you choose and bring into your organization.

Keep in mind, there is no prototype of the perfect producer. Successful people come in all shapes and sizes, from all kinds of backgrounds, with varying degrees of educational attainments, and with assorted business histories. However, your top producers will have certain traits and abilities in common that you naturally should look for in prospective individuals. Among the more important:

- The ability to plan intelligently.

- Good work habits; a capacity for keeping steadily at it.

- A keen desire to make good, and a powerful urge to lead.

- Sales-minded, but service-oriented, attitude stemming from an innate and deeply-rooted empathy.

- Emotional maturity and a high tolerance for frustration.

- Acceptance of your organization's philosophy.

- A singleness of purpose and a driving ambition.

- Some measure of financial stability.

- Good health and physical vitality.

- Facility of expression; a clear articulation of meaning.

- Be coachable; able to accept suggestions and follow directions.

- Have a competitive spirit and optimistic outlook.

- Enthusiasm and a positive demeanor.

Obviously, the recruiting of quality people in sufficient numbers is crucial to your success. Recruiting enough of the right kind of individuals must be your persistent concern.

Four Sales to Make

Your job of recruiting becomes easier as you gain experience and as you understand there are really four "sales" in the recruiting process.

1. The first and biggest sale is selling candidates on the need to consider a job change, and to take the time to contemplate our opportunity seriously and with an open mind. If there is no thread of discontent, there will likely be no movement.

2. Next, you must sell your candidates on you and your ability to bring success within their reach. Ultimately, the decision as to

whether they join your organization may hinge on their reaction to you.

3. Then comes the career "sale." Your candidates must be sold on the career and the benefits it offers.

4. Finally, you must sell them on your organization and its future. Candidates must be sold on the team they are joining. Almost everyone you talk with is interested in belonging to a winning outfit. They want to have pride in the outfit, and they want to be with a leader in whom they can place full confidence.

Recruiting high potential individuals for your organization is a dynamic, ever-continuing and ever-challenging process. Essentially a creative function, it is motivated by ceaseless drive on your part toward developing a recruiting process that consistently attracts enough of the kind who stick and stay.

In presenting the opportunity, remember to:

• Review prior interviews.

• Respond to key questions.

• Reveal problem areas.

• Respect associates' opinions.

• Deliver your "Sunday Punch."

Based on the foregoing, resolve right now to construct a convincing presentation that will attract high potential individuals in sufficient numbers and on a sound basis.

RECRUITING ENOUGH OF THE RIGHT KIND MUST BE YOUR PERSISTENT CONCERN.

VAL'S VIEWS ON RECRUITING

Recruiting is the momentum builder. It's the one management task we have performed successfully each year. It's been the key to our spectacular growth.

Past performance tends to be the best predictor of future performance. That's why it's an excellent investment of time and effort to check the history when choosing producers for your team. There is no substitute for experience and judgment in recruiting the right people.

Project a professional presence. Look like the kind of businessperson prospective producers want to emulate.

Learn about your "keepers." Decide who succeeds in your organization. We always think about our response to this question: "Is this someone we would invite to our home for dinner?"

Build your Recruiting Effort Formula. We believe strongly in automatics. For example, we send out 25 prospecting letters every Friday; all of the prospects are then called the following week. Reliably, that gives us two immediate appointments and five call-backs. Keep recruiting as your number one priority. Recruit even when you are doing joint field work.

Believe passionately in the opportunity you are presenting. That part has been easy for me. Thirty years ago I was working three jobs and earning a total of $8,000. I didn't know this business existed. You can imagine how excited I am now to show recruits a W-2 form that lists earnings over $2 million.

Make prospective associates' first visit to your office a special occasion. Ensure that they see evidence of success. Make it a practice to leave your office to greet them. As you return to your office, you will be able to introduce your star performers to the recruits. Those informal encounters will prove to be valuable impression builders.

Examine the prospects' experiences. Solicit assistance from everyone in your organization. Respect your associates' opinions.

Chapter Thoughts and Ideas
I'm Using or Planning to implement

√ Understand the Sales Force Model.

√ Search for talent.

√ Uncover the Thread of Discontent.

√ Maintain a reservoir of possibilities.

√ Look for a key producer.

√ Attract your kind of prospect.

√ Sharpen your script.

√ Develop your Sunday Punch.

Chapter 4 /*EDUCATING*

The finer Japanese restaurants typically put multicolored fish in small ponds. They are like giant goldfish and are beautiful to watch. These colorful fish are referred to as "Japanese carp," but are more properly known as koi.

> *Knowledge always shows up around success.*

The interesting thing about the koi is that if you keep it in a small fish bowl, it will grow to be two or three inches long, at most. However, when placed in a huge lake where it can really stretch out its territory, this unique fish will grow to more than three feet in length!

The same is true for our associates. If we put boundaries in their minds, or ours, as to what they can or should do, think and become, they might never reach their true potential. Their professional growth is determined by the size of their expectations and ours. The size of their world is directly defined by how they choose to look at it, and the expectations they perceive we have for them.

If we think *small*, they might never achieve the level of success they might otherwise achieve. If we discipline them to think *big*, like the koi in a huge lake, they can truly stretch their limits to levels of production they never thought possible.

The several strategies we examine in this chapter will help your producers "stretch in a much larger pond."

THE CHALLENGE OF EDUCATING TOMORROW'S TOP PRODUCERS IS BALANCING THE PAST WITH THE FUTURE. WE MUST HAVE THE COURAGE TO STOP TEACHING THOSE THINGS THAT NO LONGER WORK, AND THE CONFIDENCE TO RESIST TEACHING THOSE THINGS THAT DO NOT YET WORK.

Gary Schulte

EDUCATING IS LEADING

An important part of being an effective leader is being an effective educator. One time we heard Dr. Howard Hendricks say, "The key to becoming a good educator is to never stop studying. An educator is a student among students."

It's the ultimate goal of every teacher, coach and agency leader to have his students and followers take the lessons they've learned in the classroom and apply them in the marketplace. The goal of educating producers must be about more than just selling and generating commissions. It must also be about teaching those character traits that endure and cause your associates to succeed in life.

John Wooden was one of the greatest college basketball coaches of all time. He won ten NCAA titles in twelve years—seven titles in a row. Coach Wooden considered himself more than a coach; he measured himself as an educator. You want to be more than an agency leader. You, too, want to be an educator.

Those who played for Coach Wooden had this to say about their coach, the educator—the man.

In our opinion, there has never been another coach like John Wooden. Quiet as an April snow and square as a game of checkers. His loyalty was to one woman, one family, one school, one way.

He'd spend the first few minutes of the opening day of practice teaching his men how to put on a sock. "Wrinkles can lead to blisters," he'd warn.

His players would sneak looks at one another and sometimes roll their eyes. Eventually, they'd get it right. "Good," he'd say. "And now for the other foot." Of the 180 players who played for him, Wooden still knows the whereabouts of 172. Of course, it's not hard when most of them call, checking on his health, secretly hoping to hear some of his simple life's lessons so they could write them on the lunch bags of their kids—who probably roll their eyes.

"Discipline yourself, and others won't need to," Coach would say. "Never lie, never cheat, never steal," Coach would say. "Earn the right to be proud and confident."

If you played for him, you played by his rules. "Never score without acknowledging a teammate. One word of profanity and you're done for the day. Treat your opponent with respect."

Wooden believed in hopelessly out-of-date stuff that never did anything but win NCAA championships; there was no dribbling behind the back or through the legs. "There's no need to be fancy," he'd say.

No UCLA basketball number was retired under his watch. "What about the fellows who wore that number before? Didn't they contribute to the success of the team?"

"No long hair, no facial hair. They take too long to dry and you could catch cold leaving the gym," he'd say. That one drove his players bonkers. One time, All-American center Bill Walton showed up with a full beard. "It's my right," he insisted. Wooden asked Walton if he believed that strongly in his conviction—Walton said he did. "That's good, Bill," Coach said. "I admire people who have strong beliefs and stick by them. I really do. We're going to miss you!" Walton shaved right then and there. Now Walton calls once a week to tell Coach he loves him.

We've said many times that education takes place in the classroom. Training takes place in the field under live conditions. Selling techniques and selling skills are more caught than taught. That's why joint selling is so important.

However, you must also teach the philosophies. You teach the process. You teach the product. Classroom education is important because when the producer is in the field under live conditions, the philosophies, the systems, the knowledge learned in the classroom will surface in front of the prospect.

WATER THE PERFORMANCE YOU WANT TO GROW

Producers respond, learn and perform best when:

- They receive training in manageable amounts.

- They participate.

- There is repetition.

- They can see a "model."

- They can see favorable consequences and immediate results.

- They anticipate follow-up supervision to measure their results.

NOTHING HAPPENS WITHOUT ACTION

Everyone looks for that one key to success, the one secret that perhaps can make an immediate impact and will almost guarantee success. Well, there might not be a "silver bullet." As we have written in previous books, there are no secrets. There is one valuable truism, however, that cannot be denied.

Desire, motivation, goal setting, commitment, energy, product knowledge, persuasive skills, positive mental attitude, and preparation are useless – unless you put them into action. As the greatest teacher of all, the Carpenter from Galilee taught, "As ye sow, so shall ye reap."

Your sales success will be directly proportional to two things: the *quality* and *quantity* of your daily activities. How well you perform your activities does depend on everything from desire to attitude and may render them interdependent. Yet, one thing is clear—*nothing happens without action.*

TODAY'S TOP ACHIEVERS MUST BE EQUAL PARTS MARKETER,
SALESPERSON AND BUSINESSPERSON.

Steven Craig, CLU, ChFC

LEARNING TO PUT IN A GOOD DAY'S WORK

Educating producers must always begin with instructing them on how to put in a good day's work. Here are the three master keys you want to move front and center in your educating system.

Key No. 1. Do the right activities!

There are an infinite number of things that producers can get caught up doing each day, and it is easy for them to confuse movement with achievement. It's also easy for producers to feel like they've accomplished something each day because they were busy, but there is a big difference between busywork and effective work. Busyness and effectiveness are not always the same.

Make sure you "do the right activities" each day by identifying high payoff activities ahead of time and focusing on them. If you want to see how much room or improvement there might be in producers' daily schedules, have them keep a Day Diary. Your producers can then critique themselves. If one day isn't enough, continue the experiment until they are satisfied. Teach them to ask these questions.

"What percentage of my day is being focused on high payoff activities?"

"What percentage of my day could/should be focused on high payoff activities under ideal circumstances?"

One word of caution; don't beat them up too much, or expect perfection. Try to narrow the distance between where they currently stand and the less than 100% that is attainable.

Key No. 2. Do them right!

Assuming they are getting up to bat, the next thing is to make sure they are swinging properly. First, prepare your associates by building a foundation (if they haven't already started) then continue building that foundation. Encourage them to read books and listen to audio tapes that will inspire and help them. We have a library of books and audio tapes we consider second to none. The most important point, though, is that you find the tools you believe can help your associates sharpen their skills. You may even want to engage in role-play situations that are videotaped, or enlist the assistance of a mentor or coach.

Here's a metaphor that we found interesting.

Two jet pilots take off one night from Chicago's O'Hare Airport en route to Dallas/Fort Worth. One pilot has a detailed flight plan in hand, along with complete instrumentation, compass, maps, and a full tank of gas. The other pilot takes off with just wings and prayers with no way to determine if he is on track or how to monitor his progress. Which pilot has a greater chance of arriving at Dallas/Fort Worth?

That is, of course, a rhetorical question, but why? Both pilots had the same goal, and we can only assume the same level of desire and attitude. The difference was in their level of commitment and preparation, and, most importantly, the quality of their activities. The best way to confirm the quality of your activities and to answer the question, "Are you doing them right?" is to follow a strategy we came up with years ago—Measure and monitor what matters most. We will look at this vital strategy in depth in Chapter Eight.

Jet pilots would never take off before adequately preparing themselves and going over a detailed checklist. While en route to their destination, they will always measure and monitor their progress along the way. This is sage advice. This is not to say that wings and prayers aren't necessary, but why not stack the deck in your favor? Remember, measure and monitor what matters most.

Key No. 3. Do them often!

How much is enough? Only producers, with your input, can answer that question by reviewing their own goals as well as industry statistics. Producers might want to back into their activity goals by starting with their income goals. In order to earn Y dollars you'll need to make X presentations, or closes, etc. If they don't know the appropriate ratios for closing, appointments, contacts, etc. for the industry, use whatever statistics are available for your office or level of experience. Just remember what usually separates the victors from the vanquished—the willingness to do the things that the unsuccessful were not willing to do.

The universal truth of "sowing and reaping" applies as much to the farmer as it does to the fisherman, and is true in virtually every aspect of our life. And when it comes to sales, it's very easy to prove because there is a direct connection between the quality and quantity of sales activities and results. Improved activities and results are sure to follow!

EDUCATION IS A SOCIAL PROCESS.
EDUCATION IS GROWTH. EDUCATION IS NOT PREPARATION FOR LIFE
. . . EDUCATION IS LIFE ITSELF.

John Dewey

TEACH THE HABITS OF THE PROS

Albert E. N. Gray, a Prudential vice president, spoke at the 1940 NALU Convention at Philadelphia. His inspiring message is one of the most timeless pieces of sales literature.

What did he say that caused sales organizations of all kinds to have their salespeople read and listen to his speech now, more than 60 years later?

Mr. Gray's speech, like most all great speeches, had one dominant theme.

The secret of every man who has ever been successful lies in the fact that he formed the habit of doing things failures don't like to do.

Producers are creatures of habit just as machines are creatures of momentum. Educate your producers early about forming the habits the pros form.

√ Wake up employed.

√ Believe in total preparation.

√ Picture yourself as a problem solver.

√ Hone your probing and listening skills.

√ Give the buyer a reason to say, "Yes."

√ Sell what you own.

√ Narrow your focus.

√ Leverage your key skill.

√ Never waste time with those who waste your time.

√ Be determined to be the best in your field.

√ Become influential.

√ Take 100% responsibility for your results.

INTRODUCE ACTIVITY MANAGEMENT EARLY IN THE CAREER

The principle of activity management is so powerful that we have spent a great deal of time researching ways that can help you use it. If you're looking for productivity planners, the best tools we've been able to uncover are produced by Sales Activity Management, Inc., Oak Brook, Illinois. These are the finest books designed specifically for the insurance and financial services industry we have ever seen. They are available off-the-shelf or customized.

As the talented Mickey Straub, founder and president of SAM, Inc. says, "You can't measure what you can't see." One of the main tricks for having an effective coaching session is getting accurate information (performance data) recorded and collected. This is where these books come in. If you need assistance in training, consulting, or software that allows you to scoreboard results, they can help there, too! Sales Activity Management can be reached at 1-800-254-4SAM, or visit their Web site at www.sambook.com. Also, we like their slogan: "Don't leave success to chance."

The late Earl Nightingale, who was both a close friend and mentor, delivered an inspirational speech over the radio back in the 1960s entitled, "The Strangest Secret." It became the first inspirational audiocassette of its kind to achieve gold record status and remains today the only non-musical audiocassette with that distinction. Earl went on to become one of the most inspirational speakers of our time and a pioneer in the self-help industry. His message continues to inspire people with one simple, timeless message—"We become what we think about"—because it's as appropriate today as it was when it was first recorded. Its influence can also be seen throughout the planners we just mentioned.

Our associates, like each of us, do become what they think about. They will always move in the direction of their most dominant thoughts. If we can keep their goals before them, both activities and results, success will most certainly be theirs.

BUILD "REPLACEMENT VALUE"

One time in Fort Lauderdale over lunch, Earl Nightingale steered the discussion to this interesting concept of "replacement value."

"You fellas are engaged in very important work. You're providing a much needed service. Have you ever thought about it?" he asked. "You're coaching people on how they can improve their 'replacement values.' The more indispensable they become, the more difficult they are to replace, and the more money they earn."

That's an interesting thought, isn't it? It's one we've never forgotten.

The parking lot attendant can be replaced somewhat easily and quickly. That is not so for the heart surgeon, or for the effective, professional financial services producer. Income potential is determined by "replacement value." This helps us understand the wide-range of incomes among our associates. Those who are students of the business and who dedicate themselves to becoming more effective at what they do become more indispensable. And it's reflected in their paychecks.

THE WHOLE IDEA IS TO SOMEHOW GET AN EDGE. SOMETIMES IT TAKES JUST A LITTLE EXTRA SOMETHING TO GET THAT EDGE, BUT YOU HAVE TO HAVE IT.

Don Shula

Here are seven practical ways to increase the indispensability of those you coach.

1. Teach them to know and know they know.

    People today want informed advisors. Encourage associates to add credentials behind their names.

2. Make certain they focus on the Key Result Areas (KRAs).

    Never, ever let producers confuse activity with accomplishment. Keep them productive, not busy.

3. Start with high potential, motivated individuals.

    Earn the reputation for being a connoisseur of talent.

4. Coach them on listening actively to what is being communicated.

    They can learn to listen with three ears. Ear number one lets them hear what prospects say. Ear number two helps them hear what prospects don't say. Ear number three lets them hear what prospects would like to say but can't quite express.

5. Be an encourager.

    Your associates need booster shots regularly.

6. Lead them to become influential, to become known for what they know.

    Let their reputations precede them.

7. Encourage a high level of energy.

    Often overlooked, this one can make a big difference in what associates produce.

    Take inventory of where each stands. What is happening to their "replacement value"? Are they doing the things that will make them more indispensable? The answer to these questions is the answer to their current earning potential, and their future level of success.

> *Perhaps the most valuable result of all education is to make you do the thing you have to do, when it ought to be done, whether you like it or not. It is the first lesson that ought to be learned. And however early a man's training begins, it is probably the last lesson he learns thoroughly.*
>
> Thomas H. Huxley

STARTING WITH THE END IN MIND

Here's what the profile of a career associate should look like after completing five years in your educational system.

Selling

- Uses the complete sales cycle with confidence.

- A total needs producer who leans on process, not product.

- Is prepared through licensing and training to sell your product line.

- Is a client builder, i.e., a large percentage of new business results from repeat sales and client endorsements.

- Has consistent monthly production.

- Qualifies for company conferences and MDRT.

- Earns a gross income in excess of $100,000, adjusted for inflation, with 2002 as the base year.

- Maintains good persistency, i.e., National Quality Award qualifier with 90% persistency.

- Develops strategic alliances with accountants, lawyers, trust officers and other financial professionals.

- Has identified a specialty market niche, i.e., business planning, estate planning, family planning, charitable giving, etc.

- Adds a minimum of 75 new clients each year.

Managing the Business

- Accepts personal responsibility for effectiveness.

- Understands and uses the Professional Planning Process (referred to in Chapter One).

- Monitors, evaluates and rewards his own performance.

- Established organizational procedures to support the sales efforts.

- Developed expertise to maximize the use of facilities, resources, and support services.

- Accepted personal responsibility for Client Relationship Management.

- Has a growing net worth and income.

- Has a growing estate value in a life insurance program.

- Invests a percentage of income for personal development.

- Uses a personal accountant.

- Has an administrative assistant.

Marketing

- Has a functioning marketing assistant.

- Brand positioning and visibility in the community are improving.

- Contributes to the agency and community beyond production.

- Participates in joint selling.

- Sends a newsletter to the target market.

- Projects a distinct and unique image in the community.

- Has built an effective prospecting foundation.

Living in Balance

- Has a strong, healthy self-image.

- Maintains a self-development program.

- Manages finances properly.

- Career and personal goals are in harmony.

- Stays physically fit.

Neophyte Producers

Entry-level producers are receptive and eager to learn. Seldom will they have reservations relative to their need for continuous study. Throughout their induction period, as pointed out previously, you will have made it clear to them that they would secure the minimum amount of working knowledge, but that it would enable them to achieve a successful production level. It would also provide them with the foundation upon which to build further technical knowledge. Early field selling experience should arouse their interest to know more.

New producers should soon discover that their most successful associates are well-informed. However, many factors will combine to make it easy for new producers to break their study habits. Because of this, you'll want to consider setting up a basic educational series as soon as they have completed their pre-contract requirements. Exhibit 4.1, Educational Sessions, gives you an example of the kind of format many agency heads use.

These educational classes are conducted from 9:00 A.M. until noon weekly in your agency conference room. Individual assignments should be carefully coordinated with the 12 session topics. The completion of a variety of assignments, along with the lectures, makes possible specific opportunities for a sense of accomplishment and the building of competence.

IN A WORLD OF CHANGE, YOU ARE NEVER COMPLETELY EDUCATED. YOU HAVE TO KEEP EDUCATING YOURSELF INTO THE CHANGES. THE MORE YOU LEARN ABOUT YOUR PARTICULAR JOB, THE LESS FEAR THERE IS. FEAR IS BORN OUT OF IGNORANCE.

James A. Lovell

Exhibit 4.1 / *EDUCATIONAL SESSIONS*

EDUCATIONAL SESSIONS
9:00 A.M. – NOON

Session Topic	Date Completed
1. Orientation to agency, company and industry	_____
2. Concepts and product line	_____
3. Ethics and professionalism	_____
4. Variable products	_____
5. Underwriting	_____
6. Self-organization ideas	_____
7. Proposal design	_____
8. Computerized services	_____
9. Group insurance	_____
10. Money management	_____
11. Building clients and centers	_____
12. Professional competency	_____

THE GREAT AIM OF EDUCATION IS NOT KNOWLEDGE, BUT ACTION.

Herbert Spencer

Later in your new producers' "freshman year," we recommend you provide a "Big Picture School." This school, as the name implies, should give new producers a big picture of the several advanced markets. It's here that you leverage their contacts and link them to an experienced producer for joint selling.

You can introduce the new producers to educational materials—audiocassettes, video tapes and CDs—and perhaps a few carefully selected outside guest speakers. This school should be designed to run three full days. Again, its primary objective should be exposure of new producers to the higher income markets.

Experienced Associates

Obviously, there are limits imposed upon the variety of programs that can be offered and properly taught in an agency. Some companies maintain a staff of marketing specialists who can serve as instructors when needed. Others have wholesalers who can be of great help to you and your agency members. The characteristics of your agency and the structure of your company will determine the wisdom of including experienced producers in the educational programs we recommend.

Many agencies use Wednesday morning producer groups to discuss innovative concepts of the sales process or to further increase their experienced producers' technical skills. Experience has shown that producers who expand their professional knowledge and skills have a direct impact on the agency's growth, as well as their own bottom line.

It's usually the role of the agency's marketing manager to provide the materials that will afford producers the necessary educational foundation on which the training of skills and habits can be built.

The National Underwriter Company, for example, has numerous continuing education materials and learning options that cover a wide range of topics in the financial services business. A new course, such as *Introduction to Life Insurance*, could begin on the first Wednesday of each month. Usually conducted by an experienced producer, the course might include a presentation by one of the agency's associates who is successfully working in that particular market. This procedure is especially effective if the associate has increased his production or market awareness because of what was gained from taking the course. Once the educational objectives have been met, *Introduction to Variable Life Insurance* could be the next logical area for consideration. In this way, knowledge can be built upon the previous subject to form a more comprehensive and seamless understanding of the business.

Many of The National Underwriter Company courses are designed for advanced producers. However, the flow of the material is designed so even a selected, inexperienced associate will benefit from an early introduction to the subject matter. To aid in the learning process, each course contains a list of objectives, key terms, self-help quizzes and exam services that are provided either online or through print options.

Be reminded that a hands-on, practical application of the tools and techniques presented during the training session is the key to having successful learning experiences.

Tom Miller, a Top of the Table producer in Los Angeles and a long-time client of ours, founded The VisionLink Advisory Institute. This advisory group teaches the principles and techniques of comprehensive compensation consulting to successful financial services professionals. Growth-oriented businesses are constantly seeking effective ways to tie their compensation programs to the strategic goals of the organization.

Mid-sized, privately-owned companies have few places to turn for assistance in designing innovative and cost-effective incentive compensation programs for their key employees. Participants in the institute's training program acquire the skills and tools to market unique, comprehensive, fee-based services to their existing and new clients. It's well worth investigating at 949-794-1037.

WHEN ARISTOTLE WAS ASKED HOW MUCH EDUCATED MEN WERE SUPERIOR TO THOSE UNEDUCATED, HE SAID, "AS MUCH AS THE LIVING ARE TO THE DEAD."

Ray J. Groves, Chairman
Ernst & Whinney

Exhibit 4.2 / *DEVELOPMENT CHECKLIST*

PROFESSIONAL DEVELOPMENT CHECKLIST

- ↻ Do you have a marketing plan?
- ↻ Do you have written goals for business, family, income, physical, spiritual, self-development, etc.?
- ↻ Do you have a written business plan and have you carried out a SWOT (strengths, weaknesses, opportunities, threats) analysis in the past 12 months?
- ↻ Do you have monthly financial statements?
- ↻ Do you have a personal budget or do you spend less than you earn?
- ↻ Do you have a client database?
- ↻ Does each client have an annual review date and receive a call at least once a year?
- ↻ Have all clients been graded A, B, or C?
- ↻ Has a review been carried out in the last 12 months as to whether clients are still A, B, or C?
- ↻ Do you have, in writing, what a current A, B, or C prospective client looks like?
- ↻ Do you show your ideal prospect description to clients, centers of influence, and friends in order to obtain referrals?
- ↻ Are you an effective NetWeaver?
- ↻ Do you keep accurate records of calls, selling appointments, sales, etc.?
- ↻ Do you measure your results against your key ratios?
- ↻ Have you conducted an information and technology audit of your business within the last 12 months?
- ↻ Do you delegate all duties, except for planning, presenting, and calling key clients and new prospects?
- ↻ When you are working, do you use a daily "To-Do" list?
- ↻ Do you have written staff job descriptions?
- ↻ Do you have competent administrative and marketing assistants?
- ↻ Do you have action plans and checklists for frequent tasks programmed on your computer?
- ↻ Do you lead a balanced life?

Learning From Consultants

Among the highest paid consultants to the financial services industry are Melvin I. Weiss, Esq., Ron Parry, Esq., and Robert K. Scott, Esq. They were paid substantial fees because each had been the litigants in numerous class action suits against the life insurance industry during the last twenty years.

Inasmuch as they were paid those fees, we thought it might be smart to pay attention to their conclusions.

INSURERS SHOULD CHANGE ADVISORS' COMPENSATION BY ELIMINATING THE INCENTIVE TO CHURN AND SELL PRODUCTS BECAUSE OF THE FRONT-LOADING OF COMMISSIONS.

Melvin I. Weiss, Esq.

COMMISSION DISCLOSURE WOULD CAUSE POLICYHOLDERS TO BE MUCH SMARTER AND LOOK AT THE WHOLE TRANSACTION WITH A LITTLE MORE SCRUTINY.

Ron Parry, Esq.

ADMIT IN PRINT THAT THIS IS A RISKY INVESTMENT. INTEREST RATES ARE SUBJECT TO FLUCTUATION; AS WILDLY AS INTEREST RATES GO UP, THEY CAN GO DOWN. THAT KIND OF 'STEP BACK AND LOOK AT THE BIG PICTURE' WOULD BE A PRODUCTIVE THING TO DO.

Robert K. Scott, Esq.

Stepping back and looking at the big picture is exactly what producer education is all about today. It's exactly what our long-time colleague, Ben Baldwin, is trying to do in *The NEW Life Insurance Investment Advisor* (McGraw-Hill, Second Edition, 2001). The original *The Life Insurance Investment Advisor* (Probus, 1988) was printed in hardback and paperback and was used in The College for Financial Planning's masters program. Over 50,000 of those books have been sold and widely used in producer education classes taught by Ben Baldwin.

According to McGraw-Hill, those books have been, and continue to be, the most widely read books by both producers and consumers on financial services ever published. That demonstrates the need and desire on the part of both producers and consumers for education on how to properly use life insurance, in general, and variable universal life insurance, in particular. One reason Baldwin's book has been successful in helping producers use those products profitably for their clients' benefit is his no holds barred, tell it like it is—and tell it so consumers can understand it—manner.

Companies and organizations use this book to educate their producers on how to use variable universal life productively in their clients' estate and financial plans. Baldwin's aim is not only to grow sales as a result of increased producer confidence, but also to stress how disastrous it can be to both producers and insurance companies to have clients who are disappointed in their life insurance purchases.

We recommend you read and inwardly digest this thought-provoking piece of writing.

Holding Annual Conferences

An increasing number of agency heads are holding annual conferences for their associates. These can be the high point of agency calendars each year and we recommend them to you.

Select your conference sites carefully. In fact, we suggest that you "raise the sights" of your agency members by taking them places they probably would never go on their own. Plan these exciting experiences in quality settings; you'll find the additional cost a valuable investment.

The primary purpose of these uplifting, educational events is to improve selling results. The themes and programs should be focused on elevating the knowledge and selling techniques of those who have qualified to attend. In addition, the conference delegates and their spouses should derive the enjoyment, relaxation, and inspiration that comes from attending well-organized meetings in quality locations with excellent resources.

Always arrange for a formidable array of talent to appear on your programs. Conference mailers can be provided for each delegate well in advance of the meetings so they may be properly addressed for mailing to clients and prospects from the meeting sites. Business sessions can be held both mornings and afternoons. The evenings can then be free for recreational and entertainment activities. Conference group photographs should always be taken and a copy mailed to each delegate as a memento of the meetings.

Exhibit 4.3 / *CONFERENCE MAILER*

CONFERENCE MAILER

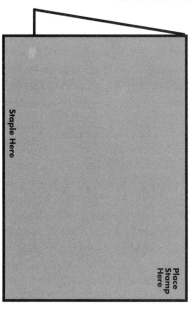

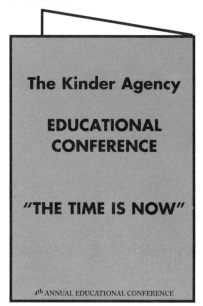

The Kinder Agency

EDUCATIONAL CONFERENCE

"THE TIME IS NOW"

4th ANNUAL EDUCATIONAL CONFERENCE

BACK   FRONT

4TH ANNUAL EDUCATIONAL CONFERENCE

The Kinder Agency
August 17-20 – Hershey Hotel
Hershey, Pennsylvania

Hershey, Pennsylvania has come to be known as "Chocolate Town, U.S.A." and offers the beautiful setting for this year's Educational Conference. Some 120 leading life insurance salesmen from Akron, Ohio and Detroit, Michigan are gathered here for the Kinder Agencies 4th Annual Conference.

A few highlights of our meeting appear on the opposite page. In these sessions, I seek to gain new knowledge about life insurance to better serve you, and to continue my personal growth as an individual. After I return from Hershey, I hope I will have an early opportunity to tell you about my experiences – and discuss some of the ideas that I think you will find of particular value.

PROGRAM HIGHLIGHTS

MANAGING YOUR LIFE
Widely known lecturer and life insurance consultant Charles "Tremendous" Jones will provide ways of better developing the person in salesperson.

THE CAREER SALESMAN
Nationally leading Trainees will discuss attitudes, skills and beliefs that have helped them develop into professionally competent financial advisors early in their careers.

BUSINESS USES OF LIFE INSURANCE
Panel discussions by MDRT Producers will inform how life insurance serves the business and corporate needs in such areas as . . . Group Insurance, Keogh Retirement Plans, Succession Planning and Pension Programs.

EFFICIENT CLIENT SERVICE
In addition, several outstanding, experienced practitioners will lend stature to the conference by sharing their experiences in life and in life insurance.

INSIDE

Plan carefully for each conference to be an exciting experience for all who attend. This will make your associates look forward to future conferences and improved selling results for the privilege of attending. You'll find it takes meticulous advance planning and imagination to manage these yearly conference events—but it pays big dividends!

THE MEDIOCRE MANAGER TELLS. THE GOOD MANAGER EXPLAINS. THE SUPERIOR MANAGER DEMONSTRATES. THE GREAT MANAGER INSPIRES.

William Arthur Ward

You Can't Shortcut Time

Driving through mountainous West Virginia en route to an agency conference we had at The Greenbrier, we saw this sign: "Antiques made here . . . while you wait." It seems to us that this announcement expresses pretty well the temper of our time.

Certainly we do not discount the value of things that have been accomplished through such an accelerated process. However, we feel the very nature of the financial services business, and the kind of clientele who must be served, preclude producers from becoming instant, permanent successes. Even so, we see young trainees entering the business every day convinced that they can skip the basics and become advanced underwriting successes almost overnight.

We recommend you tell producers joining your agency that it will take them four years to complete their apprenticeship, that is, learn the basic, essential elements financial services producers must accomplish, and get their feet firmly planted in the business. Tell them it will probably take another five years or so of building relationships with clients and completing their credential work to become finished, permanently established professionals.

Help each individual recognize that the usual producer achieves unusual early success only by seeing a high quantity of people, selling a large number of cases, and selling at least 50% of the time on a joint basis.

YOU HAVE AN OBLIGATION TO YOUR CLIENTS TO IMPROVE YOUR KNOWLEDGE AND SKILLS CONTINUALLY.

Exhibit 4.4 / *EVALUATION*

PRODUCER COACHING EVALUATION

Inventory of selling skills and determination of performance/potential gap in associates' role. On your personal visit, rate your associates as accurately as possible. You may wish to have the producers complete this exercise in advance. Later, you can compare their scores with yours. If mentors are involved, you'll find their evaluation to be of value.

5-Superior, 4-Good, 3-Fair, 2-Needs Attention, 1-Defective

1.	Displays a professional presence.	1 2 3 4 5
2.	Sets reachable goals with deadlines.	1 2 3 4 5
3.	Plans priorities the previous day.	1 2 3 4 5
4.	Is becoming credentialed.	1 2 3 4 5
5.	Has a strong "commercial."	1 2 3 4 5
6.	Effective at probing.	1 2 3 4 5
7.	Sales presentation effectiveness.	1 2 3 4 5
8.	Confidence in closing.	1 2 3 4 5
9.	Monitors Market Effectiveness Activity (MEA) weekly. (See Chapter 8.)	1 2 3 4 5
10.	Leverages key skills through joint selling.	1 2 3 4 5
11.	Gains endorsements.	1 2 3 4 5
12.	Develops administrative assistant.	1 2 3 4 5
13.	Develops marketing assistant.	1 2 3 4 5
14.	Sets up mentor alliances.	1 2 3 4 5
15.	Student of the business.	1 2 3 4 5
16.	Maintains physical fitness.	1 2 3 4 5
17.	Manages financial affairs.	1 2 3 4 5
18.	Client Relationship Management (CRM)	1 2 3 4 5
19.	Becomes influential.	1 2 3 4 5
20.	Takes 100% responsibility for results.	1 2 3 4 5

TOTAL POSSIBLE SCORE   **100**

PRODUCER'S SCORE   _____

PERFORMANCE/POTENTIAL GAP   _____

VAL'S VIEWS ON EDUCATING

Bob Love, the Chicago Bull All-Pro, spoke to the MDRT conference in Toronto, Canada, a few years back. He talked about the old-fashion, simple education he received from his grandmother. At a young age, she taught Bob to remember the five rules of life.

1. When the ball comes your way, catch it.

2. If you drop it, pick it up.

3. If you lose, practice harder.

4. When you win, be a good sport.

5. When the coach speaks, listen!

Educating today's producers needs to be kept just that simple. Never let producers get ahead of their learning. They must put knowledge into action for it to be profitable.

As you learned in this chapter, you must respect individual differences. To be effective, your educational system must be flexible to allow for these differences.

Modern technology makes it possible to develop a superbly informed sales team in a short period of time.

CHAPTER THOUGHTS AND IDEAS
I'M USING OR PLANNING TO IMPLEMENT

√ Environment should lead to "stretching."

√ Expect things to be done right.

√ Build "replacement value."

√ Learn from mentors.

√ Teach producers to put in a good day's work.

√ Don't leave success to chance.

√ Define producer profile when educated.

√ Build a sales library.

Chapter 5 /*TRAINING*

Warren Buffett, the well-known investor, has three qualifications for judging his investment opportunities. He never invests with anyone he doesn't trust, respect, and like—regardless of how good the numbers look.

> *Keep it simple.*
> *Say it often.*
> *Make it burn.*

How many times have you heard it said, "When all things are equal, prospects have a strong tendency to buy from individuals they trust and like best"? This is easily understood. The interesting point is this: In this age of relationship marketing, should things not be equal, prospects show the same tendency. Like Mr. Buffett, they still tend to buy from salespeople they trust, respect, and like.

RESPECT RELATIONSHIP SELLING

As we move through the 21st Century, the competitive edge will come to those producers who are effective relationship builders. Relationship building is a skill you can teach and develop.

It's important, then, to establish an atmosphere where selling is viewed by your associates as a problem solving situation. When prospects perceive producers to be advisors—problem solvers—they stop thinking they are there to sell them something. To do this, emphasis must be placed on the kind of services being offered. First impressions form quickly and change slowly. It's to the producer's advantage to establish a relationship as a friend and a problem solver.

Relationships form the foundation; they are the all-important base upon which ultimate sales are built.

A sure way to improve the odds in selling is for producers to cultivate the art of getting people to like them. Here are the strongest ways for producers to accomplish that.

1. Make favorable impressions. There is no second chance to make a good first impression. The prospect focuses on the producer before he focuses on what the producer is selling.

2. Remember names.

3. Discover common interests.

4. Be a "compliment carrier." Never miss the opportunity to compliment the prospect's actions and accomplishments. Use quoted compliments.

5. Cultivate the quality of being interesting.

6. Offer encouragement regularly.

7. Practice liking people until it becomes second nature.

As you will see, the first few minutes of an interview are crucial to success. The initial impression made on the prospect has a great impact on the remainder of the interview.

DELIVER WHAT COUNTS MOST

What counts most in building a high performing sales force? Consider the following.

1. As we said earlier, recruit individuals who have demonstrated a high need for achievement. These kinds of producers thrive in a system in which the effort they put forth relates to measurable results.

2. Demonstrate the "how to" of putting in a good day's work. Many give our business a timid, tentative try and leave unsuccessful. Oftentimes, they did not "catch on" quickly enough to the "how to" of being a productive entrepreneur.

3. Communicate a clear methodology for selling. It always ensures a relationship between effort expended and actual results. A defined selling system makes it easier to develop measurement procedures.

4. Supervise effectively. In recruiting, educating, and training producers, managers invest a fair amount of time and money, a good deal of which is often wasted due to ineffective supervision.

5. Earn respect. This requires meeting certain expectations of associates. The modern day producer expects you to:

    • Conceive the strategy for marketing and selling.

    • Be predictable, dependable, and available.

    • Be interested in them as individuals.

    • Believe in them.

- Tell them how they're getting along.

- Tell them in advance about changes that will affect them.

- Make the most of their potential.

BUILD A WINNING ATTITUDE

There is no known law by which your associates can achieve selling success without first expecting it. Sell this philosophy first. Superior selling results are produced by the perpetual expectation of attaining them. Despite natural talents, thorough training and education, individuals seldom rise higher than their expectations. "They can who think they can; they can't who think they can't," is an inflexible, indisputable law of selling and, actually, of life itself.

Self-confidence is the one quality a producer can *never* afford to surrender. Your associates must have the belief they can get the job done. In our business, enthusiasm can turn a one-talent producer into a multimillion dollar producer. Without that enthused, confident attitude, however, a ten-talent producer remains mediocre.

The individual who is self-reliant, positive, optimistic, and assured charges the atmosphere with electricity. This kind of producer has an aura of command that helps convince prospects he or she can deliver. Set associates' minds so resolutely, so definitely, and with such determined expectations toward MDRT production levels that nothing will sway their winning attitude.

Remember, it all starts with attitude!

> *THE GREATEST DISCOVERY OF MY GENERATION IS THAT A HUMAN BEING CAN ALTER HIS LIFE BY ALTERING HIS ATTITUDE.*
>
> *William James*

DECIDE UPON A PROCESS

We asked Guy Hatcher, a perennial Top of the Table producer, this question: "If you were charged with the responsibility of teaching producers how to sell today, what would be the main thing you'd stress?" Guy said, "That's an easy one. I'd get them sold, right from the start, that the main thing in selling is the process. The process is far more important to stress than product."

Sell the process, not the product. That makes a big difference to the prospect, doesn't it?

The sales process developed in this training system helps associates build relationships with their prospects. It causes prospects to participate in the buying process by making a series of decisions in favor of the action being proposed.

Whether producers are selling the planning service, life, long-term care, disability, health, annuities or investments, there are six sales that must be made in developing a satisfied client from the name of a person. Regardless of the market, the sales you must demonstrate and coach are those shown in Exhibit 5.1, The Client Building Process.

Sale Number 1 – Set an Appointment

Sale Number 2 – Develop Need Recognition

Sale Number 3 – Gain Agreement to Take a Serious Look

Sale Number 4 – Secure the App and Check

Sale Number 5 – Establish a Client

Sale Number 6 – Get Endorsements

Mastery of these six steps assures producers of having an effective selling strategy that can be adapted to any service or product your organization sells.

Remember, there are very few professional buyers of insurance. For the most part, prospects must be educated and "assisted" to make the buying decision. *KinderTrac,** the generic label we give to the selling process, helps producers accomplish this.

Exhibit 5.1 — *CLIENT BUILDING PROCESS*

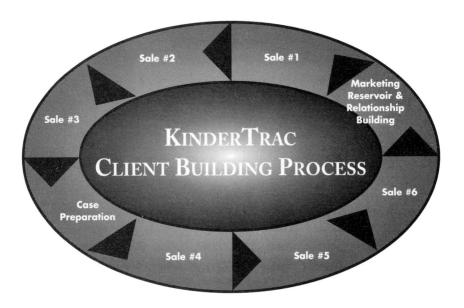

RECOGNIZE THE SALE BEFORE THE SALE

The sale before the sale is quite likely the single most important one your associates will ever make. It's staying sold on their ability, their future in selling and the absolute need to master a sales process.

The six sales are all made with words—carefully selected words—words that have motivational strength. Let's look at these words and how you persuade others to believe in them.

*If you would like additional information on customizing this process, call our office at 972-380-0747.

As shown in Exhibit 5.2, *KinderTrac* is a complete selling track that producers can use with confidence throughout their career. Study the teaching tool shown in Exhibit 5.3. You'll find it very useful in building producers' confidence in the selling strategy.

The ideas and words presented in this sales track have been proven over time. They have been used to develop some of the most successful professionals in the financial services business today. Several companies that use this method refer to it as their national sales strategy.

EARN A REPUTATION FOR TRAINING YOUR PEOPLE WELL AND YOU'LL NOT ONLY MAKE MORE PRODUCTIVE USE OF YOUR TIME, BUT YOU'LL END UP WITH THE MOST PRODUCTIVE PEOPLE. THE STAR PERFORMERS WILL GRAVITATE TOWARDS YOU.

Mark McCormack

Build Professional Relationships

This organized procedure builds a strong relationship between producer and prospect. Moreover, it enables producers to present ideas logically and to concentrate their attention on the prospect and what he or she has to say.

Again, to be of lasting value, the details of *KinderTrac* must be mastered, perfected, and naturalized. The words and the expressions must be practiced until they become a natural part of your selling style.

Whether it's a "demand" product sale or a multiple-interview sale, *KinderTrac* develops a sense of helpful, unhurried service to the prospect in providing for his basic needs. It recognizes a principle established by a poll taken a few years ago which indicated the best competitive tool is the "personal relationship between the prospect and the producer." The personal relationship in selling is all-important. Consequently, the key to your associates' successes is recognizing that most of their time must be spent marketing and arranging interviews so that they present recommendations and proposals to people who can and will buy their services and products.

Exhibit 5.2 / *THE KINDER TRAC*

THE KINDERTRAC

Marketing	Build Your Prospecting Reservoir of Warm Prospects	Organize the names of Qualified Leads where you have relationships or endorsements.
Sale No. 1	Set an Appointment	Make contact to establish the time and location for your initial interview.
Sale No. 2	Develop Need Recognition	Present trust-building "commercial." Use point-of-sale visual to uncover facts and feelings. Decide upon the need, establish money commitment, and decide upon decision-maker.
Sale No. 3	Gain Agreement to Take a Serious Look	Explain your unique service.
Case Preparation	Prepare Recommendation	Send a follow-up letter to the prospect. Study and analyze information. Develop the personalized recommendation.
Sale No. 4	Secure App and Check	Review the previous interview. Review your Agenda page. Present your customized recommendation and close the business.
Sale No. 5	Establish a Client	Make the sale solid.
Sale No. 6	Get Endorsements	Make the sale productive.

Exhibit 5.3 / *POCKET PROMPTER*

POCKET PROMPTER

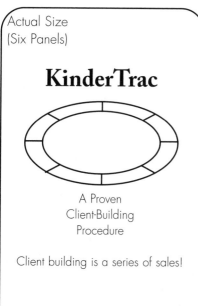

Actual Size
(Six Panels)

KinderTrac

A Proven
Client-Building
Procedure

Client building is a series of sales!

*Ad-libs are for Amateurs.
The Pros master and perfect the words
and expressions they use.*

You'll find it helpful to develop a pocket prompter to assist associates in learning their lines.

This can be referenced during "down-time" to transfer the words and expressions that make up the selling strategy. It has six panels – one for each of the six sales that comprise the client-building procedure.

You'll discover this to be a most effective teaching tool.

Becoming a successful professional, as a rule, is not a short-haul proposition. Building a career as a professional in selling is a long-term process. As time goes on, your producers are constantly capitalizing on their past efforts, improved skills and enlarged clientele.

Honest, intelligent effort is always rewarded. The "intelligent effort" requires the mastery of a proven, professional procedure. That's what this training system is all about.

GREAT LEADERS ARE ALMOST ALWAYS GREAT SIMPLIFIERS WHO CAN CUT THROUGH RESISTANCE, DEBATE AND DOUBT, TO OFFER A SOLUTION EVERYBODY CAN UNDERSTAND.

Colin Powell

SALE NUMBER 1 – SET AN APPOINTMENT

Set an appointment refers to pre-approach calls that are made by telephone or in person to arrange initial interviews. Keep in mind, the purpose of the call is to sell an interview, not to sell a specific recommendation.

The most important idea to teach about Sale No. 1 is that if enough interviews are arranged, proposals will be shown and the necessary number of sales will be made.

The number of pre-approach calls made each week is very important. In fact, the financial services business is one which stresses the law of averages. This principle is used in determining appropriate premiums for policies. This same law of averages applies to producers as well. Honest, intelligent effort is always rewarded. *Pre-approach calls initiate nearly all the good that happens in selling.* Believe in the law of averages and sell that belief to your associates. They will reap the benefits in the consistent sales results which always follow.

Use a Standard Pre-Approach

The words used must be practiced and rehearsed until saying them becomes as natural as breathing. Producers cannot over-rehearse. Knowing exactly what they are going to say will give them confidence and allow them to express themselves effectively.

"Hello, Bill? [Response.] This is Tony Lyman with (company). I'm calling at the suggestion of Bob Allen. Is this a convenient time for you to talk?"[Response.]

"Bob asked me to contact you and I promised him I would. Bill, (company) has designed an unusual and unique service to help our clients better plan and organize their insurance and investments.

"Bob was impressed with the kind of work we did for him and encouraged me to call and find a time when I could get on your calendar and show you what we do. In your line of business, Bill, when would be the best time to see you? Are mornings or afternoons better for you?"

Teach the newer producer not to be rushed in getting off the phone. Have them linger a bit by repeating the time of the appointment, the exact location, directions, etc. They will improve their "kept" ratios by doing that. Another strategy for improving kept appointments is to make this suggestion:

"Bill, let me suggest setting our appointment between 2:00 P.M. and 2:20 P.M. I'm not quite sure how to gauge the traffic and I do not want to be late for our appointment."

This statement adds formality to their setting of appointments. The aim is to set appointments that will be kept!

Handling Early Resistance

Your producer's attitude toward the response given by a prospect is a most important factor in his or her success in securing appointments. It must always be, "I will maintain poise. I will refuse to argue. I will ignore any early resistance." Explain that what a prospect says during the early minutes of the initial contact is seldom an accurate measure of his or her rating as a prospect.

Here's a three-step method you can teach your producers for handling early resistance.

1. "That's all right, Bill. I can understand why you might say that. Let me take that into consideration when we get together."

2. If the same objection persists, move ahead by saying, "May I ask, why do you feel that way?" Draw out the prospect with a question.

3. If the prospect still objects, move forward by saying, "I'm respectful of what you're saying and your time constraints. However, Bill, based upon what Bob has told me about you, I'm confident you'll find our service to be of interest. I'd appreciate your courtesy in giving me 20 minutes to meet with you and show you the kind of work I do."

The tone of voice should always communicate a positive expectancy. Continue to strengthen with your associates how important it is to develop solid endorsements.

Of course, the important factor in selling is intelligent activity. Intelligent activity is the by-product of having a marketing strategy that develops endorsements—lots of them! Demonstrate and coach the three-step, "bounce-back" strategy for coping with resistance. Your reward will be improved ratios and lots of kept appointments by your associates.

SALE NUMBER 2 – DEVELOPING NEED RECOGNITION

The two-fold objective of the first face-to-face interview is to make a favorable impression and to determine whether this individual has the qualities necessary to make him a prospect. The producer is there to impress, build confidence and qualify or disqualify. When the producer determines that he has a qualified prospect, he then gathers full and complete information with the promise it will be studied carefully and a recommendation (proposal) will be prepared for the prospect's consideration.

This opening interview must arouse the prospect's interest and turn needs into wants. If conducted properly, it will also develop important information that allows your producer to answer the key qualifying questions:

Is there a relationship of trust being built? Is there recognition of a need? Is the prospect insurable? Is there a "hot button?" Can he make the sale?

Asking probing, interest-arousing questions assists the prospect in making certain decisions in the producer's favor, one decision at a time. A most important decision has already been made—the decision to give the producer an appointment. The prospect has made that decision; the key sale in the series of sales has been made.

The approach is the name we've given to the first stage of the probing process. Presumably, it's the first actual meeting between your producer and the prospect to discuss financial services and products. The approach has two chief objectives:

1. To make a favorable impression upon the prospect and secure favorable attention.

2. To gain positive interest in responding to the fact-finding, picture-taking questions and in the services the producer can provide.

During the approach, an atmosphere of trust must be built so the prospect will have an open mind to the producer's ideas and thinking. The prospect must be motivated to listen and respond to the fact-finding questions. The prospect must be conditioned to logically consider the producer's services, recommendations and products.

Remember Impression Builders

Here are some practical ways in which your associates can be taught to make favorable first impressions.

- Be punctual.

- Believe you are worth meeting, knowing, and listening to, and you will be.

- Display a clean and businesslike appearance.

- Project a pleasant disposition.

- Remember names and use them.

- Have a confident, enthusiastic manner.

- Never miss the opportunity to pay a compliment.

- Be well-mannered and courteous.

- Develop an insight into your prospect's known and probable needs.

- Be comfortable to deal with so there is no strain in doing business with you.

Future presenting and selling interviews will generate results in direct proportion to the effectiveness of the all-important first contact call. Train your associates to make their "commercial" and approach count.

Remember, there's no second chance for your associates to make good first impressions.

PEOPLE CANCEL PURCHASES BUT THEY DON'T CANCEL THEIR GOALS.

R. Dale Preater, CFP

Approach Language

After passing the pleasantries, the approach begins using this outline.

"As you know, Bill, I'm in the financial services business here in (city) with (company)." (The influence of an endorsement is used here, when appropriate.)

"The Commercial"

"May I take just a few minutes to give you my "commercial"? (State how and why you joined your company.) You may be wondering why I left the (previous) business and how I decided to join (company)."

Key Phrases

- I liked the job I had . . .

- I believe they liked me . . .

- I had several promotions . . .

- My first contact with (company) came. . .

- I liked what he (or she) had to say. . .

- I had a number of interviews. . .

- I took a battery of tests. . .

"This had all the earmarks of being a career opportunity. Bill, that's why I'm committed to make it."

Sell the Company

"(Company) has been in business since (year). We have pioneered many developments in the insurance industry (elaborate). Our office here in (city) has served this area (give details)."

Review and study carefully Exhibit 5.4, before teaching associates to script their opening "ice-breaking" remarks.

RESEARCH SHOWS THE ONLY FACTOR THAT CORRELATES CONSISTENTLY WITH A SUCCESSFUL SALES EXPERIENCE IS THE ONE THAT TRADITIONALLY TENDS TO GET OVERLOOKED—THE AMOUNT OF TIME SPENT ASKING QUESTIONS, GETTING THE PROSPECT TALKING, AND LISTENING.

Dan Richards

Exhibit 5.4 / *COMMERCIAL*

COMMERCIAL

How producers communicate the kind of business they're in and what they believe, determines the level of success they will achieve. The Commercial positions the salesperson for success. Somewhere along the way the prospect must make a decision to listen, consider and act on recommendations. A well-expressed Commercial helps this along.

SCRIPT

(First name), may I take just a few minutes to give you my commercial? (Briefly describe your biographical sketch, your successes and how you came to consider the opportunity in the financial services industry. Be sure to indicate *"the more I listened and explored, the more certain I became that this had all the earmarks of a career opportunity – and that's exactly what I intend to make it!"*

Just out of curiosity, (name), how many accountants and attorneys do you have? How many dentists and family doctors do you have? (Normally one of each.) *Our clients discover it makes good sense to have just one professional for their insurance and financial matters. The area where you most likely spend more dollars than all the others combined is one where we specialize.*

I'd like to apply for the job of keeping you current and informed. The chances are you haven't purchased all of the life insurance you'll ever buy, or made all of the deposits you'll ever make on your pension plan.

If I do the professional kind of job I intend to do, when you think of these future purchases, you'll think of me.

May I ask, with what companies do you own your life insurance?

TRANSITION

At the end of the approach, your producer asks probing questions to develop the prospect's recognition of a need.

1. "May I ask with what companies do you own life insurance?"

2. "Why did you buy that kind of insurance?"

3. "How do you have the important settlement options arranged?"

4. "What formula did you use to arrive at the amount of life insurance you own and the annual payment you make into your pension plan?"

5. "May I ask, if you were to change, modify, or add to your program today, what would that be?"

At the start, a manager or an experienced producer should accompany a new associate. In those instances, this transition should be made.

"I have asked (name) to come with me. (Name of manager), by the way, is an experienced manager. If it's all right with you, I'm going to 'toss the ball' to (name), and I'm going to sit back and listen and learn, too."

Obviously, this approach is designed for someone who is relatively new to the business. As associates progress and see more prospects on an endorsement basis, they will no longer find it necessary to explain why they entered the business. At that point, they will change their approach to keep their prospects or clients current as to their standing in the insurance business, i.e., designations, MDRT qualifications, and NQA status.

Sample Approach for an Experienced Producer

"Before I tell you about the kind of work we do at (company), you may be interested in some important information about my insurance career. I'm a member of the Million Dollar Round Table and have qualified for the National Quality Award. That means at least ninety percent of all my clients have continued doing business with me. I have my CLU designation which stands for Chartered Life Underwriter, similar to a CPA in the accounting field. (Include comments on other credentials, college degrees, club and civic activities, if appropriate.) I feel that I am well-qualified to be judged a professional at what I do."

"(Company) has been in business since (year). Our office here in (city) has served this area with more than (amount) clients."

"My purpose in seeing you today is to explain an unusual service designed by (company) that helps our clients to better plan and organize their insurance and investments."

"We believe at (company) that we have one of the finest insurance and investment services available."

Recognize Advantages of Probing

The best way to get prospects to think and recognize a need is to ask questions, relevant questions. In many cases, it's the only way to persuade the prospect to think.

Again, prospects seldom buy anything unless they feel it's in their best interest and benefit to do so. One of the surest ways to increase selling effectiveness is to learn more about what prospects want. Strategic, probing questions develop that kind of information.

There are a number of details producers gain by developing a probing attitude. It helps:

- Prospects discover a need.

- Avoid talking too much.

- Avoid arguments.

- Crystallize a prospect's thinking in that the idea becomes his or hers.

- Give prospects a feeling of importance when respect is shown for their opinions. Then, prospects are more likely to respect and act upon opinions and recommendations.

Study carefully Exhibit 5.5, "Developing Need Recognition". You'll pick up some questions to share with your associates.

> YOU CAN'T CHANGE ANYTHING BY FIGHTING OR RESISTING IT.
> YOU CHANGE SOMETHING BY MAKING IT OBSOLETE THROUGH
> SUPERIOR METHODS.
>
> *Buckminster Fuller*

Exhibit 5.5 / *DEVELOPING RECOGNITION*

DEVELOPING NEED RECOGNITION

To help prospects *recognize* and discover what he or she *wants* to do to satisfy a need, these probing questions can be asked:

- **OWNERSHIP**
  May I ask, (name), in addition to your group insurance and any term insurance you have, with what companies do you own your personal, permanent life insurance? Why did you buy that kind?

- **RETIREMENT PLANNING**
  Are you satisfied with your preparation for retirement?

- **MORTGAGE ACCELERATION**
  What do you want done with your home mortgage if something should happen to you?

- **SURVIVOR BENEFITS**
  How much income do you want to provide for your family in the event you die prematurely?

- **FAMILY COVERAGES**
  How do you feel about purchasing life insurance to cover the lives of your children?

- **EDUCATIONAL FUNDING**
  What type of education do you plan for your children?

- **ESTATE PLANNING**
  Who will benefit the most when your estate is settled, your family or the federal government? What planning have you done to minimize estate taxes?

- **LONG-TERM CARE**
  Have you or someone you know had any experience with long-term care? Tell me about it. How do you feel about your children or your spouse taking care of you if you become ill?

- **DISABILITY INCOME**
  What would your income be if you were sick or hurt and couldn't work?

- **ANNUITY INCOME**
  Are you aware of the interest rates being paid on annuities and the tax advantages of annuity income?

- **OTHER INTERESTS**
  If you could change, modify or add to your program in some way today, what would that be? How do you have the settlement options arranged on your contracts? What kind of a formula have you been using to decide upon the dollar amount you'll invest in life insurance, retirement and investments?

Uncover Feelings

Creative selling depends upon uncovering prospects' feelings about certain needs. Producers find it helpful to involve prospects in completing a "feeling-finding" exercise like the one shown in Exhibit 5.6, "How Do You Feel?"

Exhibit 5.6 / *HOW DO YOU FEEL?*

How Do You Feel?

Please check the box that most closely describes your feelings about each statement. (A) Essential; (B) Important; (C) Unimportant.

	(A)	(B)	(C)
1. Professional assistance in planning my insurance and financial matters is	❑	❑	❑
2. Owning adequate life insurance on my life is	❑	❑	❑
3. My spouse believes an adequate insurance program is	❑	❑	❑
4. Arranging to maintain my family at their standard of living after my death is	❑	❑	❑
5. Paying off the mortgage on my home in the event of my death is	❑	❑	❑
6. Planning retirement income is	❑	❑	❑
7. Having income to replace my earnings if I become sick or hurt is	❑	❑	❑
8. Financial planning, including estate planning, asset protection and long-term care, are	❑	❑	❑
9. Wills and will planning are	❑	❑	❑
10. A good understanding of my needs, objectives, and priorities by my insurance advisor is	❑	❑	❑

Exhibit 5.7 / *INVESTMENT QUESTIONS*

PROVEN, PROBING INVESTMENT QUESTIONS

1. What has been your most successful investment? How much have you invested and kept invested in the last five years?

2. How do you reduce your taxes?

3. What are you doing to maximize return on your bank savings or money-market accounts?

4. What are you doing to generate meaningful capital gains?

5. What are you doing to provide for your retirement?

6. What services of your investment advisor have you found the most useful?

7. What investments are you concerned about?

8. How could your investment advisor improve his or her service?

9. What kind of overall annual return on your investment do you feel is realistic?

10. What are your most important investment priorities at the present time?

Exhibit 5.8 / *BUSINESS QUESTIONS*

KEY QUESTIONS FOR BUSINESS OWNERS

1. What is your exit strategy from your business either during your lifetime or when you die?

2. What plans have you made regarding your retirement?

3. What are your plans for your business?

4. What plans have been put in writing regarding the transfer of ownership, control, and management of your business?

5. Who will run your business when you are no longer involved?

6. Who runs the business now when you are on vacation or away from your business?

7. If you had died last week, who would be running your business now?

8. What plans have been made to ensure that your spouse has an adequate income in the event of your death?

9. To what extent will your children be involved in your business?

10. What steps have you taken to ensure that your children are treated fairly in terms of dividing your estate?

11. What have you done to ensure that your business can repay loans and have adequate working capital in the event of your death?

12. How will the estate taxes and related costs be paid without forcing the sale of valuable growth or income-producing assets?

13. How much do you think your business is worth? How did you arrive at that number? What impact would your death have on the value?

14. What special compensation plans are you using to recruit, retain and reward key people?

15. What challenges does your business face?

16. Are there any other special concerns that you have regarding your business?

Obtain a Money Commitment

To solidify your producer's position, a money commitment or dollar range must be decided upon. We suggest this statement when asking for the commitment.

"If you feel the recommendations we develop for you are logical in meeting your needs, what monthly dollar amount can you set aside to accomplish your objectives?"

When the prospect makes a money commitment, your producer will have gained a definite and positive sign of favorable action. That is why obtaining the money commitment is one of the most important elements of the entire selling process.

Many times, the prospect is slow to commit and may say he has not given the amount any thought. Teach the producer to respond by asking, "Could you set aside $2,500 a month?" The prospect's answer may be, "No." "Could you be comfortable with investing $50 a month?" The prospect's quick reply is, "Yes." The producer's response can then be, "Somewhere between $50 and $2,500 is a monthly amount with which you can be comfortable. Why don't we work with $250 a month?"

How does the producer arrive at a $250 monthly amount? By paying attention and by making a studied judgment of the prospect's investing potential.

Build a Competitive Edge

The business climate in which the producer sells financial services and products today requires becoming more than a "policy peddler." We strongly endorse multiple-interview selling.

As producers gain experience and build a solid clientele base, they may sell an occasional product on a single interview. However, even the most seasoned professional sells most of his services and cases using a multiple-interview strategy.

Selling in an unhurried, professional manner develops confidence, stronger presentations, bigger sales, and improved persistency.

All of that spells a competitive edge!

Build Relationships

If we could sum up all the cardinal rules of selling financial services and products into a single expression, it would be this: build relationships. Every bit of research indicates the buyer buys what we sell because of a relationship with a professional.

Little can be accomplished in a selling situation until a relationship is established. The problem, though, is that most every sales encounter begins with some tension. No matter how effectively a producer tries to convince a prospect that the purpose of his contact is not necessarily to sell products, the chances are the prospect's mind is still occupied with being "sold."

In building rapport, the goal is to build the "you attitude." Producers must find a way of sincerely expressing to prospects that they are important individuals in whom they are interested. Throughout the interview producers should express ideas from the prospect's viewpoint. This is the "you attitude." It must become an important and natural part of the producer's selling style.

Remember, when producers make friends, they make sales!

Sale Number 3 – Gaining Agreement to Take a Serious Look

The producer moves forward and makes Sale No. 3 if, and only if:

- A relationship of trust has been established.

- A need has been recognized by the prospect.

- A dollar commitment has been decided upon.

Assuming these conditions exist, we recommend the following script for the producer.

"Rather than come to you today and tell you that you need this or that, quote you some prices, and sell you something on that basis, we at (company), in situations like yours, do the opposite."

"We ask, 'Have you made provisions in your life insurance and investment programs to maximize your monthly pension income when you retire? At your death, what sort of income do you want guaranteed for your family? How do you want to handle the mortgage on your home if something happens to you? If you become sick or are injured and can't work, what sort of income will you need? What kind of education do you want for your son and daughter? What asset protection do you feel you should own in the form of long-term care?'"

"We take your responses to these and similar questions back to our office. There we study, analyze, and review your situation. With the assistance of our technical resources, we individualize your case and personalize a recommendation for your consideration. In a few days, we will present our recommendations to you. If you like it, we'd like to have you as a client. Of course, you're under no obligation."

"Here is what I'd like to do. [Lean forward and lower your voice.] I'd like to gather this information. I'd like to pick up your policies, take them to our office where we will individualize your case. We will look at your income and your obligations. We will review the insurance you already own, the kind it is and what it's doing for you. We will then prepare our personalized recommendation."

"When we next meet, I'll give you information and ideas that will be helpful to you now and in the future. You'll probably see some things you haven't had a chance to see before. Again, there's no obligation."

"That's fair enough, isn't it?" [Nod your head to assist your prospect in making a positive response.]

Record Data

The next step is to collect full and complete information. Exhibit 5.9 is an example of a simple but detailed fact-finder that we use. Your compliance department should approve any form you decide to use.

As the producer moves to collect the data, he should say to the prospect,

"To do the best job possible for you, I'll need to record the information we've been discussing. Naturally, this will be held in strict confidence."

Teach producers to always conclude this discussion by asking the prospect if there is any additional information that needs to be considered.

THE "ACID TEST."
WHAT DOES THE PROSPECT WANT?
WHAT DOES THE PROSPECT NEED?
WHAT CAN THE PROSPECT AFFORD?

Exhibit 5.9 / *FACT FINDER*

FACT FINDER

Name		DOB	Social Security	N/S (Y) (N)

Prospect _____

Spouse _____

Children _____

_____

Home Address _____ Home Phone _____

Employer/Position _____ Work Phone _____

Annual Earned Income: Prospect _____ Spouse _____ Total Net Worth _____

Annual Unearned Income: Prospect _____ Spouse _____ Tax Bracket _____

Mortgage Balance _____ Outstanding Indebtedness _____

Will/Trust: Prospect (date) _____ Spouse (date) _____

         (type) _____ (type) _____

CURRENT LIFE INSURANCE

Insured	Amount	Company	Type	Premium	Objective
1.					
2.					
3.					
4.					

CURRENT DISABILITY INSURANCE

Insured	Income	Company	Type	Premium	Company Benefit
1.					
2.					

CURRENT INVESTMENTS

Cash/Checking _____ Annuities _____ IRA/SEP _____

Bonds/Bond funds _____ Mutual Funds/Stock _____ 401K _____

Savings, CDs _____ Real Estate _____ Pension _____

INVESTMENT RISK TOLERANCE   ( ) Conservative   ( ) Moderate   ( ) Aggressive

SOURCES OF RETIREMENT FUNDING

    ( ) Pension   ( ) Social Security   ( ) Mutual Funds

    ( ) Savings   ( ) 401K/IRA/SEP   ( ) Other

OBJECTIVES TO BE MET WITH INVESTMENTS AND/OR INSURANCE

Product	Objective	Time Horizon	Source of Funds

Strengthen the Commitment

It's the little things that count most in being an effective producer. The producer should make it a practice to follow this strategic, three-step procedure after obtaining the necessary information because it will strengthen the case. At the conclusion of the first interview:

- Gather detailed medical information about the prospect's personal history and have it verified by the prospect. This should be done regardless of age because it helps solidify the case and also provides valuable insights. For example, a medical problem might be uncovered or the producer might discover there is competition. If there is a medical situation, the prospect should be scheduled for a physical evaluation to order out a policy from the underwriting department. This will produce a definite competitive edge for the producer since the first completed medical almost always wins!

- Next, the producer should move forward to set up the next interview. The time lapse between interviews should be as short as possible and practical. The prospect should be assured that:

  "We'll thoroughly review the information you gave us and your recommendation should be prepared within a week. Would a week from now be a convenient time to get together to present our recommendation and review it with you? Is the time we met today a convenient time, or would you prefer another? Let's plan to meet in our offices, where we will be free from interruptions and where we have all the resource materials and computer assistance we might need."

- Ask for two promises.

  "I'd like you to promise me a couple of things. First, I'd like an assurance from you that you will not consider a purchase until I return with our recommendations."

  This indicates to the prospect that the producer feels he or she is a good prospect. Also, it secures from the prospect the important obligation not to buy anything until the producer returns for the next meeting.

"Second, during our next meeting, you will be able to study our personalized recommendations with an open mind and make your decision at that time."

Encourage your newer producers to gain both these commitments from their prospects.

Deserve the Prospect's Business

Only a thin line separates those who aspire to excellence in selling from those who attain it. Preparation is usually the quality that makes the difference. Superior sales success is generally preceded by superior preparation.

When the qualifying interview is completed, your producer has taken an important step toward making the big sale. But only one step has been taken. Now the producer must generate an interest and strong feeling for:

- Preparing the qualified prospect for the next step in the sales procedure.

- Preparing the recommendations.

- Preparing for the next interview.

According to the laws of cybernetics, the results our producers can expect from any sales presentation are usually in direct proportion to what they have contributed through their preparation. The preparation process helps producers use all of their "selling equipment" in an effort to deserve the buyer's business.

> THERE IS NO ROYAL ROAD TO LEARNING; NO SHORT CUT TO THE
> ACQUIREMENT OF ANY VALUABLE ART.
>
> *Anthony Trollope*

Prepare the Prospect

Following the first interview, a letter, like the one shown in Exhibit 5.10, can be sent. After allowing time for the prospect to receive the letter, a call should be made to confirm the time and location of the next appointment. This letter does much to build a good relationship and to prepare the prospect for the buying interview. The brochure mentioned in the letter should be attractive and informative. It might include a code of ethics, some biographical information, or a record of the producer's achievements. Also, a list of available financial services and products can be highlighted. Remember, all of your materials must be approved by your compliance department.

Exhibit 5.10 / *LETTER*

(Date)

Bill Yoder
25 Bay Street
City, State, Zip Code

Dear Bill:

It was good being with you and having the opportunity to discuss your financial situation. Thank you for allowing me the time to explain the professional procedure we use in our organization to help our many clients improve their financial positions.

As I indicated, we are looking for clients we can serve at a profit — to them and to us.

In order that you might know a little more about our professional operation, I'm enclosing a brochure that gives you background information and shows you the things we are doing to provide a complete financial planning service for our many clients.

As we discussed, we'll be prepared to present our recommendations to you on (day), (date). By then, the work that we do to individualize your case will have been completed.

Looking forward to seeing you then, I am

                                        Respectfully,

                                        Tony Lyman

                                        TL/lf

Pave the Way

A key point to remember is that the prospect eventually will need to justify, either personally or to his or her company, the purchase made from your producer. Anything producers can do to strengthen their position before asking prospects to buy is good psychology. Enclosing an appropriate article or brochure can be very effective in smoothing the path to the prospective client. Again, any type of enclosure must be approved in advance by your compliance department. Most business and professional prospects today receive many such items every month. Very few pieces are carefully read unless they highlight a specific subject and can be immediately related, in a non-technical manner, to one of the prospect's problems.

Whenever you see an interesting article, request permission to reprint it, gain compliance approval, and have copies made for your associates.

Understand the Buying Motives

What motivates one prospect to act on a certain suggestion might not be sufficient reason for another to act. Buying motives can arise from two viewpoints:

1. the positive side, which is the prospect's impulse to gain something or to improve what he already has; and

2. the negative side, which is the fear of losing what he already possesses.

All of the lesser reasons for buying can be classified under the major headings that follow. Some prospects will buy because they want the monetary gain they receive today from interest-sensitive policies, from universal life, variable life, and equity products. They want to profit from and add to their money values. Others are principally interested in preventing a financial loss. These are the prospects who buy protection and fixed annuities.

Prospects often buy what we sell because of love of family, love of self, or love of charity. They buy because of the fear of a loss by death or disability. Prospects might buy because of a tax advantage. Their motivation might be pride of ownership. At times, they are even motivated to buy because someone they know and respect made a decision to buy.

There is always a motive behind the buyer's decision to take action on your producers' recommendations. Teach them to position themselves to uncover the motive and focus on it.

How the Buyer Buys

Positioning assists the prospect in making certain decisions in the producer's favor, one decision at a time. When the prospect has made them all, he or she has bought our products or services. But what is the buying process? How does the buyer buy? The buyer buys by making four decisions.

1. I will listen to this advisor.

2. I recognize I have a need.

3. I will look at a solution.

4. I will act now.

These four different, but important, decisions must be reached by the prospect, and they are made in a logical, orderly manner.

Why the Buyer Buys

The buyer buys because he or she likes your producer. Research reveals that favorable feelings toward the salesperson are the principal reason the buyer buys, becomes a client, and offers endorsements. Throughout their selling careers, producers must constantly learn more and better ways of making good first impressions and building relationships.

Another reason the buyer buys is because he or she sees and understands a definite owner benefit. In addition, the buyer buys because he has been assisted in making each of the buying decisions. In a very real sense, your producer must play the role of being an assistant buyer.

Case Preparation

The recommendation may be prepared in the form of a proposal. It may be a computerized printout or it may be prepared in a form recommended by the company or the compliance department. However it's prepared, in most cases, the producer should get back with the prospect within a week. Also, remember a promise has been made to study and personalize the prospect's case. The recommendation won't produce a sale unless it is built around the prospect's interest. Don't forget, prospects buy only if they feel it is in their best interest to do so. The prospect must see the owner benefits that will be his by acting on the recommendation. That is why the recommendation must be prepared to convince the prospect of the specific benefits it will provide.

The information obtained on the confidential fact-finding form used to determine what the prospect needs and wants to accomplish should be reviewed and studied.

Your producer has many services and products to offer. During the fact-finding discussion, several possible concerns were discussed with the prospect. The presentation must zero in on those areas where a need has been recognized and the prospect has expressed interest or concern.

EFFECTIVE PEOPLE ARE NOT PROBLEM-MINDED; THEY'RE OPPORTUNITY-MINDED. THEY FEED OPPORTUNITIES AND STARVE PROBLEMS.

Stephen Covey

Anticipate Objections

What are the problems the prospect might have in buying that could preclude him from acting immediately? For one thing, determine how the prospect is going to pay the premium. Most prospects won't object to owning the additional products recommended, but they may object to the financial outlay it requires. If producers leave the problem of finding the required dollars to the prospects, they leave them with the most difficult job of all. It's usually unreasonable to expect the prospect to work it out. The producer must determine for the prospect how the premium can be paid; perhaps by transferring capital from some other asset, moving a certificate of deposit, eliminating corporate dividends, using an annual bonus, or any number of other ways.

Some objections can be anticipated. In those instances, the producer should prepare to answer them before they are expressed.

Preparing the Producer

No matter how long a show plays on Broadway, the actors continue to rehearse. They are professionals; they consistently and conscientiously seek perfection. They practice their lines and their every move because each has an important purpose. They know exactly what they are saying. They understand the responses and reactions they must receive from their audiences.

Preparation means teaching your producers to be so well organized that they know before they make the presentation that the prospect will buy. Some objections can be anticipated so you should equip your producers with the ability to answer them before they are expressed.

Producers should call a day or two in advance to confirm the appointment tentatively set in the previous interview.

"Bill, I have the recommendations I promised we would develop for you. We had agreed upon (day) at (time) in (place) as the best time for us to get together. Is that still convenient for you?"

Make sure the prospect can be there at the designated time. Be certain that all the dominant parties will be present. By dominant parties we mean those who have a part in the decision to buy and pay for the recommendation, i.e., a spouse, parent, advisor, or business partner.

The producer must have all the essential materials in a file for the interview. The materials will include papers from the opening interview, the prospect's file and application forms, the agenda page for this session, as well as any policies taken during the first meeting.

Presentation Essentials

The producer's effectiveness will always be measured by the number of satisfied clients developed. Prior to making presentations, your producer invested many hours and successfully made several sales in the client building process. The earlier sales in the process are important but they lead nowhere if the producer can't sell recommendations and persuade the prospects to act without delay.

The presentation must be designed from the buyer's point of view. In other words, the presentation must give the kind of information the prospect wants and needs to have before he is willing to buy. It must make the prospect understand, agree with, and act upon the recommendations. Knowing how to develop and deliver a convincing presentation is one of the surest and quickest ways for the producer to reach the top of your company's honor roll.

No matter what kind of product producers are trying to sell, it's necessary to understand these four essentials of a result-producing presentation.

1. It must capture the prospect's instant and undivided attention.

2. It must arouse interest by describing owner benefits and the advantages to the prospect.

3. It must build desire by winning the prospect's confidence.

4. It must motivate the prospect to take action immediately.

TELL THEM AND THEY MAY FORGET. SHOW THEM AND THEY MAY REMEMBER. INVOLVE THEM AND THEY WILL UNDERSTAND.

Chinese Proverb

Proven Presentation Principles

Whether or not the prospect is willing to buy depends largely on his or her internal feelings during the presentation. Those feelings are strongly influenced by the prospect's perception of what is said. Therefore, the producer must form the habit of saying and doing those things that prove he or she is trustworthy, knowledgeable and professional.

Let's examine ten proven presentation principles. Ask your associates to study these carefully. Make them a dominant part of their presentation strategy.

1. **BUILD CREDIBILITY.** This starts with the review of the minutes of the previous meeting. It's here the producer again builds the trust level. It brings the prospect's level of interest to where it was previously.

   The producer has developed enough information to be fully convinced that what is being recommended is in the prospect's best interest. A promise has been made to individualize the prospect's case. The producer must look for ways in which the attractiveness of the proposal can be enhanced. Perhaps the producer will have the proposal bound or maybe the prospect's name will be embossed on the cover.

2. **BE WELL-MANNERED.** Liberal use of phrases such as, "May I ask . . ." or, "If it's all right with you . . ." or, "Let's . . ." tend to win the confidence of the prospect. These words will build the producer's image as a mature, likable person.

3. **SIMPLIFY SUGGESTIONS.** The power of the recommendations always lies in its simplicity.

4. **SPEAK THE PROSPECT'S LANGUAGE.** Teach the producer to stay away from industry jargon. Explanations should be kept simple as the focus stays on the owner benefits.

5. **SPEAK AS ONE HAVING AUTHORITY.** Show enthusiasm for the suggestions being made. Human emotions are highly transferable. Your producer should look and speak in terms of success. Prospects like to buy from producers they perceive as being professional and successful.

6. **SELL AT THE BUYER'S PACE.** Producers should be willing to let prospects interrupt them, but producers should never interrupt prospects. Interrupting implies that the producer has something more important to say. The most important person in the room is not your producer; it's the prospect. The prospect can sense whether or not this is understood.

7. **USE REPETITION.** Repetition overcomes communication difficulties. Producers should make the meaning clear by giving more details, by furnishing examples, and by making analogies. Repeated assertion is hard to resist. The initial reaction of the human mind is to reject anything new. This natural, instinctive reaction is a healthy one because it causes the prospect to think of the pros and cons of the idea and to avoid impulsive decisions he might later regret. However, if something is repeated over and over, the prospect's "natural defenses" tend to weaken because the idea is no longer new. The tendency is to then admit "it might be a good idea," and the prospect moves closer to acceptance.

8. **MAKE IT THE PROSPECT'S IDEA.** Each of us is best convinced by reasons we discover for ourselves.

9. **SUMMARIZE STRATEGICALLY.** "Let's examine again . . ." Cement the owner benefits. Make certain prospect understanding has been achieved.

10. **BE PERCEIVED AS A PROBLEM SOLVER.** When this is done the prospect views the producer as an advisor and not as someone who's trying to sell something.

Review these ten presentation principles frequently with your associates. They go to the heart of the process the prospect moves through when deciding whether or not to buy what the producer recommends.

WE ARE WHAT WE REPEATEDLY DO. EXCELLENCE THEN IS NOT AN ACT, IT IS A HABIT.

Aristotle

SALE NUMBER 4 – SECURING THE APP AND CHECK

Confidence is the single most important ingredient in making sales. It's not the prospect. It's not the computerized printout. It's not the interest rate or business conditions. It's your producer, the key player, the individual who assists the buyer in making the decision to act immediately. How do you assist the buyer in this way? The producer must be confident enough to make the prospect feel secure with the recommendation.

Let's face it, confidence is the fuel that powers persuasiveness. Where does confidence come from? It is the product of preparation, procedure and product knowledge. Producers must place the agenda page in front of the prospect and themselves. Having an agenda keeps producers on the right track and lets prospects know the importance of the meeting. Exhibit 5.11 is a sample of a Closing Interview Agenda.

To be sure, there are myriad products being sold today that are new and different, all the way from low-cost annual renewable term to universal life, variable life, long-term care, annuities, and equity products. Yet, the principles by which these modern plans are sold are still the age-old strategies of consultative selling which we are detailing in this system.

The ability to persuade and close sales is still the most important factor in any producer's career. Closing requires persuasiveness. The words and expressions used must motivate the prospect to act favorably on the recommendations now. There must be no hesitancy, no apology or timidity. Even though the producer handles other steps of the selling process perfectly, the sale falls apart if it's not climaxed with a moving presentation and persuasive closing actions.

Most insurance sales do not close themselves; your producers must do the closing. Nothing is more important during this part of the selling process than confidence, born of thorough preparation in the time-proven five-step strategy for closing.

Exhibit 5.11 / *CLOSING INTERVIEW AGENDA*

JOHN SMITH
Closing Interview Agenda
Date

- REVIEW OF MINUTES

- REVISIT YOUR NEED

- EXPLANATION OF SOLUTION

- PRESENTING NUMBERS

- QUESTIONS ANSWERED

- APPLICATION

- CHECK TO COMPANY

Step 1 – Owner Benefits

Make summary statements regarding owner benefits.

"We feel, and we think you'll agree, Bill, (company) has developed this plan on a very flexible basis. We feel it will do for you all the things you want to accomplish."

"First, this plan guarantees you that money will be accumulated and available for future delivery when you become too old to work."

"Second, our plan provides a guaranteed monthly income to your family at your death."

"Finally, the plan provides an accumulation of funds that will be available for financial opportunities or contingencies in the years ahead."

Step 2 – The Final Look

"I want to be certain you understand our recommendation. Give this a *final look* and determine if there are any questions you have that I haven't answered."

The producer places the proposal in front of the prospect. That makes it possible for the prospect to show positive buying signs. It is time now to keep quiet and listen and watch for opportunities to encourage and reinforce the prospect's "discoveries," realizations regarding various facets of the plan's owner benefits. During this time, the application and an uncapped pen are positioned in front of the prospect. *The producer is asking the prospect to give the recommendation a final look.* Ask the prospect to check the names for correct spelling and determine if there are any questions yet to be answered.

The producer then lets silence go to work. To use silence requires confidence and practice. Be aware that the proper application of silence can do much to help your producers close sales.

In some cases, a buying signal will be received by the producer; in most cases, especially with first-time buyers, it won't. Prospects will need to be assisted in making the decision. This requires that producers continue with the five-step closing strategy which has been practiced and perfected. Already they have handled the first two steps—summarizing the benefits of the plan, then asking for the prospect's questions and the use of silence.

I DISCOVERED I'M LEARNING ONLY WHEN ASKING QUESTIONS
AND LISTENING.

Larry King

Step 3 – The Strategic Move

"If you have no further questions, there are two questions I'd like to ask of you. The first is about the plan. How do you like the work we've done [pick up or point to the proposal] and the manner in which we have customized our recommendations to you and your family?"

This is a controlled question; the response is predictable. This question almost invariably gets a favorable response. When the prospect nods and indicates approval of the plan, the producer moves to the application and records the name of the plan on the app. The producer then proceeds by saying:

"How about the amount we are recommending? Do you feel it's about right, an amount you'll be comfortable with, Bill, based upon your current budget and dollar range you gave us to work with in our discussion last week?"

When referring to the amount, it is either the premium or the volume. Producers will often meet some resistance when asking about the amount. However, the producer is positioned to close the sale when the initial favorable response to the plan is received so he then begins to fill in the app. Now, the prospect must stop the producer; otherwise, he is giving the producer the implied consent to finish filling in the app.

179

Again, the important attitude to develop and maintain is that the sale must be closed; it seldom closes itself.

Step 4 – The Prospect's Idea

Let's assume the decision regarding the premium amount was resolved and the producer records the amount on the application. Next, move to secure consent on a number of minor questions, shifting the prospect's attention to little decisions. In effect, control of the idea to take action on the recommendation is now being given to the prospect, thus making it the prospect's idea. Teach your producers this script.

- "Bill, would you prefer to handle the premium annually or through our monthly check-o-matic?"

- "Bill, we have the beneficiary set up to be (name of beneficiary); you may wish (alternate name) to be the beneficiary for these reasons . . ."

- "Bill, we have you as the owner, but you could make (name) owner for these reasons . . ."

- "Would you like to receive your correspondence here at your business or at your home?"

Again, the response is recorded on the application. People love to buy but are reluctant to be sold. In this step, the producer is letting the prospect buy when he responds to the choices offered. The prospect can ask about the beneficiary arrangement, additional features, such as the option to purchase additional insurance, waiver of premium, and accidental death. In each instance, give the prospect a choice. On each of these minor points, continue to acknowledge both actual responses and implied consent by recording them on the application. Let the prospect buy!

Step 5 – App With the Check

Next, the producer marks an "X" on the application next to the signature line and hands the prospect the pen, saying:

"I need to ask you to write your name here, Bill, if you will, please."

Never ask the prospect to *sign* an application. Most people have been taught since an early age never to sign anything, but they will "write their name" on almost anything. After the app is signed, move ahead with this statement:

"Bill, please make your check for $1,027, payable to (company)."

Next in importance during the early minutes of the initial contact is the time when the producer asks for the check for the initial premium. This should be done in a very matter-of-fact manner.

Your producer is now properly positioned to complete the application in its entirety. This is simple to accomplish after having the app signed and obtaining the check for the initial premium.

Be Aware of the Buying Signs

The most important signs to watch for are the words and the questions the prospect might use. What the prospect says and how he says it can be most meaningful. Questions can nearly always be interpreted as buying signs as well as indicating an interest. An example might be, "What is the additional premium for the waiver of premium feature?" A question as pointed as that one tells you the prospect is waiting to bring the interview to a close.

Most prospects betray their thinking through their eyes and in their expressions. Teach producers to watch their prospects' eyes for a look of interest. Many effective producers feel the eyes tell you more than the words.

The prospects' tone of voice can also be a buying sign. Even a slight change of raising or lowering the tone of voice will give producers an indication of interest.

The prospect's attitude often betrays his interest. For example, the prospect leans forward. A prospect who rubs his chin, pulls at his ear or scratches his head might be revealing an "almost persuaded" attitude. Likewise, whenever the prospect reexamines something that references the proposal, the time has arrived for the close. The important point is to emulate the successful closers. Teach your producers to do that by staying alert, paying attention and mastering the closing strategy.

GOOD MANAGEMENT CONSISTS OF SHOWING AVERAGE PEOPLE HOW TO DO THE WORK OF SUPERIOR PEOPLE.

John D. Rockefeller

Master the Strategy

Next to the early minutes of the initial contact, the most important part of the sales interview is the time when producers close the sale.

The object of any sales effort is to motivate the prospect to make a decision now in favor of your producer. No one buys anything unless he feels it is in his best interest and benefit to do so. This is one of the reasons summary statements are so important. They must convince the prospect of the ways in which the recommended plan will benefit him. Prepare to make it much more reasonable for the prospect to say "yes" rather than "no" to what is being recommended.

Prospects are people. Their emotions drive them into decisions which will give them security, pride of ownership, respect, and a full range of mental benefits. Prospects might be convinced by facts and logic that what is being said is true, but it takes the spark of emotion to arouse them to action.

That's why in closing, nothing is more contagious than your producer's enthusiasm. Professionals who go to the top and stay there are genuinely excited about what they sell.

The secret of closing more sales is found in the building of an assertive attitude of expectancy coupled with a planned strategy. Require your producers to master and perfect the five-step strategy.

Finally, as you help producers develop their skill as a closer, also teach them to develop the ability to win the confidence of those whom they call on and meet as prospects. The big job in attaining career success as a professional financial advisor is to build a clientele rather than just sell policies.

You've discovered the way to close, now you must teach it to your associates and have them master it!

Handling Objections

How to handle resistance and objections is one of the most widely discussed topics in the field of selling. For the inexperienced producer, the skeptical tone of a prospect's objection is too often interpreted as a refusal to buy. In the face of objections, the rhythm of a presentation is broken, self-confidence wavers, and conviction is often lost.

Two factors will determine success in meeting resistance and overcoming objections: attitude and strategy. As with any part of the selling process, strategy can be learned and mastered through practice. First, though, it's important to develop an attitude that puts objections in their proper perspective.

All too often, objections are viewed as major obstacles to closing the sale. When you teach your producers the skills to handle them, you'll find producers will begin to view objections as a welcome part of the sales process. In fact, often the toughest prospect to sell is the one who gives too little or no feedback. It's hard to tell where he or she stands. The same applies to the prospect who appears to agree with everything being said. For these reasons, the correct attitude toward objections is to welcome them.

Objections provide a clue to the prospect's thought process. Teach producers to fish for feedback early in the sales presentation to determine the prospect's thoughts and feelings about the points being presented. Welcome that as useful information. When a prospect provides an objection, that is valuable feedback, too. Producers are receiving direct thoughts from the prospect about their recommendation. Objections can serve your producers well if you teach them to welcome them and have the strategy for handling them.

Once producers have the right attitude toward objections, they can develop a strategy for handling them effectively. To do so, however, producers must first determine whether they are genuine or insincere. The insincere objection, known as sales resistance, is generally illogical and cannot be answered. It's expressed in alibis, excuses, or stalls.

The prospect may give fictitious reasons to hide the genuine objection. For example, "I'm tied up at the office right now; I just don't have the time." "Your plan has a lot of merit, but I'd like to think about it." "I'd like to shop around and do some comparing."

By contrast, the genuine objections have the ring of truthfulness. In these instances, the prospect feels there's a valid reason for not buying at the present time. Examples include: "The need is an obvious one, but I have some bills I must handle first." "Frankly, I feel as though I can invest my money better in my own business." "It's just too expensive for me right now; there's no way I can afford it."

These objections are not excuses. They are genuine doubts in the prospect's mind and producers can handle them. As experience is gained, it will become easier for producers to distinguish between genuine and insincere objections. Eventually, they'll have heard them all. Like an actor in a long-running play, they'll soon know not only their lines but the lines of all the other performers as well.

No matter how skillful producers become at anticipating and answering objections before they come up, some will still surface. When they do, handle them in one of three ways: ignore them, defer them, or answer them.

Since most people tend to react defensively early in a buying situation, it's best to manage any initial resistance by ignoring it completely. In other words, don't try to counter it with logic. Teach producers to maintain their poise and build the prospect's confidence by displaying empathy and patience.

"I can understand how you feel," or, "That's all right," are good examples of managing the circumstances. Then move ahead confidently to ask for the appointment, adding, "I would appreciate very much your courtesy in giving me thirty minutes—just thirty minutes—to show you the kind of work we are doing for our clients today." You'll find this an effective way to counter early resistance.

The second method of handling an objection is to defer it by simply asking permission to answer it later. When an objection is delayed during the presentation, you rob it of its potential strength. Also, the delay keeps your presentation on track. Best of all, delaying an objection often "tables it" permanently.

As producers move to the close of the presentation and a genuine objection surfaces, it must be answered to the prospect's satisfaction. To hesitate or be evasive might magnify the objection in the prospect's mind and block the close. The sense of personal selling power derived from confidence in having a strategy for handling objections is an invaluable asset. Once the strategy is mastered, producers will be able to remain poised and react calmly when confronted with objections.

The Five-Step Strategy for Handling Objections

STEP ONE: LISTEN TO DIMINISH.

There should be no knee-jerk responses, no quick moves. Producers should never interrupt the prospect even when they know what's coming and have a response in mind. Be encouraged that the objection is being voiced; it's evidence that the prospect is listening and thinking. An objection focuses attention on those areas where the prospect requires more information and understanding. Listening to the objection establishes empathy and how producers listen is critical. Teach your producers to lean forward, nod their heads in agreement with the prospect and let their facial expressions register, "I'm taking your objection seriously." All this earns respect.

STEP TWO: RESTATE TO CLARIFY.

"I want to make certain I understand how you feel and this is what I hear you saying . . ." Paraphrase and, in the process, clarify. This does several things. It tells the prospect you have been listening and that you understand what was said. Also, it makes it clear that the objection is not accepted as final. It gives the producer time to recognize his thoughts which can be helpful.

Restating the prospect's comments or concerns puts your producer in step with the prospect and helps avoid arguments. No one ever convinced a prospect by arguing, so stay in the prospect's corner. Guide him to better understanding by providing more information. Do that by tackling the objection, not tackling the prospect.

STEP THREE: ISOLATE TO IDENTIFY.

"If we could handle this to your satisfaction, is there anything keeping you from moving forward today?" This helps determine if the prospect's comment is the only objection as well as if it is the real objection. There are always two reasons a prospect has for not deciding upon the recommendation: the reason that sounds good, and the real reason.

STEP FOUR: MOTIVATE TO ACTIVATE.

Use an illustration, example, or story. The objective in this step is to make sure there is now a prospect who is sold on the recommen-

dation. This prospect may or may not be ready to buy, but he or she is sold.

STEP FIVE: POSITION TO ASSIST.

Since the prospect is now sold, producers are positioned to play the role of an assistant buyer. This positions them to move to Closing Step Number 3, The Strategic Move. The only reason for answering an objection is to complete the sale. Properly executed, the first four steps have moved the prospect into a position where it is more reasonable for him to say "yes" than to say "no."

Again, the most important factor in stimulating action is your producer's confidence. Teach producers to always assume the prospect is going to buy now. Proceed as if all they must do is settle the few questions of minor importance. Producers' attitudes can make this closing sale easy and natural.

MAKE YOUR PROCESS SO SIMPLE THAT WHEN ORDINARY PEOPLE FOLLOW IT, THEY PERFORM IN AN EXTRAORDINARY FASHION.

Michael Gerber

Three Basic Reasons

When genuine objections are encountered near the close of the presentation, remember that the prospect is really saying, "I'm not sold, at least not yet." There are three basic reasons for the objections.

1. There is something that is not understood. A better job of explaining the recommendation in relation to the prospect's needs or desires must be done.

2. There is something the prospect does not believe. Sufficient evidence has not been produced to convince the prospect of the true benefits and value of the proposal.

3. The objection may mean there is something the prospect is trying to cover up. When this is sensed, your producer must be

considerate. Attempt to build confidence and reduce the prospect's anxiety.

Prospects will follow willingly on those things that happen to be in accord with their own desires. However, they must be *directed, assisted*, and *persuaded* if the action and cooperation you desire for their benefit is to be taken.

Some people, who seemingly should buy, simply will not. On the other hand, some prospects will buy despite their own objections. Why? Because they discover a reason for buying that exerts more pressure and influence than any of the negative reasons.

In today's sophisticated, fast changing marketplace, prospects look to producers for information and guidance. They expect producers to engage in consultative selling. This means they want both creative suggestions and assistance in helping them make decisions.

Power Phrases

Your producers should build an inventory of phrases that move and motivate. Make them accessible by putting them in writing on three-by-five index cards. Reviewed regularly, these power phrases will become part of their selling style. To get started, have your producers consider the following.

NO NEED

- Life insurance is really nothing but money. You don't need more life insurance, but you do need more money. If you live, we call it thrift; when you die, we call it life insurance.

- Intelligent people buy life insurance—when they don't need it.

- You say, "I don't need it." With all respect, I ask you, could you change the "I" to "we" and still make that statement?

- You'd give your life for Mary and Bill. Why not insure it for them?

- No need, true. If you needed it, you couldn't get it.

NO MONEY

- Don't be afraid to pay yourself first.

- No money. You don't want that to be permanent, do you?

- Earning money is easy; managing it successfully is hard. Life insurance makes its owner a successful manager of money.

- It's best to save first and spend last. There's no better time to begin that strategy than now.

NO HURRY

- Every seventeen minutes someone buys life insurance who will not live to pay the second premium.

- The only time people buy life insurance is when they think they need it. When they know they need it, they can't buy it.

- I never met a person who planned to fail. I have met many people who have just failed to plan. Why not start planning now?

INFLATION

- A widow doesn't ask what kind of dollars, just how many.

- Inflation is the reason you should have purchased this last year.

- Inflation of prices means inflation of income. Increased income into insurance will keep pace with inflation.

- Life insurance is inflation proof.

- Life insurance is inflation reactive.

- I don't have to read the *Wall Street Journal* each morning to learn what happened to my cash values; I know they went up.

WANTS TERM BUT NEEDS PERMANENT

- Will Rogers said, "I'm not so much interested in the return on my money as I am on the return of my money." You can't solve a permanent problem with temporary insurance.

- Buying and owning your home makes sense; it's better than renting. The same is true of life insurance.

- Term insurance is rented insurance and, therefore, the most expensive kind.

DISABILITY INCOME

- Consider this: The chances of the average policyholder having a homeowner's claim within a year come to only one in twelve hundred. There's one chance in two hundred and fifty of an auto claim, and the odds are one hundred and fifty to one against the policyholder dying. But, there's one chance in thirty that he or she will suffer a long-term disability. That statistic speaks for itself; why not let it speak for you?

BUSINESS INSURANCE

- Do you own the business, or does the business own you?

- If a key employee isn't worth insuring, that person isn't a key employee.

Words With Special Power

Effective closers weigh every expression. They always try to use words that will be acceptable, words that will have positive, rather than negative, impact in the prospect's mind. Producers want a "yes" response, so they must keep prospects in a frame of mind in which they will agree, rather than disagree, with what they say. Keep them answering, "yes, yes, yes," and you keep them buying.

A few key words have extraordinary power to influence people (see Exhibit 5.12). One of those is the word *why*. *Why* is one of the hardest of all questions for the prospect to answer without making a commitment. If producers learn to use *why*, they will draw out the true reason the prospect is hesitant to "write his name" on the application.

Let's is a useful word in closing sales because it implies mutuality. "Let's move forward on this basis," makes the prospects feel it's as much their idea as it is the producers, and motivates them to cooperate.

Another word with motivation strength is *how*. When New York Life's Ray Triplett says, "I'm going to show you how to make deductible gifts to your grandchildren in such a way that they will never forget you," he arouses a sense of curiosity. Prospects want to hear the rest of the story.

How to Handle Frequently Encountered Objections

DECIDING ON THE AMOUNT

The life insurance purchase is much like the story told of the Arabian horseman. Riding by night, he heard a voice of authority commanding him to dismount and pick up pebbles. "In the morning you will be both glad and sad," the voice said.

At daybreak, the horseman awakened to discover that the pebbles he picked up were precious stones. Immediately, he was reminded of what the voice had predicted.

He was glad that he had gathered some, but sad he hadn't gathered more.

ASKING THE SPOUSE, "WHAT DO YOU THINK?"

"Mary, before you respond, let me say this. Most spouses I talk with think their husbands own enough insurance. But, Mary, I have yet to talk with the first widow who thought her husband owned enough insurance."

"Mary, in answering the question, 'What do you think?', let me ask you, do you think this would be enough to take care of you and the children if something happened to Bill?"

THINK IT OVER

"I want to make certain I understand how you feel. You feel you need more insurance and you can afford it. It's just that you want to think it over. Is that right? In addition to that, is there any other reason why you wouldn't want to buy this plan this afternoon?"

"I think that's smart. You should never buy a plan this important without thinking it over. I wouldn't want you to ever buy anything that wasn't right for you. So, why don't we think this thing over together. Now, what questions do you have that we should think about?"

NO NEED

"The life insurance purchase is much like buying a parachute. You don't buy a parachute when you need it. You buy one when you don't need it. You make the intelligent decision to buy the parachute when you don't need it so you'll have it when you do need it. If you need it and don't have it, you can't get it! It's the same with life insurance. That makes sense, doesn't it?"

COMPARE

"I want to make certain I understand how you feel. You like the plan, you feel you need more insurance, and you can afford it. It's just that you would like to compare, is that right? In addition to that, is there any other reason why you wouldn't want to buy this plan this afternoon?"

"I think that's smart. You should never buy a plan this important without comparing. But you know what would make me feel bad? If, while you were comparing, something happened that subsequently prevented you from qualifying for this preferred rate or, perhaps, any rate. Or, if while you were comparing, something happened to you."

"Let's move forward on this basis. You give me a check and I'll put your plan into effect today. Then, you go ahead and compare. In fact, I would compare this plan with two or three companies. If you find a plan as good as this plan along with another financial advisor who will take care of you like I will, then go ahead and buy it and I'll give you your money back."

"That's fair enough, isn't it?"

I'm Not Certain About Making a Financial Commitment Now

"(Name), let's assume you are going to drive from (city) to (city). You wouldn't wait until all the traffic signals were green before you started. Rather, you'd start when you saw the first green signal. It's the same way with an individual starting on a program like this. If you wait until you can see all the way to age sixty-five, you will never have a program of any sort. But, (name), in almost every instance, when a person is doing the right thing and starts out, the lights work in his favor. Is there any better time for you to get started on this plan?"

Cautious About Making a Mistake

"(Name), whether you buy this plan or not, you are going to make a mistake. If you buy it and don't need it, because you don't die or have plenty of income from some other source in later life, then you might have made a mistake. You have saved (dollar amount) in premiums. We will refund (dollar amount), which is a mistake that has earned you money. But maybe you could have earned more elsewhere if you had conscientiously saved the same amount on the same regular basis. To that extent only, it has been a mistake."

"If you don't buy it, and your family needs it, then your mistake has cost them (face amount). Have you ever tried to wiggle out of a (face amount) mistake? Since the choice is yours, wouldn't you prefer a mistake that returns to you more than you put up, rather than a mistake that cost your family (face amount)?"

THE PRODUCERS' "STOCK-IN-TRADE"

Professionalism in selling insurance and equity products requires prompt, personal follow-through. As Dr. Mike Mescon, former Dean of the Business School at Georgia State University, says, "Good or bad, right or wrong, clients are most likely to recall the last, not the first, experience. They remember the end of the story, not the beginning. Clients want consistent service from start to finish." As a professional, your producers want to deliver consistent service and achieve client satisfaction.

Teach producers to strive to make client satisfaction their "stock-in-trade." How do producers do that? Quite simply, by making certain their prospects receive more in the way of service from them than they expect; making certain they get more than they pay for; and making sure they provide more in the way of client service and information than they can possibly realize from competitors.

"Spoil your clients," says Calvin Hunt, a highly respected producer in south Texas. "Give them more and better service than they thought was possible. Everybody gets an annual review from me, either by letter, telephone, or in person. I send birthday cards with personal notes in them, and Christmas cards. I want clients to know I appreciate their business and confidence. Repeat business comes easy when you go out of your way to spoil them."

Exhibit 5.12 / *POWERFUL EXPRESSIONS*

POWERFUL EXPRESSIONS

Words That Probe

Why?
How?
What is your opinion?
What do you think?
Can you illustrate?
What do you consider?
What were the circumstances?
How do you feel about . . .?
Could you explain?
Which would be best for you?

Words That Motivate

Thank you	*Flexible*
Congratulations!	*Value*
Let's	*Profit*
I would appreciate your courtesy	*Love*
I want to make certain I understand	
* how you feel.*	*God*
Will you help me?	*Guarantee*
It was my fault.	*Safe*
I'm proud of you!	*Loss*
Please	*Qualify*
You were very kind.	*Home*
It's been a real pleasure.	*Recommend*
Growth	*Up-to-date*
Quality	*Death*

Words That Irritate

Understand?
Get the point?
Do you see what I mean?
To be honest with you
Bucks
Deal
I, me, my, mine
I'll tell you what!
You know

SALE NUMBER 5 – ESTABLISHING A CLIENT

Policyholders buy only once. *Clients buy several times.* While the difference between a policyholder and a client is often subtle, the financial difference to the producer is substantial. The professional's mission is to develop clients who become advocates.

The person who purchased the product and invested the money did so because he or she had the confidence in the producer and the on-going service that producer would provide. Whether or not that confidence will be maintained, or even enhanced, depends largely upon the producer and the manner in which the "sale after the sale" is handled.

The delivery interview presents the opportunity to build a solid relationship and to begin the conversion from client to advocate. This is one of the most important parts of the selling process. The method used, what is said and done, and the producer's approach to the delivery interview will impact persistency, renewal commissions, and future selling opportunities.

The delivery interview is an integral part of the *KinderTrac* system. It's much more than a mere formality; it's here the sale is made solid.

If producers proceed on the basis that their job has been completed when they process the signed application with the initial premium, then they are merely deceiving themselves. Available research consistently reveals that, in nearly 60% of all life insurance lapses, the policy terminates with the second premium. In fact, some of these extensive surveys conclude that after clients make four premium payments, lapses are negligible. The following are some of the post-selling strategies the producer should utilize to make sure sales stay closed.

Send a Congratulatory Letter

The producer should assure the new client that he or she has made an intelligent decision. An effective way to do that is to send a congratulatory letter. We suggest the letter be written in each instance and that the follow-up letter leave the producer's office as soon after the sale as possible. Exhibit 5.13 is an example of a letter being used by a number of successful professionals.

Exhibit 5.13 / *CONGRATULATORY LETTER*

(Date)

Mr. and Mrs. Bill Yoder
25 Bay Street
City, State, Zip Code

Dear Bill and Mary:

Thank you – and please know I appreciate very much doing business with you. As the years roll on, I assure you that both (company) and I will strive to merit your confidence.

Since changes in family and financial conditions make it desirable to review your insurance and investments periodically, I will keep in touch and call on you from time to time.

Naturally, I'll consider it a privilege to be consulted by you and your friends whenever the subject of financial services and related products comes up. I'd like very much to have you folks consider me your Financial Advisor.

Respectfully,

Tony Lyman

TL/lf

(A hand-written comment might be added to assure the client that all the necessary papers are being processed. Sometimes an appropriate, compliance-approved enclosure will serve a worthwhile purpose.)

In-Person Delivery

When the contract returns from Underwriting and Issue, it should be delivered promptly and in person. Your producer is now meeting someone who has been converted from a name to a prospect to a purchaser. *The delivery sets the stage to make the purchaser an advocate.*

The prospect has been motivated to buy and his confidence has been gained. Maintaining that confidence and increasing it begins with the delivery. This "eyeball-to-eyeball" exposure permits the producer to accomplish four important objectives.

1. To resell the needs and discuss the handling of the next premium. This helps make the sale solid.

2. To condition the client for the next purchase.

3. To obtain referral information, introductions, and endorsements.

4. To convert a satisfied client to an advocate.

Render a Distinct Service

Just as selling interviews must be held under favorable circumstances, a delivery interview should be made under conditions advantageous to the producer. A favorable delivery interview permits the producer to resell himself as a professional.

A policy summary should be professionally prepared. It should also be standard procedure to enclose the product in an attractive delivery kit. Clients recognize professionalism when they see it; they associate it with dependability. They know the disinterested, careless, complacent producer is here today and gone tomorrow. They would rather rely on a professional who renders a distinct service.

Also, personal contact provides an opportunity to resell the need for the insurance and to explain the manner in which the next premium is to be handled. This can start the client thinking about subsequent purchases.

Review Owner Benefits

Producers must take the time to review the purpose of the purchase. Emphasize the benefits and, again, how they solve the prospect's needs and wants. It's here that producers will develop the thoughts pointed out in the summation statement.

Explain the Premium Schedule

Make certain the schedule of subsequent premiums is covered carefully.

Discuss the Next Purchase

Decide upon the needs the client feels should be handled next. Decide which is the most important and set the stage for the next purchase.

The Company Newsletter

Producers should review with their new clients the quarterly newsletter they will receive from your office. Clients should be given a current copy and assured that the information will be interesting and informative.

Make Two Commitments

Tell the new client:

"Bill, I want to make a couple of important commitments to you, then I'd like you to make one for me."

"First, I'm going to keep you informed and current. I'll be positioned to advise you from time to time on changes affecting your overall insurance and investment programs. Second, I'll be personally available to review your insurance program at any time, and I'll contact you periodically to remind you of the advisability of such a review."

"Now, Bill, I'd like you to think of me whenever the subject of insurance and investments comes up. Should you be contacted by another financial services advisor, tell him or her I handle your financial matters. If the advisor has something to recommend, ask him or her to review it with me."

Set a Review Date

Schedule the review date to fall 30 days prior to the insured's age change. That provides a "motivational edge" each year when contact is made with the client.

Satisfied Clients – Your Greatest Asset

This is the follow-through sale, the "sale after the sale." It is an essential part of the *KinderTrac*. The sale should never be considered complete until the policy has been personally delivered and a satisfied client developed.

This sale includes these points:

- Send a congratulatory letter.

- In-person delivery.

- Render a distinct service.

- Review owner benefits.

- Explain the premium schedule.

- Discuss the next purchase.

- The company newsletter.

- Make two commitments

- Set a review date.

The primary objective of the post-selling contact is to build confidence in the service and make the sale solid. The greatest assets of professional financial advisors are satisfied clients.

SALE NUMBER 6 – GETTING ENDORSEMENTS

The prospect is now a client. Proper servicing of future needs ties the prospect to your producer. At the same time, it allows the producer to develop sales to the new client's contacts.

By developing endorsements, the producer is building a success pattern by gaining information and introductions to new prospects. Sales can then be made through the same steps by which the original sale was made.

Of course, producers must earn the right to receive endorsements through the prompt, courteous service they provide. This manner of conducting business results in new sales, and many of them, because the producer has won the client's confidence.

When delivering the policy, and after reinforcing the new purchase, this transition should be made.

"Bill, I need your help. We study our business closely. Our studies reveal that as much as sixty-five percent of our new business comes to us from satisfied clients, like you. I'd like to ask you to help me by giving some thought now to someone you know who appears to have a need for our services. For example, the last two times I have been to your home, I noticed that John and Mary Jones live next door. Are they the type of people with whom I should be doing business?"

When making this statement, producers turn to the prospect cards where referrals are recorded to indicate to the client that they fully expect him to provide the requested information. Secure as much pertinent information as possible. Remember, one good lead that producers can approach, develop, and sell, is much better than a notebook full of names and addresses where there is no enthusiasm to make the follow-up call.

Feed Names

The best strategy of all is to feed names to clients. Producers can do that by paying attention during interviews.

"Bill, the last time I was here you mentioned that Tom Adams was a close friend you have played golf with for years. I'm wondering if Tom is the type of individual who might be interested in the kind of work we do?"

Ask the client for information about these people. Mention names your clients know and to whom they can provide introductions. This is done by consistently paying attention to next door neighbors, relatives, friends, and business associates the client mentions in the course of doing business. After the client has been given three or four names of people who he should be referring to you, it is easy to ask him about other individuals he knows.

"Who Are Three Top . . .?"

Here is a proven way to develop strong referrals.

"Bill, I'd like to ask you to help me. Who are the three top people in business you know who I can approach about the work we do? [No pause.] When I call for an appointment I will say, 'John, I asked Bill to name the three top business people I could contact about the work I do. Bill gave me your name and told me about the fine job you do.'"

"Bill, I will not always get an appointment, but the person you refer will always appreciate your recognition of his or her performance."

This strategy can be altered to fit any kind of prospect. Just modify, for example, three top salespeople, three top coaches, etc.

Another Strategy That Works

When completing the sale, producers often ask clients if they can enter their name in a telephone directory that they probably maintain. After the producer enters his name, he should ask if there are others in the book who he could meet. At that point, the producer has in his hands his clients' best friends along with their addresses and telephone numbers.

What to Do if You Meet Resistance

If the new client should resist giving names, information or introductions, producers will need to reinforce their original referred lead approach this way.

"I understand how you feel and I'm not asking you to tell me who will buy one of our products. I've found that, on the average, out of every three people I talk with, one will be interested in one or more of my services now, and one will be interested later. So you can see that I'm not asking specifically for the names of people who want to buy now. The law of averages will take care of that for me."

Any further resistance can be met by saying:

"You see, my business is unlike any other. If I don't have people to see, I'm out of business. Most who are in my business spend ninety percent of their time looking for people to talk with and ten percent servicing their clients. I prefer to spend ten percent of my time looking for people to talk with and ninety percent servicing my clients. Since you have agreed I'm the kind of person with whom you like to do business, you can help me. That way, I can spend most of my time working for you instead of looking for prospects."

"Bill, who are the three top salespeople who call on you?"

Develop a Possible Response

Realizing that the best time to overcome objections is before they come up, the final step is to instruct the producer to develop with the client the possible response to be expected from the individual being referred. Also, cultivate any interests or affiliations of the referral prospect that might be helpful in developing a relationship quickly.

Producers should thank the clients for referring prospects and also let them know that they will be informed of any developments. Be certain producers follow up. Every time! It will do much to strengthen their relationships with their clients.

Sale Number 6 makes the sale productive and keeps our producer on "the selling track." It keeps the producer excited because he has qualified prospects to see—lots of them!

REMEMBER, THE BETTER THE PRODUCER, THE HIGHER THE PERCENTAGE OF HIS OR HER BUSINESS THAT IS DERIVED FROM SATISFIED CLIENTS.

Make the Sale Productive Every Time

Producers are interested in referral information, introductions, and endorsements. "Who can I sell a bit easier now because I was successful in making this sale?" That's the key question to resolve.

A survey of 4,165 households showed that two out of three had never been asked for referrals. Yet, the majority of the people interviewed said they would have given referrals if they had been asked properly. The reasons are simple.

First, new clients probably have a trace of buyer's remorse. "Did I buy the right kind? The right amount? From the right source?" If individuals they respect make a similar purchase, they have a better feeling about the decision they made. Additionally, many individuals like being a strategic matchmaker—matching up people with problems with people who have solutions.

One time we heard a marketing specialist, Eric Wiltshire, in Detroit, say something about the referred lead technique that you'll want to remember. "I have never met a professional salesperson or even heard of one for that matter, who obtained anything more than an average success without having developed a strong endorsement developing strategy. They let their customers do the selling for them!"

Professionals are entitled to referred leads. They've earned the right to ask for and receive them. After all, they have provided the prospects or clients with profitable service. Clients know, and producers know, that our services have helped them. Endorsements come for the asking.

Securing endorsements makes the sale productive—every time!

VAL'S VIEWS ON TRAINING

Personalized sales training ignites producers.

We believe training begins at the initial meeting. It's here that we set the stage by defining what our kind of training is all about. Training is making sure the strategy is understood. This is done best in live demonstrations.

Never teach in the office what you do not plan to demonstrate at the point of sale.

Training is closely observing the sales performance of the individual. It's identifying weak spots and providing personal coaching to improve needed skills.

We've discovered that videotaping, supported by CDs, has revolutionized training in our business today. These sales support tools are portable and predictable. They never change their lines or grow stale.

We videotape the new associate making the contact call, interviewing the prospect and closing the sale. Often, the effectiveness of the taped performance is so bad that we do not let the producers view it. Ninety days later, we tape them again. What a confidence builder it is for them, and the trainer, to witness the great improvements they have made.

Remember, training producers is the work you perform to help them improve their attitudes, skills, and knowledge. Training and coaching are important developmental activities that are within the scope of each of us as managers.

CHAPTER THOUGHTS AND IDEAS
I'M USING OR PLANNING TO IMPLEMENT

√ Teach relationship selling.

√ Expect mastery of the sales process.

√ Teach fact-finding and feeling-finding questions.

√ Transfer presentation essentials.

√ Utilize "pocket prompter" training tools.

√ Strengthen producers' commercials.

√ Make certain buying motives are understood.

√ Teach the "feed names" strategy for generating endorsements.

Chapter 6 /*MARKETING*

*THE SECRET OF STAYING AFLOAT IN BUSINESS IS TO CREATE SOME-
THING PEOPLE WILL PAY FOR.*

Thomas Edison

On a foggy Fourth of July morning in 1952, 34-year-old Florence Chadwick waded into the water off Catalina Island, California. She wanted to become the first woman to swim the Catalina Channel. Millions watched on television as she began to swim toward California.

Create prospect attraction and trust.

The water was numbing cold that morning. The fog was dense. Florence could barely see the boats in her own party. Several times sharks approached her and had to be driven away with rifle shots.

Fatigue had never been her biggest problem in these swims, rather, it was the bone-chilling cold that challenged her most. More than fifteen hours later she succumbed to the icy water and asked to be taken on to one of the boats.

Her trainer and her mother told her they were near land. They urged her not to quit. When Florence looked toward what should have been the California coast, all she could see was the dense fog. A few minutes later, she was taken out of the water.

It was not until hours later, when her body began to thaw, that she felt the shock of failure. She had quit just one-half mile from the California coast! She told a reporter, "Look, I'm not excusing myself, but if I could have seen land, I may have made it."

Florence reflected that she had been licked, not by fatigue or even by the cold. The fog alone had defeated her; it had obscured her goal. It had blinded her eyes, her reason, and her heart. It was the only time she ever quit.

Two months later, Florence Chadwick swam across the Catalina Channel. This time, she made certain that conditions were favorable for her. The day was bright and clear—no fog would obscure her view this time. She knew she had to be able to see her goal. Not only did Florence Chadwick become the first woman to swim the Catalina Channel, but she beat the men's record by two hours!

Florence Chadwick discovered what all effective leaders already know: What you see is what you get. We trust this important system will assist your associates in seeing clearly the power of effective marketing. Help them become known for what they know. Their reputation will precede them, and their production will jump.

Expect to discover the many ways you can accomplish this with the marketing strategies developed in this chapter.

YOUR CHIEF CONCERN

Today your tough-minded "boss"—the situation—unmistakably requires the moving of producers into higher levels of production and sophistication earlier in their careers than ever before. This need becomes crystal clear to us in the management seminar work that we do throughout the country.

Mike Cataldo, the talented Jefferson-Pilot vice president, shared with us the results of a recent producer survey. One hundred successful producers were asked this question: "If you were making a company change today, what would be the single most important thing you would like to find in your new relationship?"

According to Mike, nearly 90% of those polled had the same response: "I'd like to find a leader-type manager who will show me how to move to a substantially improved level of production."

Perhaps this explains the chief concern among agency heads today: "How can I do a better job of upgrading; of moving my associates to the next level of production?"

EVERYONE LIKES SOMEONE WHO HAS IDEAS THAT CAN MAKE THEM MONEY.

Leigh Steinberg

MARKETING DEFINED

Marketing is arranging new interviews under favorable conditions, in sufficient numbers, each week in the marketplace where the producer wants to operate.

New interviews can be brand new prospects or interviews with current clients regarding a different line of business. It can be setting up an interview to convert term insurance or adding to current coverages for a client's family or business partners.

Marketing is the activity that takes place before the selling process occurs. Marketing can be done through seminars, advertising, letters, telephone calls, or face-to-face contacts.

Your job as the agency builder has not changed much in the last 50 years, but it has expanded. It's expanded dramatically in the areas of compliance and marketing. You must become the chief marketing officer of your agency. Bill Pollakov, a past president of the General Agents and Managers Association (GAMA), made this statement: "One of the most important jobs for an agency builder is to become the agency's chief marketing officer. You must set the marketing example. You must show your associates that marketing is not something they *should* do, but something they *must* do on a consistent basis if they are to move to the next level."

Marketing involves building relationships with target markets, i.e., CPAs, attorneys, doctors, bankers, etc. It can be the life specialist in a property & casualty firm where the producer has a strong relationship with the owner. You position your producer inside the organization. This can also be done with mortgage bankers and other organizations that have regular contact with clients and feel a need for providing financial products and services.

Prudential Financial great, Dalton Raymond, shared this marketing strategy with us. Dalton says, "I can't sell Dalton Raymond to prospects nearly as well as others can, especially my clients. Some years ago, I recognized a marketing edge I could have by building what I call my *Third-Party Referral Book.*"

Today, Dalton has in his collection more than 300 endorsements. He draws selectively from his referral book to "warm up" prospects during the initial interview. As a token of appreciation for the endorsements, one of Dalton's assistants presents a monogrammed Mont Blanc pen to the individual during a scheduled visit.

WEALTH WILL NEVER BE ACHIEVED WHEN SOUGHT AFTER DIRECTLY…IT ONLY COMES AS THE BY-PRODUCT OF PROVIDING USEFUL SERVICE.

Henry Ford

External Marketing vs. Internal Marketing

It's important to establish a marketing plan for every producer, every year. Base your plan on external and internal marketing.

External marketing is marketing by producers to prospects who are not currently personal clients. In the early years, this requires a high percentage of the entry producers' time.

As producers grow and gain experience they'll do more and more internal marketing. Internal marketing is marketing to those who are already personal clients—individuals they've already sold. For example, orphan policyholders are considered as external marketing because the current producer did not personally sell the policies.

It's important for producers to distinguish between ways to market to their present client base and ways to add new clients through referrals, personal observation and target marketing.

The longer producers are in the business, the larger and stronger the personal client base will become. At that point, they should have a budget and a plan for client events. Producers can offer seminars for clients. A golf outing might be sponsored. A "Thank You Brunch" around the Thanksgiving season will prove to be popular. Call it public relations, business promotion—call it what you want: You need to keep sharpening your skills in this important area of marketing.

Today Marketing vs. Tomorrow Marketing

In addition to external and internal marketing, there is today and tomorrow marketing. Today marketing is setting up interviews with prospects who make quick decisions on purchasing products. Tomorrow marketing is spending time and energy with people who are going to take longer to develop.

Client Relationship Management

Ed Morrow, CLU, ChFC, CFP, RFC, President of Financial Planning Consultants, is based in Middletown, Ohio. Ed is a consultant to financial advisors in the areas of practice management and computerization. He's the author of seven software programs including the *Text Library System*, and a recent book, *Personal Coaching for Financial Advisors* (Financial Publishing Centre, Middletown, Ohio). This is what Ed had to say about marketing action plans, or as he refers to them, marketing sequences.

MARKETING SEQUENCES

A client relationship management (CRM) system requires action plans or marketing sequences to automate the nurturing process. Most of the very best prospects are not instantly ready to meet with a financial advisor on the day of the first contact. Successful, affluent people are busy. They have a full schedule and their concentration is occupied by pressing matters.

The owner of a mid-sized manufacturing company helped attract a new firm to town since they were a major parts supplier for his firm. He mentioned this to his life producer/advisor and also to his property & casualty agent who was also getting into financial planning. The life advisor sent a standard referral letter, made a follow-up phone call but did not get an appointment because the businessman was occupied in the renegotiation of critical clauses in his new lease agreement.

The property & casualty advisor sent a similar referral letter but, because he was very busy, did not place a call. His staff placed the name into an automatic process, classifying the recipient as a business owner prospect. A series of letters were sent out on the agency's stationery, accompanied by an article selected to be of interest to a business owner, as opposed to one intended for a young couple or a retiree. After five such mailings, at three-week intervals, a staff person called the business owner. Again, he was too busy for an appointment, but did not object to the articles he had been receiving. Then, after receiving nine follow-up letters and articles, one arrived that caught his attention. He called the advisor and made an appointment.

The life advisor spent about a dollar for the referral letter but received nothing in return for his effort. In fact, he was a bit disappointed and disheartened not to have scheduled an interview with someone his client had referred to him.

The other advisor spent about $10 for the initial referral letter and nine follow-up letters and articles. His return was over $15,000 in commissions.

The critical issue is that conditioning the suspect into being a prospect and developing the prospect's confidence and interest into becoming a client takes time. In addition, frequently a good deal of material must be carefully prepared, personalized, and sequenced.

There are several components to a CRM marketing sequence, all of which build and strengthen brand recognition.

- The letter text.

- The accompanying information.

- Periodic telephone scripts.

- The plan that triggers actions.

The financial Text Library System has several campaigns or sequences that are included as part of its powerful CRM component. For more information on the Text Library System and how it can work for you and your agency, contact: Ed Morrow, Box 42430, Middletown, Ohio 45042, or by e-mail at edm@financialsoftware.com.

RELATIONSHIPS . . . NEVER TAKE THEM FOR GRANTED. NOURISH THEM AND BE WILLING TO GO THE EXTRA MILE TO STRENGTHEN THEM.

Ken Miller

How NetWeaving™ Can Assist You

All leadership begins at the top and permeates downward. Agency builders who embrace NetWeaving™ as part of their agency culture are making a statement about who they are and what they stand for. NetWeaving is a term coined by the well-known Atlanta, Georgia consultant and writer, Bob Littell. His book, *Power NetWeaving* (published by The National Underwriter Company, Erlanger, Kentucky), is must reading for all sales professionals and agency builders who are interested in sharpening their relationship marketing skills.

NetWeaving is really "marketing according to the Golden Rule." Agency builders who teach this strategy are saying, "We're going to train our associates how, by serving others in unique and sometimes totally unexpected ways, good deeds will come back to them in a big way."

Bob Littell points out that NetWeaving is an altruistic, gratuitous form of networking that concentrates on WIIFY (What's In It For You) rather than WIIFM (What's In It For Me). The two skill elements of NetWeaving are:

1. learning how to become a strategic matchmaker by putting other people together in win/win relationships; and

2. learning how to position yourself as a strategic resource to others, either by providing the resources yourself, or surrounding yourself with a resource Rolodex of experts in a variety of areas in the financial services arena.

Your value to your associates and the agency's clients increases exponentially by virtue of the resource network you create or can supply.

Bob goes on to say, "Not only do the long-term benefits from NetWeaving far exceed those of traditional 'networking,' but the positive benefits of becoming an advocate and spokesperson for

NetWeaving has tremendous public relations value within your local community, or even nationally."

From an agency builder's viewpoint, there are a few caveats about NetWeaving which, if not understood, can sour the producer on the concept. The benefits of NetWeaving, with some exceptions, are long-term in nature. Some newer producers can become so caught up in the positive energies created by NetWeaving, both people and information, that they forget they must first survive in the business long enough for their NetWeaving efforts to have the time necessary to percolate and come back around to benefit them.

The elements of Bob Littell's NetWeaving that newer producers should be coached on include:

- Incorporating the philosophy of NetWeaving into their practice and daily lives.

- Building upon some of the basics of NetWeaving. For example, establishing the simple habit of introducing people to other people, tuning their listening skills to pick up hints of client needs and problems for matchmaking opportunities, and, especially, establishing a network of resources.

- Learning how to expand their professional knowledge so they become a more valuable resource to their prospects and clients.

Noted author, Bob Burg, in a speech to the Million Dollar Round Table, identified a key question. This one will set you apart from everyone your prospect will ever talk to: "How can I know if someone I'm talking to would be a good prospect for you?"

Obviously, Bob Burg believes in NetWeaving.

Agency builders who mentor their associates in NetWeaving will cultivate better human beings as well as creating better producers.

Giving Back

You received assistance, advice, and ideas from others as you advanced in your management career. You may feel as if you owe many people. How can you pay them back? By doing the same in return. It does take time to invest in others, but you should always be ready to give back; give back to clients, give back to the profession, give back to your community, and give back to individuals.

Try some of these ideas:

- Mentor someone.

- Volunteer in a social service organization, civic group, or children's group.

- Serve on local government or civic boards.

- Provide pro bono work for a local nonprofit organization.

- Send a thank you card.

- Volunteer to serve on a committee for your professional association.

- Volunteer to speak at your local professional chapter meeting.

- Speak at your local high school's career day.

- Start a scholarship fund.

All of these will prove helpful in your marketing efforts.

Be and stay a respected, knowledgeable, well-balanced agency builder. Be all the things that you are capable of being. Astound yourself! Your associates will follow your lead.

"Capturing Mind Share"

Market access is the number one problem that keeps producers from succeeding and moving to the next level. Bob Krumroy, in his fine book, *Identity Branding* (published by Lifestyles Press, Greensboro, North Carolina), says, "If you can't get in, your selling skills are useless. In order to get in you need to create a visible distinction, something that is creatively consistent and attracts the prospect before your call. This is called 'capturing mind share.' It is the key marketing skill."

Providing a Climate of Success

In addition to developing producers themselves, successful management provides the kind of climate that consistently breeds independent, responsible producers. Your agency should look the part of an outstanding business organization. Its prospects and clients should be able to tell from its location and layout that competent, professional advisors are housed there.

Clearly, the principal objective of successful agency management is the efficient building and economically justified maintenance of a professional, high performing sales force. As you move toward the achievement of this goal, however, you must recognize that the same high standards that characterize your interest in the individual producer must also apply to the organized facilities and support services you provide.

THE PRICE OF GREATNESS IS RESPONSIBILITY.

Winston Churchill

Again – It's Those Little Things

Many times it's the little things that count the most in setting the stage for higher productivity. Your agency quarters should be maintained in the best dignity of professional offices. It should never be referred to as "a shop;" it's a financial services organization. You should be conscious of what goes on the walls. Producers should be known as associates both within and outside your agency.

There are some little things you should do for new associates in advance of their starting date. Consider the following.

- Place the associate's name on the agency directory in the lobby.

- Give the associate's name, with the correct pronunciation, to the receptionist and telephone operator.

- Place a nameplate on the associate's desk.

- Secure business cards for the producer and have announcements prepared.

- Personally introduce your new associates to the office staff members and agency associates whom the producer has not previously met.

- Arrange for a personal letter to reach the producer from the appropriate upper management official of your company extending a warm welcome.

- Furnish the new producer with an attaché case that contains specially selected materials and forms that he or she will need in starting the selling career in an organized and businesslike manner. The contents of the attaché are intended for the new producer's initial usage. Among the items included in the case are selected information bulletins, prospecting cards, applications, proposal requests, service forms, promotional materials, rate book information, and the monthly appointment book.

These are small items, but they make a difference in setting the stage for early success. The materials are significant and they have an impact on new associates. They project a positive image of the agency and they start building pride in the outfit and confidence in your style of leadership.

Proven Marketing Strategies

Born out of our experience in the many MDRT Accountability Study Groups we've moderated in recent years, our recommendation is that you consider promoting one or more of the following marketing strategies. Coach your associates on how they can effectively implement these strategies.

DEVELOP PROFESSIONAL COMPETENCY

Become known for what you know. Earn the right to a continuing relationship. When you deliver proposals and policies to your clients, package them attractively. Initiate more follow-up activities on existing clients. Establish regular client communications through materials of your choice. Keep clients aware of their needs and of your services.

STANDARDS OF ABSOLUTELY FIRST-CLASS, PRISTINE PERFORMANCES DON'T SPONTANEOUSLY EMERGE. FIRST-CLASS SALESPEOPLE COMMITTED TO THE NOTION THAT SECOND BEST SIMPLY WON'T DO CULTIVATE STANDARDS OF EXCELLENCE.

Michael Mescon

JOIN A STUDY GROUP

Form a "fraternity relationship" with other producers to foster a combination of creative ideas for penetrating higher income markets.

CREATE A BIOGRAPHICAL BROCHURE

An attractively done brochure with your picture, background, credentials and record of achievements, plus a list of the services you provide, can be a most effective way of building relationships with prospects and upgrading your clientele.

ESTABLISH A CLIENT BUILDING NETWORK

These once a month meetings produce contacts and endorsements—lots of them. Prospects for your network include CPAs, real estate salespeople, florists, property & casualty sales representatives, bankers, etc. Share endorsements while respecting the "Privacy Act" guidelines.

THINK BIGGER

Show at least one $1,000,000 illustration monthly. Never underestimate premium-paying ability, especially among two income families. There is more discretionary buying power around today than you can possibly imagine.

CALL ON AGING, GRAYING AMERICANS

The over-65 population is growing 26 times faster than younger segments. Older prospects have more premium dollars than younger prospects.

"VULNERABLES"

Contact the "vulnerable." At least once a week, call on the small business owner. Those who survive are "money machines" who need your good counsel. The MDRT refers to this high potential prospect as a "vulnerable." That means the business owner is a likely prospect for everything we sell.

X-DATE TUITION TERMINATIONS

When the tuition payments stop, substantial premium dollars have been located.

Get in the Seminar Selling Business Fast

Seminar selling is a developing idea whose time has definitely come! P.J. Shevlin, the National Life of Vermont general agent and son of the GAMA Hall of Fame member, Paul Shevlin, is one of several agency heads we know who has successfully upgraded the selling results of his associates through the vehicle of seminar selling.

P.J. tells us the seminar selling strategy accomplishes a number of desirable objectives for the agency's producers.

- It enhances the producer's reputation as a financial advisor.

- It provides a positive platform for presenting sophisticated information and ideas.

- It opens up the opportunity for the producer to develop a relationship with CPAs, attorneys, doctors and trust officers.

- It develops higher income market business and better quality clients.

Look for Multiple Sales

Look for the extra sale in every interview. Sell the spouse and children. Look for the critical illness, disability income, major medical, long-term care, or property & casualty sale, if you sell those products.

Develop a "Learning Center"

You can have one of these in your automobile simply by keeping appropriate cassettes or CDs with you. There is a wealth of information and inspiration available through the MDRT Center for Productivity.

Keep Educationally Active

Be an active participant in any educational courses provided in the agency, or by the local estate planning council.

CREATE AN IDEA BOOK

This collection will help advisors improve present sales methods, enter new markets, conduct successful presentations, and make bigger sales. When you see articles or hear talks that provide new selling ideas, add those to your collection. Periodically review your ideas to determine just how many you are implementing.

INVEST IN CLIENT APPRECIATION EVENTS

These can range from a Thanksgiving season brunch to a golf outing that your associates promote for their better clients. Of course, as the agency leader, you can often take the lead.

Andy Martin heads up the largest sales organization at Protective Life. Andy has developed a marketing program entitled, "Moving to the Next Level" that is available on audiocassette and video tape. The "idea count" is high. For example, Andy conducts an annual golf outing for all of his producers and prospective producers which is almost entirely funded by contributions from vendors. It has become a big event each year and has proven extremely profitable to his organization's members.

WRITE ARTICLES

There is always a demand from company and association publications for well-written articles about financial problems and their solutions. This is another way of becoming known for what you know. Reprints of these articles can be secured and they make excellent sales support items to use with your prospects and clients.

LET NO ONE EVER COME TO YOU WITHOUT
LEAVING BETTER AND HAPPIER.

Mother Teresa

Another Profitable Marketing Strategy

One of the best decisions your associates and your organization can make is to begin networking with CPAs and other advisors. They have already established a client base that trusts them with their personal financial information. You gain control once you have this type of relationship secured. The CPAs' clients, small business owners or high income earners are the types of clients you regularly target. You and your associates can spend a great deal of money on marketing and never reach these prospects.

The hard part is already done when a CPA refers you to a client, or sets a meeting and brings your associate in as the expert. The CPA will know more about the client's financial situation than anyone. When they understand the services you offer, they will be better equipped to market products and services to those clients.

When your associates have control of the decision maker, they will have success in securing action on their recommendations. As the old saying goes, "If you can't beat 'em, join 'em." When you recruit or network with CPAs you put yourself in a much better position for the sale. We know that no matter how good the sales presentation is, if the CPA doesn't agree with the proposal, you will probably lose the sale anyway.

At the time we developed our popular CPA sales support program*, there were 190,000 career agents. The number of CPAs in the United States is approaching 400,000 with many of those CPAs working for the government; scores of them are in-house CPAs. A large number of accountants work for the top 100 companies. Nonetheless, it's estimated that 162,000 CPAs are independent or work in small firms. They are probably your best prospects.

The American Institute of Certified Public Accountants (AICPA) has been quoted as saying, "We will control the financial services industry

---

*You can obtain more information on this program by calling 1-800-372-7110.

in five years." That might or might not happen, but we do know the number of CPAs who currently have their insurance license is over 100,000. We know that individuals and small businesses would likely buy their insurance from their CPA.

MORE AND MORE CPAs ARE FINDING THEIR CLIENTS ASKING, "WHY CAN'T YOU MANAGE MY INVESTMENTS FOR ME?"

There is no question that CPAs are the most trusted financial advisors. They are influential in personal and business decisions, and they have accessibility and credibility. They can help your organization shortcut time when it comes to marketing.

Increasing Your "Professional Equity"

Jim Cathcart, author of *The Business of Selling*, refers to "professional equity" as the degree of ownership producers acquire in their careers. That can be considered their professional net worth, according to Jim. The assets that make up their "equity" as producers include their relationship building skills, their credentials, their product knowledge, and their contacts.

Here are three ways producers can be coached on enhancing their "professional equity."

1. Build Relationships.

    Many say it's not what you know, it's who you know. When it comes to prospective buyers, it's not who producers know, it's how producers are known. Having contacts in the upscale marketplace is desirable. However, your associates must have credibility with those prospects. Prospects and clients must like and respect producers.

    Relationship building is a skill that can and must be developed. It requires producers to be mindful of things they can do or say to build confidence and establish trust. Examine each of these proven methods for building relationships. Again, they are NetWeaving actions.

- **LOOK FOR COMMUNICATIONS OPPORTUNITIES.** There are many ways to send business, prospects, or information to prospects and clients. Producers should ask this question regularly, "What can I do to help my prospects' and clients' businesses?"

- **MAKE PROSPECTS FEEL IMPORTANT.** Producers must look for ways in which they can genuinely compliment prospects on their intelligence, appearance, achievements, or possessions.

- **JOIN THE CLIENT ADMIRATION SOCIETY.** Here, producers make it a practice to acknowledge or admire significant details about members of their clients' families. As Mark McCormack says, "If you have a client you want to impress, do something for a member of the family."

- **BE A WELL-WISHER.** Suggest that producers deliver one birthday greeting every week—in person.

Coach producers on practicing these techniques until they become second nature.

2. Acquire Symbols of Excellence.

The financial services industry prides itself on keeping standards high for the various awards it has developed. Your producers must earn professional degrees and strive to achieve the awards that are identified with excellence. Those credentials will cause them to become known in their marketplace and will lubricate all future introductions.

Encourage producers to become ten-letter producers as early in their careers as possible. They can do that by putting CLU, MDRT and NQA behind their names. In today's environment, adding ChFC, CPCU, CFP and RHU will enhance their credibility, too. These degrees and awards identify producers who are competent, competitive, and consistent.

3. Stay Contact-Conscious.

Nearly all high performing producers are involved in their community. They are active members of church, civic, cultural, and local business organizations. They tend to assume leadership roles, being communicators rather than passive observers.

Andy Bluestone is a leading general agent for Mass Mutual in New York City and has always been active in civic affairs. That provides a good example for his associates as well as helping his recruiting efforts. Andy purchases season tickets for the Knicks basketball and the Mets baseball teams, entertaining his leading producers and selective clients regularly at those games.

Andy knows the financial services business is a contact business. Breakfast and luncheon clubs offer a network of business and social contacts. They usually feature a program, sometimes with outside speakers. These clubs can also widen a producers' contact base.

Producers also need to become involved with the professional community. The well-known financial consultant, Dr. Robert Oberst, speaking at the International Association of Financial Planners (IAFP) Conference, explained the value of his membership in the Red Bank, New Jersey, Estate Planning Council. Similar councils around the country are made up of trust officers, accountants, insurance professionals, attorneys, and financial planners. Dr. Oberst stated,

"By becoming involved in these types of organizations, you accomplish several things. One, you learn a great deal. Where else can you sit next to a skilled attorney and exchange ideas with him or her on estate matters? Furthermore, the professionals in the council will discover that you are interested. You want to learn. You have a good working knowledge of your own specialized profession."

"If you can contribute something meaningful, the accountants and attorneys will come to you for advice on matters where they know you are trained and skilled. Then they will begin referring clients to you."

THE ONLY CERTAIN MEANS OF ACHIEVING LASTING SUCCESS IS TO FORM THE HABIT OF GIVING MORE AND BETTER SERVICE THAN IS EXPECTED OF YOU.

Og Mandino

Creating an Image

Help producers determine what kind of an image they want to develop in the minds of their prospects and clients. How do they want to be perceived? The National Association of Insurance and Financial Advisors (NAIFA) spends nearly one-half million dollars each year to build the public image of its members. The financial services industry spends millions of dollars each year to build a favorable image of their products, services, and producers. It's up to you and your associates to reinforce these positive impressions through relationship building. When prospects, clients, and community leaders are surveyed, your producers want their names to be put in the same category as other professionals—the doctor, accountant, banker, lawyer, or minister.

Building a professional image tends to soften producers' markets. It facilitates the process of turning prospects into clients and of making additional sales to existing clients. Building a professional image brings growth to your producers and your business.

Increasing Producers' Effectiveness

As a general rule, producers are underpaid for the amount of sales effort put forth during the first five years. After those apprenticeship years, they tend to be overpaid. There are several reasons for this. Selling and marketing skills take time to develop. Knowledge and confidence grow along with those skills. The experienced producer is better disciplined and, obviously, has a more extensive referral network. Studies have shown that only 15% of producers' success will be determined by technical knowledge. This means that 85% of their effectiveness is determined by their ability to manage themselves and their skills in meeting and dealing with prospects, and the joint selling activity they produce.

Providing Marketing Leadership

You need to have a strategy for moving producers into advanced markets. That strategy must be personalized to the producer. Change, progress, new product lines, and competition have made marketing savvy compulsory for producers wishing to sell more with a lighter workload.

ANALYZE WHERE THEY HAVE BEEN

Personalizing the producers' marketing plan begins with an in-depth study of their last 200 sales. It might be they will want to take a look at last year's sales only. Producers will see a good picture of their selling patterns by looking at their last 100 sales, or even the last 50. We recommend producers look at either the last 200 sales, or last year's sales.

Producers will want to study sales according to the source, the occupation, the time of day the sale was made, as well as the age and income level of the client. Then have them take a look at their selling methods and note whether it was business, health insurance, or special markets.

A KEY COMPONENT TO GROWING OUR AGENCY FORCE BY TWENTY-FIVE PERCENT OVER THE LAST FOUR YEARS WAS TURNING OUR SALES OFFICES INTO MARKETING FIRMS.

Bill Cuff, Vice President
New England Financial

Exhibit 6.1 / *ANALYZE LAST 200 SALES*

ANALYZE LAST 200 SALES

Source	Sales	Lapses
Policyholder		
Personal Observation		
Referred Leads From Close Friends and Centers-of-Influence		
Referred Leads From Policyholders		
Other		
Occupations		
Attorneys		
Doctors/Dentists/Veterinarians		
CPAs		
Other Professionals		
Business Owners		
Executives		
Salespeople		
Spouse/Child		
Other		
Time of Day & Week		
Day		
Night		
Weekend		

Exhibit 6.1 cont'd / *ANALYZE LAST 200 SALES*

ANALYZE LAST 200 SALES

Age	Percentage	Cumulative
Under 30		
30 - 34		
35 - 39		
40 - 44		
45 - 49		
50 - 54		
55 - 59		
60 - 64		
Over 65		
Annual Income	**Percentage**	**Cumulative**
Under $50,000		
$50,000 - $75,000		
$76,000 - $100,000		
$101,000 - $125,000		
$126,000 - $175,000		
$176,000 - $250,000		
Over $250,000		

Exhibit 6.1 cont'd/*ANALYZE LAST 200 SALES*

ANALYZE LAST 200 SALES

Sales Method	Applications	Commissions
KinderTrac		
Personal Family Planning		
Personal Estate Planning		
Business Planning		
Business Life Insurance		
Sole Proprietor		
Partnership		
Corporation		
Business Health Insurance		
Disability		
Group Life/Medical		
Group Pensions		
Other		
Special Markets		
IRA		
HR-10		
501(c)(3)		
401(k)		
Payroll Deduction		
Other		

CONSTRUCT THE PLAN

Once producers have taken a look at their past sales and where they stand now with qualified leads, it's time to look forward to the construction of a marketing plan. The marketing plan can be constructed by completing Exhibits 6.2, 6.3, and 6.4.

Exhibit 6.2 / *THE MARKETING PLAN*

CONSTRUCTING THE MARKETING PLAN

_____ Annual Reviews   _____ Client Greeting Cards

_____ Term Conversions   _____ Family Birth Dates

_____ Age Change Notices   _____ Thank You Cards

_____ Social Security Audits   _____ Quarterly Professional Newsletters

_____ Client Acquisition   _____ Annual Personal Newsletter

Strategies to support this effort:

_____

_____

_____

_____

_____

_____

_____

_____

_____

_____

Exhibit 6.3 / *DEVELOPING MARKETS*

CONSTRUCTING THE MARKETING PLAN
MARKETS I INTEND TO DEVELOP

_____ Family Planning	_____ Group Insurance
_____ Spouse Insurance	_____ Deferred Compensation
_____ College Planning	_____ 401(k)
_____ Retirement Planning	_____ Worksite Marketing
_____ Estate Planning	_____ Group Carve-Out
_____ Charitable Giving	_____ Qualified Plans
_____ Equities	_____ Corporate-Owned Life Insurance
_____ Small Business Owners	_____ Professionals by Degree
_____ Professionals by Performance	_____ Inherited Wealth

Strategies to develop these markets:

_____

_____

_____

_____

_____

_____

_____

_____

Exhibit 6.4 / *PROSPECTING PLANS*

CONSTRUCTING THE MARKETING PLAN
PROSPECTING PLANS

_____ Natural Markets   _____ Direct Mail

_____ Endorsements   _____ Mass Mailing

_____ Key Centers of Influence   _____ Seminars

_____ Telemarketing   _____ Trade Shows

_____ Association Marketing   _____ Orphan Leads

Strategies to develop these prospects:

_____

_____

_____

_____

_____

_____

_____

_____

_____

_____

DECIDE BEST PROSPECTS

Producers now make a list of their best prospects by recording the names in each of the categories.

Exhibit 6.5 /*BEST PROSPECTS*

BEST PROSPECTS

	Prospect #1	Prospect #2	Prospect #3	Prospect #4	Prospect #5
$15,000 FYCs					
$10,000 FYCs					
$ 5,000 FYCs					
Profit Sharing & Pension Plans					
401(k)					
Defined Benefits & 412(i) Plans					
IRAs and SEPs					
Retirement Plan Rollovers					
Group Insurance					
Key Person Insurance					
Split Dollar/Corporate					
Split Dollar/Personal					
Deferred Compensation					
303 Stock Redemption					
Family Planning					
Spouse Insurance					
College Planning & 529 Plans					
Term Conversion					
Estate Planning					
Section 125					
Section 105					
Payroll Deduction					
Executive Bonus					
Equities					
Disability Income					
Long-Term Care					
Fixed Annuities					

Exhibit 6.6 / *IMPROVEMENT POSSIBILITIES*

EXAMINE IMPROVEMENT POSSIBILITIES
STRENGTHENING MARKETING EFFECTIVENESS

After you consider each question carefully, draw a circle around the figure in the rating column that represents your evaluation on each of the seven dimensions.	EVALUATION				
	POOR	WEAK	AVG.	GOOD	SUPER
1. GOAL DIRECTED To what extent are you focused on definite goals, more paid cases and increased commissions? Are these goals reduced to writing? Are you emotionally committed to their achievement?	20	40	60	80	100
2. PRO-ACTIVE To what extent have you earned the reputation for thinking right, selling right, studying right and living right? Are you a product of decisions or conditions? Active or passive?	20	40	60	80	100
3. EFFECTIVE To what extent do you know where your time goes? Do you plan your sales day the day before? Do you demonstrate a sense of urgency? Do you focus on the critical sales activities that produce a high pay-off?	20	40	60	80	100
4. CONFIDENT To what extent do you make your enthusiasm contagious? Do all three of your "sales companions" — enthusiasm, preparation and professionalism — show up with you on all interviews? Does your enthusiasm for your product add interest and power to all you say? Do prospects feel your self-confidence?	20	40	60	80	100
5. COMPETENT To what extent are you resourceful? Do you know your products and your competition thoroughly? Have you formed the habit of being well informed and current? Do you prepare in advance to meet situations likely to come up in interviews? Is your technical competence always improving? Do you have a true service attitude toward prospects?	20	40	60	80	100
6. CONSISTENT To what extent are you convincing in your contacts with prospects? Do you have the prospects' interests uppermost in your mind during your contacts with them? To what extent do you express absolute, unshakable loyalty to your agency and your company? Do you have the reputation for being a person with a strong sense of responsibility?	20	40	60	80	100
7. BALANCED To what extent does your reputation in the community precede you? Does your appearance attract prospects? Do you treat clients as you would like to be treated if you were in their place? Are you a good manager of your personal finances? Do you schedule "quality time" with the members of your family on a regular basis? Do you display staying power?	20	40	60	80	100

Add the circled numbers to determine your Sales Personality Evaluation. ☐

Average rating of your present Sales Personality. (Divide the above number by seven.) ☐

Exhibit 6.7 / *LOW -BUDGET STRATEGIES*

Low Budget Marketing Strategies

Marketing is the strategy used to position you to make more and better sales. Effective marketing improves your visibility and increases your contacts.

Here are twenty proven, low budget marketing strategies. They work!

1. Establish a client builder cluster group that meets each month. Exchange information, introductions and endorsements.

2. Submit press releases to the media regarding your achievements, published articles or books.

3. Send articles with information that will be of interest to your present prospects and clients.

4. Become "credentialized" to build your credibility, then announce it to your prospects and clients.

5. Collect testimonials.

6. Write articles for your professional journals or associations.

7. Have a client appreciation event, perhaps a Thanksgiving season brunch.

8. Sponsor a community event such as a 10K run or golf tournament.

9. Refer new customers to your clients.

10. Donate a service or product to charity.

11. Agree to be interviewed on radio or television.

12. Plan to meet three new people each week in every networking situation.

13. Identify and meet with "mentor type" individuals who can instruct you.

14. Speak at civic and professional organizations' meetings.

15. Send a quarterly newsletter.

16. Conduct informative seminars.

17. Take prospects to breakfast or lunch.

18. Send handwritten thank you notes.

19. Keep a supply of business cards with you. Hand them out freely everywhere you go.

20. Make friends with secretaries and receptionists, all of them!

Your Leadership is the Key

There is but one answer to the problem of improving the marketing skills and achieving vertical growth in the process. It is to be found in the strong imaginative marketing leadership you provide as the agency head.

Just as nearly every growth company in *Fortune's* 500 reflects the initiative and drive of one individual, so nearly every dynamic financial services organization achieving marketing results and satisfying vertical growth mirrors the good work of one person, its agency head.

ENTHUSIASM IS THE PRIME METHOD OF PERSUASION WITHOUT PRES-SURE. ENTHUSIASM IS THE YEAST THAT RAISES THE DOUGH. ENTHUSIASM IS THE GREATEST ONE WORD SLOGAN FOR LIVING EVER DEVISED.

Frank Bettger

VAL'S VIEWS ON MARKETING

Selling is no longer just selling. It's become, largely, a marketing event. Marketing is the ball game today. When marketing is done effectively, the producer's reputation as an advisor precedes him or her.

Identify the associate's natural market. Where is the individual favorably connected? When the market is defined, it makes it possible for management to personalize the training.

The key question to answer is, "Where will this producer be most comfortable?" When you resolve this issue, you are positioned to coach the individual on how to do those things that will cause him to become known for what he knows.

Make certain your associates understand, promote and execute the NetWeaving™ strategy discussed in this chapter. It can have a high payoff.

Chapter Thoughts and Ideas
I'm Using or Planning to implement

√ Provide marketing leadership.

√ Teach proven marketing strategies.

√ Analyze where associates have been.

√ Respect the little things.

√ Understand "Capturing Mind Share."

√ Review low budget marketing strategies.

√ Enhance producers' "professional equity."

√ Construct the plan.

Chapter 7 / INDUCTING

Og Mandino, arguably the finest self-help writer our country ever produced, was an equally gifted speaker. A few years back, we heard the late, legendary Mandino tell a story to a Dallas audience that we've never forgotten. His story drives home the theme of this chapter.

Confidence comes from successful experiences.

AT THE BEGINNING OF ANY WORTHWHILE PURSUIT,
WE ALL NEED HELP TO EARN, TO GAIN CONFIDENCE,
TO GROW, AND TO BE ENCOURAGED.

Back in the 15th Century, in a little village right outside of Nuremberg, Germany, there lived a family with fifteen children. Daddy worked three jobs just to keep food on the table for this tribe. Two of the boys had an ambition, a dream. Both had the same dream. They both wanted to go to the Art Academy in

Nuremberg, but they knew full well that there was no way their daddy would ever be able to afford to send either one of them.

So these two brothers, with similar talents and interests, worked up a pact. They would toss a coin to choose. The winner would go to the academy. The loser would go down into the mines and, with his pay, support the winner's studies. Four years later, after the first brother graduated, he would go into the mines, or use the income from his commissioned artwork, to support his brother who would attend the academy to obtain his art degree, too.

One morning they tossed the coin. Albrecht Durer won. Albert Durer lost. Albrecht went off to the academy, and Albert went down into the mines.

Albrecht was an immediate sensation at the academy. He was better than any of his professors. In his paintings, in his line drawings, in his engravings, in his woodcuts—he was just a natural. By his third year in school, Albrecht was earning enough in commissions to support himself. When he graduated, the family held a large party out on the lawn. All the children were there. Albrecht, from the head of the table, arose with a glass of wine. He offered a toast to his beloved brother, for all that Albert had done for him. He finished the toast by saying, " . . . and now, Albert, now it's your turn. You can go to the academy, and I will take care of you."

All eyes turned to the other end of the table. Albert was staring down at his hands and shaking his head saying, "No, no, no."

Finally, Albert rose, tears streaming down his cheeks. He looked down the table at Albrecht and said, "Albrecht, dear brother, it's too late for me. Look what four years in the mines have done to my hands! I've broken every finger at least once. I have arthritis in my left hand so bad that I can't even hold a piece of bread. I can't even lift my hands together so that I could return your toast properly. No, brother, I love you, but it is too late, much too late for me."

Four hundred years have passed. Albrecht Durer's artwork hangs in every great museum in the world. And yet, most know him for just one of his creations, because one day, Albrecht Durer honored his beloved brother by painting his hands.

Some of you have it hanging in your home. Or, maybe, you wear it around your neck as a charm. Maybe you have it in your office as bookends. But I know all of you know it. Today we call it "The Praying Hands."

When you look at that marvelous piece of work, study it carefully. Let it remind you of the common thread that runs through the life of every true success story in selling. No professional, no matter how great, achieves outstanding success alone. Like all the rest, he or she needs help to learn, to grow, and to develop skills.

Moving associates to a fast, confident start is an art to be mastered. In today's competitive market, and with the kind of individuals we need to attract, we must be prepared to have our new associates submit business quickly. The situation demands it, and the situation is the boss.

POTENTIAL JUST MEANS YOU AIN'T DONE IT YET.

Darrell Royal
Former Football Coach
The University of Texas

THE COMMITMENT "PLACE MAT"

The important starting point is to build a solid foundation. This is done effectively by following our structured, job description interview. This four-hour discussion is outlined with the acronym, *COMMITMENT*. The most important time you invest with a new associate is probably the time spent in this in-depth discussion just prior to the official starting day. This full and complete job description interview is outlined as shown in Exhibit 7.1. Make a copy and have it laminated so it can be referenced frequently without it becoming "dog-eared."

Place one "mat" in front of you, and one in front of your new associate. You want a responsible commitment to your proven methodology for registering entry-level individuals as performing producers early in the "ball game."

Let's spell out the job description as we might do with an entry-level producer. Keep in mind, this "Place Mat" concept can be modified and used with experienced producers, too.

CONFIDENCE IS CONTAGIOUS. BELIEVING IN PEOPLE IS THE BEST WAY TO HELP THEM BELIEVE IN THEMSELVES. THE NEXT TIME YOU ARE HANDING OUT A CHALLENGING WORK ASSIGNMENT, START BY ASSURING PEOPLE OF HOW MUCH CONFIDENCE YOU HAVE IN THEIR ABILITIES.

Rick Pitino

Exhibit 7.1 / *COMMITMENT "PLACE MAT"*

COMMITMENT "PLACE MAT" INTERVIEW
Professional Partnership Explained

COMPATIBILITY APPRAISAL

ORIGINS OF SUCCESS
> Contacts/Social Mobility
> Selling/Marketing
> Self-discipline
> Entrepreneurial
> Wife/Husband Support
> Money Management
> Staying Power

MAJOR RULES FOR SUCCESS
> Fast, Confident Start
> Daily Plan Habit
> Weekly Effort Formula
> Daily Performance Ledger
> Sales System and Marketing
> Sales Language Mastery
> Paid Cases, Club Membership
> Performance Improvement Formula (MEA)
> Professional Growth
> Personal Growth

MEANING AND PURPOSE OF THE PRE-APPOINTMENT

ILLUSTRATION OF ROLES PLAYED AND JOINT WORK GRID

THE INVESTMENTS
> Personal Product Purchases
> Association Membership
> Computers
> Sales Professional's Success Kit

MY PHILOSOPHIES AND EXPECTATIONS

EARNINGS (HOW PRODUCERS ARE PAID)

NECESSARY FAST START; 30-DAY, 90-DAY CHECKLISTS

TARGET PAID CASES/MDRT CREDITS FOR THE YEAR

Exhibit 7.1 cont'd ⁄ *COMMITMENT "PLACE MAT"*

 **COMPATIBILITY APPRAISAL**

- Is this your "final answer?" Appraise compatibility objectively. Be convinced 100% that your long-term relationship is going to be a harmonious one with this selection.

c**O**MMITMENT **ORIGINS OF SUCCESS**

- **CONTACTS/SOCIAL MOBILITY.** The financial services business is a contact business. It rewards relationship building and social mobility.

- **SELLING/MARKETING.** These skills are essential to the producer's success. Selling is what is done at the point of sale; marketing is what is done to position the producer favorably in the eyes of the potential client.

- **SELF-DISCIPLINE.** Forming the habits the professionals form.

- **ENTREPRENEURIAL.** Taking 100% responsibility for activity and results.

- **WIFE/HUSBAND SUPPORT.** Many times this becomes a critical, turning issue.

- **MONEY MANAGEMENT.** It's difficult to advise others if the producer is not managing his or her own finances properly.

- **STAYING POWER.** Define what you believe to be the apprenticeship period. Sticking with it often provides the "winner's edge."

Exhibit 7.1 cont'd /*COMMITMENT "PLACE MAT"*

　　　MAJOR RULES FOR SUCCESS

- **FAST, CONFIDENT START.** Confidence comes from successful experiences and those successful experiences must come early on. Discuss joint work and your strategy for setting up the producer for early success.

- **DAILY PLAN HABIT.** Help them see how important it is to awaken employed.

- **WEEKLY EFFORT FORMULA.** Here you explain the job description and calculate the numbers that must be reached each week.

- **DAILY PERFORMANCE LEDGER.** Stress the importance of managing actual selling time.

- **SALES SYSTEM AND MARKETING.** Review, again, the client building sales strategy and the importance of consistently generating warm prospects.

- **SALES LANGUAGE MASTERY.** The producer must become comfortable with the language in 30 days, and conversational in 60 days.

- **PAID CASES, CLUB MEMBERSHIP.** Stress the importance of the frequency of successes, reaching and surpassing your company's minimum standards of performance.

- **PERFORMANCE IMPROVEMENT FORMULA.** This is the average size sale, multiplied times closing effectiveness and the number of ask-to-buys. (This formula is discussed fully in Chapter 8.)

- **PROFESSIONAL GROWTH.** Discuss the importance of acquiring credentials as quickly as possible. Clients like doing business with competent advisors.

- **PERSONAL GROWTH.** Focus on the benefits of living the balanced life.

Exhibit 7.1 cont'd /*COMMITMENT "PLACE MAT"*

MEANING AND PURPOSE OF THE PRE-APPOINTMENT

- This activity facilitates the fast start and provides a production jump on any contract requirements. Discuss it and explain the Operation Fast Start Checklist.

ILLUSTRATION OF ROLES PLAYED AND JOINT WORK GRID

- See Exhibits 7.2 and 7.3 to focus your discussion on these two important items.

THE INVESTMENTS

- **PERSONAL PRODUCT PURCHASES.** Emphasize the importance of owning what you sell.

- **ASSOCIATION MEMBERSHIP.** Demonstrate your commitment through memberships in professional associations.

- **COMPUTERS.** Computer literacy is a mark of professionalism in today's fast-changing world of technology.

- **SALES PROFESSIONAL'S SUCCESS KIT.** This program will assist producers in developing confidence in prospecting, telephoning, and closing skills.

Exhibit 7.1 cont'd / *COMMITMENT "PLACE MAT"*

MY PHILOSOPHIES AND
EXPECTATIONS

- Cover, in-depth, your basic operational philosophies. Please refer to Exhibit 7.6, the "Personal Mission Statement." Your expectations must be carefully spelled out. Your production estimates should be reasonably high, but tempered with good judgment.

EARNINGS
(HOW PRODUCERS ARE PAID)

- Carefully explain how and when earnings are paid.

NECESSARY FAST START;
30-DAY, 90-DAY CHECKLISTS

- Review each of these important checklists, line by line.

TARGET PAID CASES/
MDRT CREDITS FOR THE YEAR

- Communicate your expectations.

THE SOWER MAY MISTAKE AND SOW HIS PEAS CROOKEDLY; THE PEAS MAKE NO MISTAKE, BUT COME UP AND SHOW HIS LINE.

Ralph Waldo Emerson

Exhibit 7.2 / *NEW PRODUCER DEVELOPMENT GRID*

NEW PRODUCER DEVELOPMENT GRID

Peter Drucker once observed, *"More and more I see managers searching for the panacea rather than developing their skills for motivating and bringing out the best in their people."*

Building Independent, Responsible Producers (IRPs) is the goal.

☐ Thinking Right

☐ Working Right

☐ Selling Right

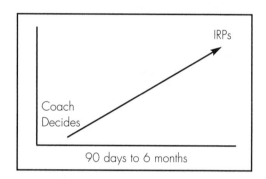

☐ Motivate

☐ Upgrade

☐ Measure

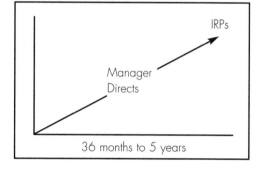

☐ Assist

☐ Inform

☐ Promote

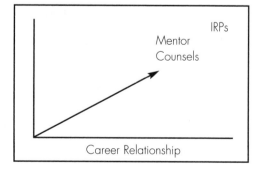

Exhibit 7.3 / *EARLY SUCCESS SETUP*

SETTING UP PRODUCERS FOR EARLY SUCCESS

Model Joint Work Schedule
(Nine Week Program)

WEEK	MON.	TUES.	WED.	THURS.	FRI.
1					
2					
3					
4					
5					
6					
7					
8					
9					

Joint Work   Independent Work   Joint Business

*Concentrated joint work and organized joint business
are the key activities in developing new producers.*

Exhibit 7.4 / *MEMORANDUM OF UNDERSTANDING*

MEMORANDUM OF UNDERSTANDING

KEEPING THE PROMISE

I, _____, recognize the importance of the 90-day Fast Start.

My 90-day production commitments are:
_____ Applications Submitted _____ MDRT Credits Submitted

COMMITMENTS

I commit to these five key activities:

1. Plan each day the day before.
2. Memorize, professionalize, and personalize the sales language.
3. Strengthen my marketing efforts; be contact conscious.
4. Have ten interviews each week.
5. Prepare for and participate in weekly PEP session.

AGREEMENT

I, _____, am determined to achieve the objectives and commitments identified above realizing that nothing happens until someone makes a responsible commitment.

_____
(Producer)

I, _____, resolve to partner with you to achieve your Fast Start numbers. I will monitor and measure your Weekly Effort Formula activities and results. Together we will form a winning team. I will prepare and conduct a weekly PEP session until you are an MDRT qualifier.

_____
(Manager)

Exhibit 7.5 / *OPERATION FAST START*

OPERATION FAST START
PRE-APPOINTMENT CHECKLIST

Name _____ Completion Date _____

- ☐ **Prospects (#_____)**
  (Include complete information.)

Attitude Builders

Read and inwardly digest the following:

- ☐ *How I Raised Myself From Failure to Success* – Frank Bettger
- ☐ *The Common Denominator of Success* – Albert E. N. Gray
- ☐ *Secrets of Successful Insurance Sales* – Jack and Garry Kinder

Skill Development (Training)

- ☐ Life and health licenses
- ☐ Series 6 and Series 63 licenses
- ☐ View tape and complete the workbook – *Developing Tele-Confidence*
- ☐ Complete Sales Professional's Success Kit
- ☐ Read *Red Letter Language* – Howard Wight

Knowledge (Education)

- ☐ Life Products
- ☐ Long-Term Care
- ☐ Annuities
- ☐ Product Solutions
- ☐ Market Analysis

People who are unable to motivate themselves must be content with mediocrity, no matter how impressive their other talents.

Exhibit 7.6 / *PRODUCER'S MISSION STATEMENT*

PRODUCER'S MISSION STATEMENT

This is an important document. This is why many management professionals spend days, even weeks, developing a statement unique to the individual producer.

This statement defines the values that represent the producer's chief aims in life, both personal and professional.

Here is a collection of beliefs to be considered in building this mission statement.

- Make good on all commitments.

- Plan tomorrow's work today.

- Show up on time.

- Manage selling time.

- Never confuse activity with accomplishment.

- Stay focused on the vital factors.

- Be orderly in person and in the work environment.

- Never compromise honesty.

- Believe honest, intelligent effort is always rewarded.

- Know your lines; ad-libs are for amateurs.

- Develop one new proficiency each quarter.

- Stay physically fit and mentally alert.

- Succeed at home first.

- Know your numbers.

- Utilize the wise counsel of others.

- Manage finances.

The vision you glorify in your mind,
The ideal you enthrone in your heart —
This you will build your life by,
This you will become.

Exhibit 7.7 /*CONTRACT STARTING DATE LETTER*

CONTRACT STARTING DATE LETTER

Date

To (your newly appointed associate):

Today you begin your professional selling career with (company). It promises to be a satisfying and profitable one.

You will want to keep in mind the basic fundamentals for achieving the right start in this business. These are the habits that will assure your success.

• Plan each day the day before.

• Memorize, professionalize and personalize the sales language.

• Strengthen your marketing efforts; be contact conscious.

• Have ten interviews each week.

• Prepare for and participate in weekly PEP session.

Our first objective, (new associate's name), is to complete the Pre-appointment requirements. Let's focus our efforts on accomplishing these, and plan to do so in the time frames we discussed. Completing all licensing requirements is at the top of our priority list.

In a recent study of MDRT members who qualified within their first two years in the business, it was found they worked an average of ten hours a day and three evenings a week. Ninety percent worked on Saturday and had five selling interviews each week. Additionally, they averaged 102 paid transactions their first two years.

Let's work closely to build your confidence in our selling strategy. Let's build and maintain a "partnership-type" relationship.

May your thoughts always be as good as mine will be for you, (name).

All the best,

Exhibit 7.8 / *30-DAY CHECKLIST*

30-DAY CHECKLIST

Name _____ Completion Date _____

☐ Prospecting Reservoir _____

☐ Production Submitted MDRT Credits $ _____

Attitude Builders

☐ Breakthrough Cassettes (Attitude Series)

☐ *How to Think Right* - Video

☐ Bob Love's MDRT Presentation - Video

SKILL DEVELOPMENT EXERCISES

☐ *How to Close with Confidence* - Video

☐ *Secrets of Successful Insurance Sales* - Cassettes (4, 5 & 6)
(Complete workbook exercises)

Knowledge

☐ Computer _____

☐ Products _____

☐ Weekly Progress Guide

Honest, intelligent effort is always rewarded.

Exhibit 7.9 /*90-DAY CHECKLIST*

THE CRITICAL
90-DAY CHECKLIST

Name _____ Completion Date _____

❒ Prospecting Reservoir _____

❒ Endorsements _____

❒ Production Paid MDRT Credits $ _____

Attitude Builders

❒ Breakthrough Cassettes (Strategy Series)

❒ *How to Sell Right* - Video

Skill Development Exercises

❒ *How to Handle Objections* - Video

❒ Breakthrough Cassettes (Strategy Series)

Knowledge

❒ Products _____

❒ Underwriting and Issue

Showing up for work, on time and attitudinally dressed,
ready to play, provides the basis for excellence in any endeavor.

INDUCTION INITIATIVES

Everything we've discussed in this system must come together in order to achieve these three initiatives.

- First, entry-level producers must be *shown* how to "put in a good day's work."

- Second, the sales strategy and sales language must be transferred.

- Third, an attitude of mind must be developed that causes the producer to "capture the magic of enjoying every sales call."

IF TALENT DOESN'T WORK HARD, HARD WORK BEATS TALENT.

Art Resnick

A Good Day's Work

The most important factor in selling success has always been, and will always be, the way the producer invests his or her selling time. It follows, as night follows day, that your biggest challenge is in showing entry-level producers how to put in a good day's work.

- We recommend you adopt this practice as a standard operating procedure. Buy or borrow a stopwatch, the kind used at athletic events. Be careful not to purchase the kind that resets to zero after every stop.

- Have producers carry the watch in their pocket every day for a week of normal selling. They are to turn it on and let it run every minute they are actually in the presence of a prospect, talking about the benefits of financial products. In other words, *while they are actually selling.* They are not to let the watch run while they are driving around deciding where to make a call. They never let it run while they are having idle conversation with a prospect, while they are wrestling with compliance issues in the office, or while they are having coffee. *In short, they don't let the watch run while they are doing anything but conducting an actual sales interview.*

- Since the stopwatch readings are for the producer, and for the producer alone, there will not be the temptation to fudge the reading. The goal is to increase the producers' incomes, not egos.

- Add up the daily readings at the end of the sales week. If they find that during the entire week they spent less than ten hours of new, creative sales effort in front of prospects, they shouldn't be discouraged! They need not be discouraged even if the readings for the week total less than six hours. They may be shocked, but not discouraged. After they recover from the shock of seeing a record of their actual selling time, they will realize they have gotten to the very heart of the production problem, and they have done it quickly. The problem is they aren't generating the sales effort and rewards they could easily learn to appreciate because they aren't spending enough hours in actual selling situations. They might be putting in the hours, but now you both know that very few of those hours are actually invested in selling.

So, what's the solution? Help producers make a strong resolve that from now on they are going to be very choosy in how they invest their time.

WATCH YOUR THOUGHTS, FOR THEY BECOME WORDS. CHOOSE YOUR WORDS, FOR THEY BECOME ACTIONS. UNDERSTAND YOUR ACTIONS, FOR THEY BECOME HABITS. STUDY YOUR HABITS, FOR THEY WILL BECOME YOUR CHARACTER. DEVELOP YOUR CHARACTER, FOR IT BECOMES YOUR DESTINY.

Sales Language Transferred

First, decide upon the sales language you will use. Again, you communicate to the producers that you want the sales language to become as natural as breathing. You want the producers to be comfortable with the language in 30 days, and conversational in 60.

You transfer sales language best through joint work efforts. That is where you make both demonstrations and observations. It helps you see that the producers are gaining an understanding of the words and the strategy.

The Pocket Prompter discussed earlier, along with CDs, video and audiocassettes, makes your job of transferring sales language much easier. Keep in mind that technology has revolutionized producer training. These training tools are always available, they never change their script, and they never lose their energy levels.

Correct Attitude Developed

Every sales call producers make, like everything else they do in life, is made up of a small amount of conscious activity plus a huge bulk of subconscious activity.

The subconscious is amazingly versatile. It handles countless demands made on it every selling day. But the subconscious mind has some peculiar sides, also. Perhaps the one that affects producers most is that terrible, consuming fear of rejection, inadequacy, and failure. It runs far deeper than most of us even suspect. It affects every detail of our waking selling lives. The cowardly subconscious will go to almost any lengths to avoid or postpone even the possibility of rejection, inadequacy, or failure. *Read that sentence again.*

Many producers have succeeded in training their subconscious to push them on instead of dragging them back. Those producers are the star performers who consistently compile impressive sales results.

> *To be tested is good.*
> *The challenged life may be the best therapist.*
>
> *Gail Sheehy*

Producers cannot make the mistake of thinking they can manage their subconscious with any process of reason or logic. The subconscious simply doesn't respond to reason or logic. For example, imagine a good, heavy plank lying on the ground, say one about a foot wide, six inches thick and twenty feet long. You could, without difficulty, walk the full length of this plank, turn around at the end, and walk back. You could do it a hundred times.

If the same plank was fastened rigidly between the roofs of two high buildings, with several hundred feet of empty space below, you might be able to force yourself to walk it, but your feelings would certainly be very different! Reason and logic tell you that you could successfully walk this plank. You could do it a hundred times on the ground. It's plenty strong, rigidly fastened, and it won't spring or sway.

Would all that reason and logic change your feelings about walking that plank high in the air?

It is important you remember that the subconscious does not respond to reason and logic. Your subconscious fear of making calls is not logical and neither is the cure for that subconscious fear.

Reason and logic tell producers there is nothing to dread about making the next call. No prospect will harm them. Humiliation and embarrassment and rude treatment doesn't harm them physically. Logically, producers should not feel any different about contacting prospects than they would feel about calling a clerk in a department store to place an order. But are their feelings the same? Why not? Can they make them the same? *The answer here is yes, they can!* But don't try to get them to do it with logical information. It's as hopeless as trying to reason them into walking the plank high in the air.

Since you cannot decrease the strong impact of the producer's subconscious by a fraction of an ounce by any process of reason or logic, what can you do? You can get them to agree that the subconscious is like a big, dry sponge. It absorbs some things like a sponge absorbs water. It absorbs imagination—in a big way. That is why many individuals spend much of their time daydreaming.

They daydream of recognition, of prestige, and of success. They daydream about MDRT status and the prestige of being the top professional in the organization. They daydream of "having it made." They even daydream about telling off an unreasonable prospect who should buy, but for no apparent reason, wants to think about it.

Does the producer's subconscious respond to these daydreams? You bet it does! So the master key becomes: *Give it something useful to absorb.* Nothing can keep the producer's subconscious from responding! If they feed it the right things it will absorb them. It must respond. The response will clear away those illogical subconscious fears of rejection, inadequacy, and failure.

Just how do producers go about feeding their subconscious something useful in place of daydreams?

The first step is for them to recall their feelings at the time when they made one of those easy, natural sales. It's important they recall their exact feelings, as clearly as they can. They must recall the actual details of their feelings. They must recall them vividly.

One of the best illustrations of how quickly and positively the subconscious responds is found in this well-known fact about selling. *The best time to make a new call is right after you have made a good sale.* At that time, producers' attitudes are perfect. By giving their subconscious something useful to absorb, they will constantly create the same kind of attitude they have when they're "hot." They will be able to heal and neutralize the limp, apologetic feeling they have when they are "cold."

The whole formula is quite simple. Before every sales call they should ask themselves, "How would I feel about making the next call if it were an easy, natural sale?"

This is the simple formula. Don't let them complicate it. Don't let them try to reason it out. They must start acting and talking in a confident, assured manner. You'll note that we did not say they are to start *feeling* that way. Rather, they are to *act* in an enthusiastic, positive way. Feelings always follow actions. Just try it! It works!

This formula will work better every time the producers use it. They can't overdo it. They can use it between every sales call. They can use it during every selling interview. This same confident manner will carry them right into the presentation and through it. Again, how would they feel if they were presenting a recommendation which they knew was the answer to the prospect's problem and the sales talk was predestined to have a happy ending?

They would be confident, but not cocky. They would be poised, confident, courteous, and mentally prepared. They would have no reason to be tense or hesitant.

Producers should form the habit of applying this formula to every selling situation. The surge of energy they experience when they act is their first glimpse of the tremendous reserve of hidden power they possess. As they experience the same surge of enthusiasm, time after time, they will begin to realize the immense size of the potential within. Producers can then enjoy every selling interview from that moment on. *The secret, the magic, depends upon their giving their subconscious something useful to continuously absorb.*

Imagination, plus the action it can stimulate, is the magic that will work for each of your producers.

IT IS THROUGH THEIR WORK THAT MOST INDIVIDUALS WRITE THE STORY OF THEIR LIVES. THEY ARE BOTH THE AUTHOR AND THE STORY'S PRINCIPAL CHARACTER. THEY ARE FREE TO BE THE HERO OR THE VILLAIN; SUCCESS OR FAILURE.

Malcolm Forbes

Exhibit 7.10 / *DO YOUR WORK*

DO YOUR WORK . . .

*Not just your work and no more,
but a little more for the lavishing sake.
That little more which is worth all the rest.*

*And when you suffer, as you must,
and if you sometimes doubt, as you will,
do your work.
Put your heart into it. Give it your best.
And the sky will one day clear.*

*Then, out of your very doubt and suffering
will be born the supreme joy
that comes from work well done.*

*In a day and time when we have grown to
almost deify leisure time,
it's good to be reminded that most
of our great satisfactions in life will come,
not from our leisure, but from our work.*

Dean Briggs, Northwestern University

VAL'S VIEWS ON INDUCTING

I've always believed setting producers up for early success was one of those management skills you and I must perfect. I'd much rather have a producer with marginal potential directed by a strong manager than have a high potential producer with a weak manager who can explain and rationalize a lousy production start with a new recruit.

To register new producers as early successes, we believe you must spell out the job description very carefully. Be sure you gain understanding. At all times, producers should know what is expected of them and how they are performing.

Explain the professional partnership concept. Reinforce how you want to serve them and assist them in reaching your expectations and theirs.

Drive home over and over again this basic philosophy. During the producers' early years, we want them to be imitators, not creators. They are not expected to be original. Their jobs are to learn how to put in a good day's work and sell business following precisely the model they will see management use over and over again.

Make your process so simple that when ordinary producers follow it, they perform in an excalibur fashion.

CHAPTER THOUGHTS AND IDEAS
I'M USING OR PLANNING TO IMPLEMENT

√ Complete the Memorandum of Understanding.

√ Explain the New Producer Development Grid.

√ Complete the joint work schedule.

√ Build correct attitudes.

√ Review checklists, line by line.

√ Focus on induction initiatives.

√ Build a mission statement with producers.

√ Review the major rules for success.

Chapter 8 / *MONITORING*

Any time we've witnessed individuals achieve the extraordinary, they have been a monomaniac with a passion. *In other words, they were focused individuals with a mission.*

In the movie *City Slickers*, starring Billy Crystal, a story evolves of a man going through a mid-life crisis. He decides to go out with some buddies and rustle cattle for a week. Crystal's

Monitor Consistently What Matters

character reports to a trail boss by the name of Curly, played by Jack Palance.

Curly really seems to have everything going right for him. Curly has his act together. Crystal keeps asking what his secret is. Curly's only reply is to hold up his index finger and say, *"One thing."*

Finally, in frustration Crystal asks, "What is that one thing?" To which, Curly replies, "That is what you must figure out. No one can decide it for you!"

Monitoring and measuring what matters always improves what matters. Monomania brings a focus to bear on those critical few things that matter.

The greatest manager who ever lived taught, "If your eye be single – your whole body will be full of light."

What do you focus on with producers? What is it that matters? This is what we'll decide upon in this chapter.

INDIVIDUAL DIFFERENCES

Effective monitoring recognizes producers have individual differences. They have different motivations, goals and aspirations. This makes it important that each producer being developed be considered as an individual.

Producers will improve their performances when they see . . .

- Need for improvement;

- Recommended changes improve their productivity; and

- Financial rewards for making the extra effort to change.

OUR CHIEF WANT IN LIFE IS SOMEBODY WHO WILL MAKE US DO WHAT WE CAN.

Ralph Waldo Emerson

ATTITUDES

Here are five sound monitoring attitudes you'll want to adopt:

1. *Producers are individual assets worth investing in.* Develop producers to become independent and responsible. Build on strengths, as you manage the weaknesses.

2. *Keep producers sold on making good on the Weekly Effort Formula numbers.* It's important that they become sold on the "law of averages."

3. *Work for the success of each producer as you work for your own success.* Treat producers as if they already were what they ought to be, and you'll help them become what they are capable of becoming.

4. *Work with producers on the same basis as you would expect them to work with their clients.*

5. *Keep producers sold on their abilities, their futures and your confidence in them.* Your greatest satisfaction will come from assisting producers in reaching their potential.

Monitoring is one of the most difficult of all managerial jobs. The ability to talk to associates frankly about their attitudes, skills and habits – and to keep them focused on the key factors that will cause improvement – is a real challenge. It requires your creative best.

PRODUCTION TRIANGLE

The ultimate result of a well-conceived monitoring system must be improved performance on the part of the individuals being monitored. There are three interrelated factors that provide the framework for achieving this improved performance. These factors provide the triangle within which you implement your monitoring system.

Exhibit 8.1 / *PRODUCTION TRIANGLE*

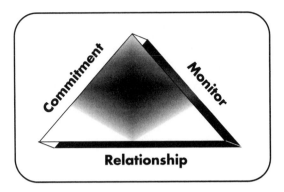

1. *Relationship building provides the important foundation.*

   Unless the foundation is built solidly, you monitor, measure and motivate on "shaky ground."

2. *Commitment is next.*

   Nothing significant happens until and unless you secure a responsible commitment. This is why mutual goal setting and intelligent planning produce desired results.

3. *Monitoring and measuring completes the triangle.*

   Monitoring and measuring, when done positively and meaningfully, always improve performance!

Keep in mind always, it's relationship building, commitment, monitoring and measuring that provide the framework for consistently achieving improved performances.

What – Where – How

What Do You Monitor?

At the start, you monitor the planning process. Next, you monitor sales activity and results. Intelligent activity produces results. Results build confidence. Selling confidence comes only from successful experiences.

Where Do You Monitor?

You monitor in the field, in live selling situations. You monitor in role-playing situations, and in joint work situations.

How Do You Monitor?

You monitor by coaching confidence. Selling the daily planning habit – following through to make certain producers are waking up in the morning "employed." This requires them to plan their activity the day before. You help producers to understand "you keep records to break records."

You make producers aware of your awareness. When they are conscious of being monitored, behavior changes and performance improves.

IT IS A GOOD RULE TO FACE DIFFICULTIES AT THE TIME THEY ARISE AND NOT ALLOW THEM TO INCREASE UNACKNOWLEDGED.

Edward W. Zeigler

Progress Guide

The Weekly Progress Guide, shown in Exhibit 8.2, is a personalized monitoring tool for producers. The report shows selling activity for the current week, the previous week year-to-date, total year-to-date, this year's goals, and what is left to go. The needs for each week remaining in the year are then calculated. It asks for pre-approach calls, appointments set, opening interviews, closing interviews, submitted applications and submitted commissions. Submitted results and paid results are also monitored. This report is completed and reviewed on a weekly basis with management. Next week's specific plans are outlined and the producer is evaluated year-to-date.

Performance Improvement Formula

Three factors make the difference in producers' incomes. *These factors should be monitored and measured closely on a weekly basis.* We cannot overstate the importance of this weekly management discipline. See Exhibit 8.3, Performance Improvement Formula.

The three factors are Market, Effectiveness and Activity. A producer's Market score is expressed as the average size MDRT Credit sale, on a rolling 50-week basis. Effectiveness is the closing ratio, again over a 50-week basis. It's expressed as a percentage. The producer's Activity number is the number of ask-to-buy attempts the producer averages on a weekly basis. Again, these numbers are all calculated on a 50-week basis. The three numbers are then multiplied. *When multiplied, the result gives you the producer's weekly commission income average.*

The performance improvement formula is M x E x A. Help the producer see that a slight improvement in any factor multiplies and will result in a substantial change in the weekly income average.

A standard can be developed for each producer. The producer's contacts, skill level and experience will influence the standard. For example, during the early years a producer might have as a standard the following:

Average Size Sale (M) – $700

Closing Percentage (E) – 50%

Ask-to-buys (A) = 4

This producer's weekly commission is $1,400. ($700 x .50 x 4)

YOU CAN'T REALLY MANAGE TIME. THERE ARE ONLY 24 HOURS IN A DAY, AND YOU CAN'T CHANGE THAT. WHAT YOU CAN DO IS MANAGE YOU'R SELLING ACTIVITIES IN RESPECT TO TIME.

R. Alec MacKenzie

Exhibit 8.2 / *PROGRESS GUIDE*

PROGRESS GUIDE

Your performance today is the key to your future.

Name _____ **For week ending** _____ **20** ____

Weeks worked this year-to-date _____ **Weeks left to work this year** ____

Sales Activity

	This Week	YTD Last Week	Total YTD	This Year's Commitment	Yet To Go	Need Each Week
Pre-Approach Calls						
Appointments Set						
Opening Interviews						
Closing Interviews						
Submitted Apps						
Submitted MDRT Credits						

Submitted Results

MDRT Credits	This Week	YTD Last Week	Total YTD	This Year's Commitment	Yet To Go	Need Each Week
• Life						
• DI						
• Annuity						
• Long-Term Care						
• Equity Sales						
• Other						
• Total Submitted						
• Endorsements						

Exhibit 8.2 cont'd / *PROGRESS GUIDE*

Paid Results

	This Week	YTD Last Week	Total YTD	This Year's Commitment	Yet To Go	Need Each Week
Cases						
Life MDRT Credits						
DI Credits						
Annuity Credits						
Long-Term Care Credits						
Equity Sales Credits						
Other MDRT Credits						
Total Paid MDRT Credits						

Clients developed this week _____   **Total clients to date** _____

Next Week's Specific Plans

Opening interviews scheduled: _____
Closing interviews scheduled: _____

Best prospects:

_____

_____

_____

Year-To-Date Evaluations
(Use rolling 50-week average)

M – **Average size sale:** $_____
E – **Closing percentage:**   _____%
A – **Ask-to-buy interviews:**   _____ =
                                              _____ FYCs/Wk.

Comments:

_____

_____

_____

Exhibit 8.3 / *PERFORMANCE FORMULA*

PERFORMANCE IMPROVEMENT FORMULA

CRITICAL SALES ISSUES

Market $_____

(Average Size Sale)

X

Effectiveness _____%

(Closing Percentage)

X

Activity _____

(Ask-to-buy attempts per week)

Equals

Weekly Commission Average $_____

Weekly, you calculate the numbers for each of your trainee producers. These numbers serve as a thermometer, which measures the well-being of the producer and the direction he or she is headed.

The numbers cannot be skimmed. They must be studied and discussed at every PEP Session.

Remember, the numbers are calculated on a rolling 50-week basis.

What Producers Expect

In implementing and improving your Monitoring System, remember producers have some common expectations about their relationship with you and what it's going to accomplish. Their list includes the following:

- Give us specific methods for improving our sales - not what to do, but how to do it.

- Show us how to apply the best planning practices to our daily work.

- Serve us instructional and educational material in easy-to-digest capsule doses – short, simplified, documented and illustrated.

- Carefully plan and conduct sales meetings to make us money. Schedule these sessions at a time other than our selling time.

- Show us, by example, how to be more effective in arousing the interest of prospects and creating their desire for our products and services.

- Help us to organize our time to maximize selling time.

- Teach us how to handle the competition. Tell and show us exactly what to do and say.

- Give us factual examples of successful selling practices used by other high-performing producers.

- Involve us in joint selling activities that will expand and improve our markets.

- Assist us and coach us in selling more effectively in advanced markets.

- Promote us in a way that will cause us to have an enhanced professional presence in the community.

Performance Evaluation and Planning Sessions

This is the most important part of the Monitoring System. When you learn to handle these sessions skillfully, you'll be on the way to bringing out the best in your producers. The ability to determine that a potential problem exists, to determine its cause and prescribe positive action is what the producer development process is all about.

The purpose of Performance Evaluation and Planning (PEP) sessions is to help you and each of your newer producers perform more effectively, while demonstrating accountability for achieving desired results.

Weekly PEP sessions should be scheduled. Once sessions are set, other activities should be planned around them.

At the start of a producer's career, you'll want to conduct these sessions weekly. Follow this procedure regularly during the Developmental Years. As the producer demonstrates maturity and effectiveness, PEP sessions can be held less frequently.

Again, keep in mind, producers achieve skill and confidence at varying speeds. This is not to imply that monitoring doesn't continue through the early years – and, in some instances, even beyond. However, as a producer develops, a different type of monitoring needs to be provided. *Let the situation be your "boss" on this matter.*

PEP Session Pattern

Ideally, PEP sessions are held at the end of each week. *Make certain there is visible evidence of the preparation you've done.* Review any notes and action plans made from previous sessions. By being properly prepared, 45 minutes will be an adequate time frame for this session.

Each PEP session should follow a definite pattern. The following will be needed for the session:

- Appointment Book;

- Progress Guide;

- Business Plan; and

- Next Week's Plan.

Look for those things you can compliment. Build on strengths. Coach confidence. Remember, individual coaching is the link between producer education and training.

Review what the producer has done during the week, as you measure activity against the Weekly Effort Formula numbers.

Review results. Discuss specifically what must happen each week for the balance of the year to reach and surpass committed objectives.

PEOPLE ARE GENERALLY BETTER PERSUADED BY THE REASONS THAT THEY HAVE THEMSELVES DISCOVERED THAN BY THOSE THAT HAVE COME INTO THE MINDS OF OTHERS.

Pascal

PEP Pointers

1. Review Weekly Progress Guide and previous plans before session.

2. Review results of the past week's activity and compliment the positive aspects.

3. Review activities that led to these results; compare with the Weekly Effort Formula.

4. Check progress toward objectives. Calculate together what must be done each week for the balance of the year to reach these committed objectives.

5. "Draw the producer out" relative to attitudes and feelings toward progress and future.

6. Role-play the phases of the selling strategy which need to be strengthened.

7. Schedule any educational or training sessions, or joint work you agree is necessary.

8. *Review average size sale, closing ratios and closing attempts (MEA).*

9. Review carefully next week's plan. Discuss in detail planned sales activity for the coming week – especially Monday. You want to expect and build consistent effort.

10. Close on a high note – make it a meaningful PEP session. The key objective of your sessions is to keep them sold on their abilities, their futures and the confidence you have in them. Make entries in your records, or in your appointment calendar immediately following the session so you will be well prepared for next week's session.

Remember the Main Thing

Your closing objective in PEP sessions is to see that producers leave your office more confident about the development of next week's business. This means the producer has specific places to go to obtain new interviews and sales. Also, this requires you to be a skillful thinker, planner and motivator.

Probe for Unshakable Facts

Do not merely have the producer report to you that so many calls were made or so many new prospects were secured or so many ask-to-buy interviews were conducted. Ask searching questions about the prospects developed each day starting with Monday. Why are these people prospects? Where did the producer get the prospects? What contact has been made? Have a probing attitude. Develop unshakable facts. Continue this process through the entire week's activities.

This probing process reveals much more to you than facts about activity. It reveals the producer's real concept of the selling job. It underscores possible problems. *Most of all, it helps producers learn to evaluate selling activities and results in a meaningful way.*

Again, stress the importance of the Weekly Effort Formula. Keep it simple! Say it often! Burn the numbers in! Help each producer understand the formula's importance, emotionally as well as intellectually. *You cannot – we repeat – you cannot stress the Weekly Effort Formula and its numbers too often.*

"Main Event"

We are strong advocates for having an agenda-driven, "Main Event" Monthly Managers' Meeting. In attendance at this meeting are all Managers, Potential Managers, Marketing Team Leaders and the organization's Key Office Person (KOP).

Your job is to work from an agenda and to be 100% responsible for the content to inform, instruct and inspire. There should be strong evidence of preparation. You must take 100% responsibility for the development of the management team.

A key happening at each month's "Main Event" is when you fix a focus on Key Result Areas. Each participating manager builds a forecast of what will happen in the next 30 days. You are to challenge these forecasts, and make them solid.

Monitoring results vs. commitment is a strong strategy for "burning in" your philosophy relative to making good on all commitments.

At next month's session, the "3Rs" are addressed by each manager:

R #1 – is a Review of forecast made 30 days ago.

R #2 – actual results are Recorded and discussed.

R #3 – a new forecast for next month is Reported.

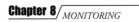

See Exhibit 8.4, Monthly Focus Report for a format you'll find helpful.

*GOOD ENOUGH NEVER IS; AND BETTER IS ONLY ACCEPTABLE IF THERE
IS COMMITMENT TO MAKE IT BETTER.*

Betsy Sanders

Performance to Potential

An excellent management development tool is shown in Exhibit 8.5
– Performance to Potential. This proficiency checklist serves as an inventory of skills and abilities you want to develop with your management
team members.

Study it closely and decide to revisit it quarterly. It will keep you and
your team members brilliant on the management basics.

Exhibit 8.4 / *MONTHLY FOCUS REPORT*

MONTHLY FOCUS REPORT

For _____

Manager

For the month of _____

KEY RESULT AREAS	MONTHLY FORECAST	(LBE)* YEAR-END
Recruits	_____	_____
(A) Class FYCs	$_____	$_____
Total FYCs	$_____	$_____
On-Time MDRTs	_____	_____

*Latest Best Estimate

THE 3Rs

Each month a forecast is developed.

The following month, this forecast is Reviewed. (R#1)

Then, actual results are Recorded. (R#2)

Also, a new forecast is Reported for next month, (R#3)

as well as the LBE for the year-end.

FIX THE FOCUS ON THE DESIRED RESULTS

Exhibit 8.5 / *PERFORMANCE POTENTIAL*

PERFORMANCE TO POTENTIAL

This proficiency checklist serves as an inventory of skills and abilities. Its purpose is to determine the performance/potential gap in your management practice.

5-Superior, 4-Good, 3-Fair, 2-Needs Attention, 1-Defective

1. Goal-setting and follow-up with associates	1 2 3 4 5
2. Achieving consistent production growth	1 2 3 4 5
3. Attracting high potential recruits	1 2 3 4 5
4. Using fast-start strategy, without compromise	1 2 3 4 5
5. Using Monthly Planning book	1 2 3 4 5
6. Teaching transferable sales system and language	1 2 3 4 5
7. Developing associates' selling and marketing skills	1 2 3 4 5
8. Monitoring weekly sales and marketing activity (PEP)	1 2 3 4 5
9. Coaching confidence, and being an encourager	1 2 3 4 5
10. Building MDRT, CLU, NQA and NAIFA memberships	1 2 3 4 5
11. Using time effectively	1 2 3 4 5
12. Building relationships with staff	1 2 3 4 5
13. Promoting activity in business, civic and community affairs	1 2 3 4 5
14. Maintaining an environment of excitement and success	1 2 3 4 5
15. Conducting effective, motivational meetings	1 2 3 4 5
16. Helping associates become good managers of personal affairs	1 2 3 4 5
17. Building the agency "self-help" library	1 2 3 4 5
18. Adhering to compliance expectations	1 2 3 4 5
19. Fostering good relationships with home office personnel	1 2 3 4 5
20. Personal planned self-improvement program	1 2 3 4 5

TOTAL POSSIBLE SCORE   **100**
MY SCORE   _____
PERFORMANCE/POTENTIAL GAP

_____

CHANGE STARTS WITH ME. I can change my professional and personal life from one of disappointment, ineffectiveness, and mediocrity to one of fulfillment and success by deliberately changing my performance score on the above career and personal concepts.

Manager's Signature: _____ **Date:** _____

VAL'S VIEWS ON MONITORING

Associates like to know that you know what they are doing. Make them aware of your awareness. It's a key strategy in bringing out the best in your people.

Supervisory strength comes from doing three things each week until they are expected. We have always called this "PRP."

- Review performance;

- Build confidence; and

- Plan next week.

Monitor the prospecting reservoir extra carefully. We remind our associates that the pharmacist has medicine and pills on the shelf; grocers have food; the clothier has suits on the rack. They monitor their inventory regularly. Diminished inventory – diminished revenues. You must watch the inventory. Producers can't afford to "run dry." Their greatest need is an "endless parade" of prospects to see.

Most important of all – when you are engaged in supervisory sessions, seize the opportunity to sell producers on their abilities, their futures and the confidence you have in them.

CHAPTER THOUGHTS AND IDEAS
I'M USING OR PLANNING TO IMPLEMENT

√   Build relationships first

√   Respect individual differences

√   Know what producers expect

√   Conduct weekly PEP sessions

√   Gain responsible commitments

√   Use Progress Guide weekly

√   Study MEA weekly

√   Fix the focus monthly (3Rs)

Chapter 9 /*MULTIPLYING*

*AN EFFECTIVE MANAGER MULTIPLIES. AN EFFECTIVE MANAGER
HELPS ASSOCIATES REALIZE THEY HAVE MORE ABILITY THAN
THEY THINK THEY HAVE. THEN, THEY CONSTANTLY PERFORM
BETTER THAN THEY THOUGHT THEY COULD.*

Charles E. Wilson

General H. Norman Schwarzkopf tells of the time he was put in control at the Pentagon. Colin Powell had to leave for an unexpected, lengthy assignment and Gen. Schwarzkopf was second in command at this time.

Multiply to maximize.

When leaving, Powell came to Schwarzkopf's office to wish him well. Gen. Schwarzkopf stopped him. "Wait a minute. What if decisions need to be made?" Colin Powell replied, "Always remember Rule 13!" The puzzled Schwarzkopf responded — "Rule 13?" Powell snapped back, *"Rule 13 — When put in command - Take Charge!"* Leaders who lead, take charge.

As he followed Powell down the hall to the elevator, he asked, "Are there any other last minute words of wisdom?" Powell responded, "Yes, remember Rule 14." Naturally, Gen. Schwarzkopf asked, "What's Rule

14?" Colin Powell said, *"Always do what's right, even if it is political-ly incorrect!"* That requires discipline. Leadership plus discipline multi-plies. Take charge and do what's right. It will catch on and multiply in your organization. Leaders who finish strong do what's right.

Leaders who take charge and do what's right, multiply!

But there's another lesson here to be learned from the Powell-Schwarzkopf confrontation that should not escape us. It is this – *having carefully selected and developed multipliers permits delegation.*

We hope this important system will help you see clearly the possi-bilities for leveraging your skills and efforts by developing multipliers you can count on – every time.

DEVELOP MULTIPLIERS

In front of the Research Center of the Firestone Tire & Rubber Company you view an impressive monument of the company's founder, Harvey S. Firestone. On a plaque that graces this statue are these words:

> "Harvey S. Firestone, born on a farm in 1868. He was rich in friendships and warmly loved by his fellow man. He believed what the centuries had to say as against the years, as against the hours. He was a courageous leader and pioneer. He trans-formed a gift of nature into a benefit for all mankind. The inspi-ration of his living is an enduring heritage. He was devoted to church and to home – *he brought out the best in others by giv-ing the best of himself."*

The best way to build responsible associates is to be a consistently responsible performer yourself.

IT IS ONLY AS WE DEVELOP OTHERS THAT WE PERMANENTLY SUCCEED.

Harvey S. Firestone

How Leaders Operate

West Point's first leadership manual coined an interesting expression – *"Be, Know and Do."* It was a succinct summation of how effective leaders operate. Also, it pointed to the central challenge of developing leader-type multipliers.

The capacity for "knowing" and "doing" is relatively easy to build up in your associates. It's a function of educating, training and monitoring. Most agency builders are reasonably good at developing the "know" and "do" skills.

But knowledge and skills are perishable. Why? Because they're not applied all the time and because they can become outdated. It's the "be" factor – their self-concept, their values, their ethical makeup, who they are – that lasts.

It's the "be" factor you must search for and evaluate when positioning your multipliers.

> *The highest reward for your toil is not what you get for it, but what you become by it.*
>
> *John Ruskin*

Management Team Multipliers

In the planning system, we show an organizational chart that you'll want to revisit. (Exhibit 1.2 in Chapter 1) At the top of the chart, reference is made to the management team.

The management team today is typically made up of your key office person (KOP), marketing team leaders, marketing director, recruiting coordinator, equities director, field sales managers and compliance officer. At the regular, monthly "main event" team meeting you will want to include each of these and a few carefully selected potential managers.

To help you raise the level of effectiveness among the members of your management team, there are five evaluation questions you want to respond to regularly:

1. Are they excited about what they're doing? And, are they perceived that way by others?

2. Are they optimistic about the future? Do they see the future is full of promise?

3. Do they make good on all commitments?

4. Do they distinguish between "busyness" and effectiveness?

5. Are they and you satisfied by what they are becoming – personally and professionally?

Key Office Person (KOP)

Successful agency builders are almost always those who have learned to make maximum use of their management time. An important factor in maximizing management time is the development of your administrative staff. In many agencies this means the selection and development of a Key Office Person (KOP). A staff need not be large to be effective. Of course, the size of your staff will depend upon your organizational needs.

Remember when building your staff, excellence requires both dedication and talent. *Start with a carefully selected KOP who will bring permanency to the assignment.* Chances are you'll be successful in developing this key person *if* the individual is with you long enough to be developed.

The *MDRT's Practice Management Guide* is the single best resource to use in selecting and developing administrative and marketing staff members.

Marketing Team Leaders

Here is a multiplying strategy whose time has come. It's not a particularly new concept, but it's one that has become necessary to maximize your agency's growth. We'd recommend you select a number of your experienced producers and form an intra-agency group, which you refer to as the "marketing team leaders." These should be producers who excel in certain markets. They might be especially competent in, say, long-term care, pension plans, estate plans, or equity products.

The Marketing Team Leader is both a team player and a high performing producer. *This individual would like to be a part of the management team, without management responsibilities.* This individual brings to the table experience, competence and a strong selling record.

Encourage these key associates to become authorities in their respective lines. Arrange for them to write articles for national publications. Help them organize PowerPoint™ presentations and talks that can be given to industry and civic groups, as well as in your monthly meetings. *Encourage and help them to become known for what they know.*

Many fast growing agencies today have on their organizational chart as many as ten Marketing Team Leaders. They make a significant contribution with little or no budget implication. Their revenues come from the joint selling they do with other producers. The customary sharing of commissions is done on a 50/50 basis.

Naturally, you'll want to encourage other members of your organization, whenever they have prospects in any one of these areas, to team up with "the expert" who is competent in that particular area. This will provide special recognition for your experienced producers, and they'll like it. Moreover, they'll stay involved and will help the new agency members become educated in advanced markets. They will become effective mentors to newer associates.

Almost without exception, the dynamic agencies we work with today are those who have a substantial amount of their revenues coming from joint selling. Review Exhibit 9.1 – The Advantages of Joint Selling, and learn what Jack Shaffer has to say about the merits of joint selling.

> *IF YOU WANT PEOPLE TO CARE, GET THEM INVOLVED. PEOPLE WANT TO GET INTO THE ACT – LET THEM. ADOPT A PARTICIPATIVE STYLE TO INVOLVE YOUR ASSOCIATES. TODAY'S TECHNOLOGY MAKES IT POSSIBLE TO PARTICIPATE AND COMMUNICATE WITHOUT A HIERARCHY OF GO-BETWEENS.*
>
> *Mike Vance*

Exhibit 9.1 / *THE ADVANTAGES OF JOINT SELLING*

THE ADVANTAGES OF JOINT SELLING

Virtually every successful producer we have been associated with has had at one time or another the assistance of an effective joint worker. It is our opinion that there has never been, isn't now, and never will be a substitute for joint selling, mostly in the field, during a producer's early training period.

Many associates at Zlotnik, Lamb & Company in Vancouver, B.C. are able to achieve TOT status because of the synergistic effect of joint selling. Jack Shaffer discussed the major advantages of joint selling with his MDRT peers at a recent MDRT meeting.

CREDIBILITY
People find advice more credible if they receive it from more than one person or if other advisors support that advice.

LARGER CASE SIZE
Joining forces with others brings different talents and perspectives to a case. The end result becomes much larger than it would have been otherwise. For example, a newer producer who is not yet experienced in a large case market may feel somewhat intimidated in presenting a large premium dictated by an in-depth analysis. The normal reaction would be to assume that the client simply wouldn't consider such an extreme price tag.

BETTER PERSISTENCY
If the solution is the best available under the circumstances, and the client appreciates this fact, the solution will persist.

IMPROVED MANAGEMENT SELLING TIME
There is a multiplier effect created by providing more time to open or deal with other cases while someone else is doing the prep work.

MORE REFERRALS
We make ourselves more referable by offering the best solution possible.

IMPROVED CLOSING RATIO
If the majority of time and effort is spent on fact-finding and offering solutions rather than attempting to get the client to take action, closing ratios greatly improve.

MORE INCOME, LESS EXPENSE
Joint selling is an efficient and effective marketing strategy that will result in more commissions without an increase in expenses.

Let's remember that most producers would rather "see a sermon than hear one any day." *The relationship between an effective joint selling record and total management success has always been great. Joint selling is one of the vital keys to success in building a master agency.* Move quickly to make yourself effective in this area of your management job.

Marketing Director

This management team member wakes up every day thinking about all of the many ways sales can be increased and improved.

The marketing director must have not only good interpersonal skills and people skills to deal with the agency's prospects and clients, but they have to know the business.

Beverly Brooks, a former President of the Society of Financial Service Professionals, says this: "There's no better way to learn the business than to make a commitment to continuing education. I recommend that Marketing Directors make the decision to obtain their credentials so they set themselves apart as professionals who have made a commitment to lifelong learning."

Recruiting Coordinator

As was expressed earlier, recruiting is the one job that must be done successfully every year. The recruiting coordinator has as a number one priority, keeping the managers' focus on sufficient activity and appointments.

Equities Director

A growing percentage of revenues today come from the sale of equity products. A knowledgeable, experienced professional in this assignment will prove to be a profitable addition in the years ahead.

Field Sales Managers (or Sales Managers)

Keep in mind the several, generally required skills and attitudes that a candidate should possess before becoming a part of your management team as a Field Sales Manager (FSM). These include the following:

√ Sells according to a sound, transferable process.

√ Displays leadership skills that develop loyalties.

√ Has good self-management and self-motivation habits.

√ Plans time and schedules activities well.

√ Stays focused.

√ Attracts quality people.

Keep score right from the start — almost from your initial recruiting contacts — to determine whether or not associates have or can develop these desired management characteristics. When individuals demonstrate they possess them, you can then add them to your "promotable" list of candidates.

Spell out FSMs' job description. We recommend your first expectation be that they stay respected producers. Encourage a consistently improving sales record. *Keep in mind that in the world of business, individuals often fail in a new assignment because they stop doing the things that earned for them the promotion.*

Exhibit 9.2, Insurance Policy for Field Sales Manager Success, provides an example of a certificate that can be put in an 8½ X 11 frame and presented to each FSM on the day of appointment to that position. The certificate outlines the ten essentials that insure an FSM's management success.

Additionally, there are two things related to Field Sales Managers that are well worth remembering.

- Their number one job is to show those they manage how to put in a good selling day.

- Field Sales Managers who perform best are always the FSMs who aspire to having a job like yours, sometime in the not too distant future.

Put these two philosophies in your "memory bank" for frequent recall.

I HAVE TO DO IT MYSELF, AND I CAN'T DO IT ALONE!

Compliance Officer

The need here is an obvious one. Compliance is installed to monitor producer selling practices to ensure the delivery of the best possible advice and service to prospects and clients.

The compliance battlecries of the 21st Century require you, the agency head, to model excellence. You must "rally the troops" around a common cause. That cause is to exceed client's expectations while consistently delivering prompt, accurate, courteous service. Quality Service is not just a slogan, but is the strategy for survival. Your ability to create compliance-consciousness in your agency is the foundation on which quality performance can be built.

Your compliance officer can help you inspire the highest standards of professional competence and behavior.

Exhibit 9.3, Customer Relationship Management, gives you several modern-day philosophies to share with your associates.

Exhibit 9.2 / *INSURANCE POLICY FOR FSM SUCCESS*

INSURANCE POLICY FOR FSM SUCCESS

BE AND STAY A RESPECTED PRODUCER. Stay in the field doing joint selling . . . Lead by example.

RECRUIT ENOUGH OF THE RIGHT KIND. Be accountable for attracting three new associates each year.

PLAY THE PERCENTAGES. Pre-contract every recruit.

DEMONSTRATE TRANSFERABLE SELLING SYSTEM. "Burn it in" during the first 90 days.

DECIDE TO EXCEL. Decide to pay the price.

MAJOR IN THE MAJORS. Stay focused.

HOLD PEP SESSIONS EACH WEEK. Evaluate results, goals and next week's plan.

CONDUCT MONDAY MORNING MEETINGS. Inform – Instruct – Inspire.

BUILD TEAM IDENTITY. Eliminate "I – Me – My."

BELIEVE IN SELF-IMPROVEMENT. Practice and promote it.

MODEL THE IDEAL SELLING DAY. Show "how to" put in a good selling day.

YOU CANNOT COMMAND SUCCESS – YOU CAN ONLY DESERVE IT.
YOU ARE MORE THAN A HUMAN BEING,
YOU ARE A HUMAN BECOMING.

Og Mandino

Exhibit 9.3 / *CLIENT RELATIONSHIP MANAGEMENT*

CLIENT RELATIONSHIP MANAGEMENT

Efficiency is doing a thing right.
Effectiveness is doing the right thing.
First-class client service requires both.

Hold yourself responsible for higher
standards than anybody else expects of you.

Everyone has an invisible sign hanging
from their neck that reads, "make me feel
important." Never forget this message
when working with prospects and clients.

Quality is the first thing seen.
Service is the first thing felt.
Premium is the first thing forgotten.

Always exceed the client's expectations.

Never let a client problem go unresolved.

A producer is essentially a teacher and advisor
to a client. It is recognized that the emphasis
can't be upon selling alone. Delivering Quality Service
to the client is the essential objective.

Accountability

As an agency builder, you can never delegate accountability for results. Though you vest an assistant with full responsibility and complete accountability, you nevertheless cannot escape full accountability for the results. And, the result produced is always the final judge.

Relationship Builders

There are a number of specific ways you can improve your effectiveness in developing each of your multipliers. According to Dr. Donald Clifton, and his associates at Gallup, the strongest are considered to be these:

√ Use people's correct names.

> How do you discover their correct names? Simply by asking. You may find that Robert prefers to be called Robert, Bob, Junior, or even "Tiny." The most important thing, however, is that you make people aware of your awareness, and this tends to build stronger relationships.

√ Ask for their opinions and advice.

√ Discover interests you have in common.

√ Search for "the turning point."

> Probe into their histories to uncover the points where their lives took on new and more meaningful directions.

√ Discover people's "hot-buttons."

> Be aware of what "turns on" each of your associates — what motivates them as individuals.

√ Learn about their successes.

> Each of your associates has done something successfully. So, here again, make them individually aware of your awareness.

√ Offer encouragement regularly and abundantly.

> Grove Patterson, the late editor-in-chief of the *Toledo Blade*, once said something that should never be forgotten by agency

heads. He said, "My years in the newspaper business have taught me many things. Among these is the fact that most of life's high achievements came about because of encouragement." He went on to say, "I don't care how great – how famous – how successful a person may be, he hungers for encouragement. Encouragement is the oxygen that keeps the soul healthy."

√ Practice emotional disclosure.

This tends to make people see you as an authentic, human and approachable person. Such disclosure leads to trust.

√ Build your capacity to care.

Minimize your self-concern and maximize your concern for others.

√ Know the individual career paths of multipliers – their futures.

Never stop being aware of what other individuals want to accomplish – what they want to become – where they want to go in their careers.

Relationship-building at its best is making others aware of your awareness in each of these areas. It's a skill that can be developed. It's a skill professional leaders must possess to develop multipliers.

UTILIZE THE TALENT

A story is told about a boy who valiantly, but unsuccessfully, attempted to move a heavy log to clear a pathway to his favorite hideout. His Dad stood quietly nearby, watching his son straining against the load. Finally, he said, "Son, why aren't you using all of your strength?"

Confused and a little angry, the boy responded, "Dad, I'm using every last bit of strength I possess!"

"No, son, you're not," his dad responded. "You haven't asked me to help!"

Effective agency builders employ "all of their strength" by recognizing, developing and utilizing the people around them. They learn how to develop effective alliances and multipliers.

NO ONE CAN BECOME RICH WITHOUT ENRICHING OTHERS.
ANYONE WHO ADDS TO PROSPERITY MUST PROSPER IN TURN.

Alexander Orndorff

Exhibit 9.4 / *MULTIPLIERS ARE SELECTED TO BE WINNERS*

MULTIPLIERS ARE SELECTED TO BE WINNERS

Winners	**Losers**
Winners respect those who are superior and try to learn something from them.	Losers resent those who are superior and rationalize their achievements.
Winners explain.	Losers explain away.
Winners say, "Let's find a way."	Losers say, "There is no way."
Winners go through a problem.	Losers try to go around it.
Winners say, "There should always be a better way to do it."	Losers say, "That's the way it's been done here."
Winners know what to fight for and what to compromise on.	Losers compromise on what they shouldn't, and fight for what isn't worth fighting about.
Winners work harder than losers, and have more time.	Losers are always "too busy" to do what is necessary.
Winners are not afraid of losing.	Losers are secretly afraid of winning.
Winners make commitments.	Losers make promises.

VAL'S VIEWS ON MULTIPLYING

Agencies are built on personality, procedures and philosophies. Only those built on a "blending" of all three multiply, prosper and stand the test of time.

Management team members, administrative personnel and sales managers must be an extension of the agency builder if multiplying is to be effective.

Know what you believe about the key elements of agency building. Then, make sure all the key players know that you know.

A powerful multiplying strategy, but one often overlooked, is to promote your multipliers. This sends an important message to other aspiring associates. Much of our success can be traced to the fact that we promoted out 25 agency heads.

Our greatest pleasures will not come from doing things for ourselves, but instead will come from the success and the things we do for others.

CHAPTER THOUGHTS AND IDEAS
I'M USING OR PLANNING TO IMPLEMENT

√ Be and stay a model of excellence

√ Develop Key Office Person (KOP)

√ Utilize Marketing Team Leaders

√ Spell out Sales Managers' job description

√ Respond to five evaluation questions

√ Develop sales-minded Marketing Director

√ Sell advantages of joint work

√ Practice the relationship-builders

Chapter 10 / *MOTIVATING*

GREAT ORGANIZATIONS CAN IGNITE PASSION.
CELEBRATIONS ARE A GREAT WAY TO ENERGIZE AN ORGANIZATION.

Jack Welch,
CEO General Electric

Years ago, Snuffy Stirnweiss, former Yankee second baseman, won the American League Batting Championship with an average of .306. Snuffy, who had never batted better than .275 before joining the Yankees, was asked how he could average 30 points better in the majors. He replied: "Wearing a Yankee pin-striped uniform is worth 30 points to anyone's batting average."

Joe Torre says, "Dress a player in a Yankee's uniform and you can expect excellence. The first time I put on the uniform, I got goose bumps. It was like wearing something sacred."

Build Pride in the Outfit and Confidence in Your Leadership

As the leader, immerse yourself in the goal of creating the type of environment where the best and brightest are attracted, retained and unleashed. Strive to provide associates with an exciting, highly motivated environment so they, too, will feel that just being a part of your organization will enhance their opportunities for superior selling success. Build the "Yankee mystique" – make it worth 30 extra points to their batting averages, just because they are proud members of your professional sales team.

Most people are presently capable of performing far better than they ever choose to do. They have the skill, the knowledge and the capacity to do a much better job. But the will must accompany the skill. They must be inspired to do it – and then they must be motivated to action.

YOUR MOTIVATING SYSTEM

We believe today's producers' desire to do a superior job is equally as important as his or her ability to do it. If either is lacking, the producer will fall short of excelling.

As a consequence, you must do your best to understand the character and motives of each of your associates. You must sincerely believe that all producers really want to perform better, think better, and live more effective business lives. That is why producers need and want the kind of leadership and environment that inspires and motivates them.

One of your chief responsibilities as a leader is to develop yourself as an effective motivator. It's to become skillful in handling the "human side" of the equation. You are the key in motivating your associates to do a superior job – to have them feel the pride that comes from stretching to do the best job possible. And motivation becomes the key factor.

MOST LIVES HAVE DEFINING MOMENTS – MOMENTS THAT FOREVER CHANGE YOU – MOMENTS THAT SET YOU ON A DIFFERENT COURSE – MOMENTS OF RECOGNITION SO VIVID AND SO CLEAR THAT EVERYTHING LATER SEEMS DIFFERENT.

President George W. Bush

The Most Important Factor

Again, we believe every producer who joins your organization wants to belong to a successful outfit and to work with a spirited leader. Producers want to be inspired and motivated to be at their best. We believe that producers like to work. They need the feeling of satisfaction that comes from doing good work. They want badly the recognition that accompanies good work. They are motivated by such recognition.

Your important role in all this, then, is to enrich the climate in your organization by providing built-in and continuous programs of recognition that inspire and motivate your associates. Look for ways to provide frequent, specially planned experiences that elevate their morale and produce excitement.

We feel strongly that the agency head's attitude is the most important single factor in providing a favorable climate, which motivates producers so they, in turn, seek high levels of performance. Superior agency heads generally do a great job of determining, understanding and utilizing whatever it is that motivates their associates to high-performance levels. More importantly, their own attitudes and styles permit them to create the relationships – the agency climate – in which their associates' desires for achievement can be realized.

THE GARDNER THOUGHT

This thought, developed by John Gardner, "strikes home" at what we are saying.

> The best kept secret in America today is that people would rather work hard for something they believe in than enjoy pampered idleness. They would rather give up their comfort for an honored objective than bask in extravagant leisure. It is a mistake to speak of dedication as a sacrifice. Every man knows that there is exhilaration in intense effort applied toward a meaningful end.

Producers must find pride in their accomplishments. If they have pride in their business and the organization, they will do a better job. We believe producers, properly recognized and motivated, will often expend extra effort for an agency cause.

Call it inspiration. Call it morale. Call it zeal. Call it job interest or drive. Call it team spirit. Call it the old "college try." Call it anything you like. It's still one of the greatest determinants of producer performance. In your agency operation, its presence can make bad procedures look good – and its absence can make good procedures look bad.

Most people are presently capable of performing far better than they ever choose to do. They have the skill, the knowledge and the capacity to do a much better job. But the will must accompany the skill. They must be inspired to do it – and then they must be motivated to action.

ELEMENTS OF THE MOTIVATING SYSTEM

There are several important elements included in an agency motivation system that is designed to create a favorable agency climate in which associates will be inspired. You'll want to include many of these in your own system. Let's examine a few.

Availability of the Leader

We feel it's important that you, as the leader, keep yourself available to associates, new and experienced alike – for any reason, business or personal.

Informal, personal get-togethers will also play a big part in your motivating system. You want all associates in the agency to know you are genuinely interested in them as individuals and in their success as individuals, as well as in their success as producers.

EXPERIENCE THE ADVANTAGES OF "SERVANT LEADERSHIP."
RECRUITING IS DONE MORE BY ASSOCIATES; MORE EXCITING
ENVIRONMENT; PEOPLE WANT TO BE A PART OF THE ELECTRICITY;
PRODUCTIVE IDEAS EVERYWHERE; JOINT SELLING BECOMES
A NATURAL PART OF THE EVOLUTION OF YOUR AGENCY.

Maury Stewart

Being intensely and sometimes unreasonably human, producers often harbor silly gripes, misgivings and misunderstandings. What they need is an interested leader upon whom they can "unload." Naturally, you can maintain an "open door" policy – and you can encourage agency members to bring their problems to you at any time. This sort of thing tends to build and maintain relationships. It motivates!

It is also good to schedule personal conferences in which producers have the time required to go over their goals, concerns, progress, and the things they want to accomplish. A pat on the back from you, as the leader – or just your allowing them to "dump their bucket of concerns" – often may be worth far more than money to them. Such conferences might take place in the office, on the golf course, at lunch, at the athletic club, or in your home.

Nothing can replace this "availability" factor. Its favorable impact on the motivation and morale of producers is immeasurable.

Regular Sales Meetings

Sales meetings afford an excellent opportunity to provide meaningful motivation for people in your organization. Steve Worthy, the effective speaker and agency builder at Charlotte, expresses a strong belief in using meeting exposure for motivation purposes. Steve builds his sales meeting agendas to include the current high achievements of his agency associates.

Motivation of this type, in the presence of peers, can often be the strongest kind.

Tom Bullock, the agency builder at New Orleans, promotes and gets more mileage out of his sales meetings than most anybody we've watched. Tom has this to say about meetings: *Whether it's planning an agency meeting or an agency function, make it first class or don't do it at all.*

Take care of the details well in advance. Have a printed agenda distributed prior to the meeting to let your associates know in detail what the meeting is all about. Also, have a final agenda passed out at the beginning of the meeting. Have a variety of topics and intersperse the technical with the motivational. Remember, "brains" are more receptive before lunch, versus after lunch.

So have your more technical information in the morning. *And don't forget: start on time and end on time.* If you want a top notch outside speaker, lock them in early and plan what they will talk about to get the best bang for your dollar.

Have the meeting at a first class place – a country club, hotel or an out-of-town resort.

Feed their brains and fill their stomachs! In this era of consolidation, many of your associates may have several hours to drive, so feed them a good meal. Don't have "short arms and deep pockets." Act like a "host" at your function, not the "king." Your associates like to see you working for them.

Don't have a meeting just to have a meeting. Make it worth their while. Remember, producers are self-employed business professionals. When they come to your meeting, they are not making any money. You need to have a first class meeting or they won't come back.

A PAYCHECK IS WHAT AN EMPLOYEE LIVES ON.
RECOGNITION AND APPRECIATION IS WHAT THEY LIVE FOR.

Mac Anderson

SPECIAL EVENTS

There are a number of agency functions you can stage each year that will do much to build and maintain an *esprit de corps*. We recommend the following:

Annual Kick-Off Meeting

On the 2nd day of January each year, hold an important kick-off meeting. Review the agency's performance for the year just ended, and recognize your leaders. Then formally announce your goals for the New Year. PowerPoint™ slides and posters should be prepared to make your meeting sparkle. *Seize this opportunity to build pride in the outfit and confidence in your leadership.*

Invite a company officer to your meeting – one from the advanced underwriting department – preferably, who can report on the company's results and plans. Prepare this all-important meeting to inform, instruct, inspire and motivate.

Talk about the members of your support team. Talk about the important jobs they are doing, introducing those who are attending the meeting. Recognize the members of the agency's managerial family and, of course, newly appointed associates who are in attendance.

Conclude your meeting with a luncheon at which you ask both your Junior-Associate-of-the-Year and your Associate-of-the-Year to speak. You'll want to "put a cap" on the day and close this meeting on a high note.

MOTIVATORS ARE GET-IT-DONE AND THEN SOME PEOPLE.

Annual Black-Tie Awards Dinner

The annual black-tie dinner, to which all members of your agency and their spouses are invited, should be held during the first quarter of each year. Awards are presented to all of your production leaders for the previous year, and special recognition is given to your top associates.

Present all spouses in attendance with appropriate mementos, as tokens of appreciation for the things that they do to contribute to the success of the producers. You'll get an extra dividend now and then if you make it a practice to invite the high school and college senior sons and daughters of agency members to this recognition meeting.

When you have an outstanding year, invite your company president or agency vice president to attend.

This, of course, should always be a big event in the lives of your agency members. Make careful preparations to assure the black-tie awards dinner is a meaningful and uplifting experience. It should be a great occasion.

Annual Sports Outing

A fishing trip, golf outing, or comparable event – for which producers must qualify – can be held each spring. A business-type meeting of interest can be held in the morning. The remainder of the day, then, is left open for recreation and good fellowship.

The master agency builder from Tallahassee, Lee Harrison, tells us his annual summer conference is the high-point of his year. Lee makes it a family affair. All family members are invited. However, special recognition is given to those who led in production during the agency's "Summer Show of Strength" contest leading up to the event.

Annual "Open House"

In December, you can hold an annual agency holiday party. Invite all associates and members of their families to agency headquarters for an "Open House." This permits you to put on display your fine facilities and, once each year, tie the whole spirit of things to the producers' business home. Slides of agency functions held during the year should also be displayed.

Invitations should be extended to your examining doctors, attorneys, trust officers, accountants, important clients and leading centers-of-influence.

This "Seasonal" get-together, then, can be climaxed by a year-end spiritual message given by a local religious leader.

NEVER UNDERESTIMATE THE POWER OF THE TINIEST PERSONAL TOUCH.

Tom Peters

SPECIAL GROUPS

We'd suggest you establish or promote the following special groups in your agency. They can be beneficial in a number of ways, but here we are primarily interested in the motivational impact they tend to have on agency members.

Agency Advisory Board

Here is another good recognition idea for inspiring and motivating your associates. Create an "Advisory Board" and allow all associates who have been with the agency 10 years or longer to become members. Hold luncheons, to which you invite all board members, honoring each new member upon joining this experienced group on his or her 10th anniversary.

Participation can be a powerful motivator. Motivation to accomplish sales results tends to increase as producers are given opportunities to participate in decisions affecting those sales results.

Get their advice, opinions, and suggestions whenever it is appropriate.

Leaders' Quarterly Round Table

The recognition for membership in the Leaders' Quarterly Round Table is designed to inspire and motivate your associates to maintain consistent production. Qualification is based upon production, of course, and the qualifiers are recognized for surpassing a minimum standard rather than just meeting it.

We recommend you adopt this idea and that you furnish some obvious and worthwhile reward. We'd suggest, for example, you invite each producer who qualifies to attend a luncheon with other leading producers, providing that each producer brings to the meeting a center-of-influence – an accountant, lawyer, trust officer, or banker – depending upon the outside speaker you have engaged.

In addition to providing important recognition, we believe these special groups will have a strong influence in upgrading your sales force and in improving the quality of the business produced in your organization.

INDIVIDUALS ARE ALWAYS STRONGER WHEN THEY HAVE THEIR
SUCCESSES AND STRENGTHS CLEARLY IN MIND.

Dr. Donald Clifton

Special Motivation

There are a number of ways you can provide special recognition for agency members. Here are a few we've found to be motivational.

Agency Wall of Fame

Prominently display the framed portraits of those producers who capture this coveted award. Only those associates who have demonstrated superior achievements should qualify.

Upon qualification, a producer may be presented, say, a "Blue Blazer" with your agency's insignia. Announcement letters can be mailed from agency headquarters to 100 of the producer's select clients, informing them of the selection and honor, and inviting them to visit your offices to view the wall display.

Incidentally, if you do not have an agency insignia, we'd suggest you develop one and use it. Have it professionally designed to be your agency's personalized logo. You'll find it helpful in building *esprit de corps* in many ways. The insignia can be used in all of your publications and bulletins – and, from time to time, you may wish to award cuff links, tie bars, money clips, etc., which carry the insignia of the agency.

Each year, for example, you can give money clips to your persistency winners – say, to those producers who have a minimum of 50 paid transactions in the calendar year and at least 90% persistency on their business.

Associate-of-the-Month Award

Your agency Associate-of-the-Month can be selected on the basis of MDRT credits. However, you should require that, to qualify, the producer must be a NAIFA member and have a minimum, say, of $6,000 of annualized first-year commissions during the particular month.

An attractive article with the producer's photograph can be published in the business section of the local newspaper. Arrangements can be made to purchase "slick copies" of the article from the newspaper. Copies can be made available to the producer for mailing inserts throughout the year. Also, copies of the article and an appropriate letter can be mailed from agency headquarters to 50 of the producer's clients.

Agency "Dedicator" Program

Your "Dedicator" program can provide recognition each month for those associates who produce $6,000 MDRT Credits, during the month.

An engraved trophy can be presented as a permanent possession to each producer who qualified as a "Dedicator" eight times or more during the calendar year.

Monthly Publication

Your agency publication should be completed and distributed by the 10th of each month. Its primary purpose should be to serve as the chief means of regularly reporting and recognizing noteworthy associate achievements.

This magazine should average about 20 pages an issue. Fifteen pages can be devoted solely to pictures and production records of those producers who performed in superior fashion during the preceding month. The other five pages can be comprised of articles, messages and facts that have been selected to aid your associates in their search for ways and means of self-improvement and self-education.

The underlying philosophy of your agency magazine should be to give as much personal recognition to as many different people as possible. However, the recognition must be deserved, or it will lose credibility and desired effect.

Special Announcement Releases

As we've said previously, you should send out "flash" news items whenever it is appropriate to do so. These announce special happenings in the personal and business lives of your agency members.

I OWE THE AUDIENCE MY BEST, REGARDLESS.

Frank Sinatra

Exhibit 10.1 / *WALL OF FAME*

WALL OF FAME

Members of this coveted award will be chosen from those individuals who have demonstrated superior achievement. Upon qualification, the associate will have his or her picture placed on our Agency "Wall of Fame." It will remain on permanent display. Appropriate letters will be mailed to 100 of the associate's select clients announcing the selection, and inviting the clients to visit our attractive offices.

QUALIFICATIONS

Million Dollar Round Table

- Three consecutive years
- Qualifying MDRT member five times during career

National Conference Qualifiers

- Three consecutive years
- Four out of the last seven years
- Five times during career

National Quality Award Winner

Award-Winning Supervisor

- Three consecutive years

"May we always be inspired by their achievements."

Exhibit 10.2 / *"DEDICATOR" PROGRAM*

"DEDICATOR" PROGRAM

1. "DEDICATOR" . . . $6,000 MDRT Credits in a month.

- If "Dedicator" four times in each half-year, you honor your spouse with a special gift.

- Year-ending members of the President's Cabinet and the MDRT along with our National Quality Award winners will also honor their spouses.

- If "Dedicator" eight times in calendar year, you will be recipient of engraved "Dedicator" Trophy for your permanent possession.

2. Gifts for the spouses of the above will be presented according to this schedule:

- 1st half – Educational Conference in August

- 2nd half – Agency Awards Dinner in March

"First, last and always, ours is a mental attitude business.
As we think, we travel; we are today where our
thoughts have brought us. And we will be tomorrow
where our thoughts take us."

Pygmalion In Management

Dr. David Schwartz, at Georgia State University, has said that each person wears a badge that reads, *"Encourage me – Expect well of me – Make me feel worthwhile and important."* Your associates want to feel important. They want to feel that they are making a contribution. They want you to build their confidence. When they are helped to feel competent and confident, they see themselves doing their jobs in a superior way.

In his research paper, *Pygmalion in Management,* J. Sterling Livingston develops the conclusions of a comprehensive study he performed at Harvard with a group of insurance managers. The evidence produced revealed the following:

- What managers expect of their associates and the way a manager treats them largely determines their performance and career progress.

- *The unique characteristic of superior managers is their ability to create high performance expectations that associates fulfill.*

- Less effective managers fail to develop similar expectations, and, as a consequence, the productivity of their associates suffers.

- *Associates, more often than not, appear to do what they perceive they are expected to do.*

Have no question about it - when it comes to motivating, successful leaders learn to treat their associates in ways that lead to superior performances. They build on strengths. They encourage. They coach confidence.

IF WE EVER GET AROUND TO BELIEVING INDIVIDUALS CAN'T CHANGE, THEN MANAGERS WILL BECOME EXTINCT.

John Greene,
Sr. V.P. Marketing Prudential Financial

This is Motivation

- I respect you, not only for what you are, but for what I am when I am with you.

- I respect you, not only for what you have made of yourself, but for what you are making of me.

- I respect you for the best of me that you bring out.

- I respect you for ignoring the possibilities of the fool in me and for laying firm hold of the possibilities of good in me.

- I respect you for closing your eyes to the discords in me, and adding to the music in me by listening.

- I love you because you have done more than any creed could have done to make me effective.

- You have done it without a touch, without a word, without a sign. You have done it by your example and your availability. After all, this is what being an encourager and motivator is all about.

Boss vs. Motivator

The professional manager who inspires rather than bosses earns the kind of following that is reflected in satisfying figures on the production reports. The inevitable result of good management of producers is good motivation, and the inevitable result of good motivation is increased production and improved morale.

Here are some excellent comparisons between the boss and a motivator. Which do you desire to be?

Exhibit 10.3 / *BOSS VS. MOTIVATOR*

BOSS	MOTIVATOR
• Points out weakness	• Builds on strengths
• Drives people	• Coaches confidence
• Depends on authority	• Depends on good will
• Inspires fear	• Inspires enthusiasm
• Says "I"	• Says "We"
• Says "Go"	• Says "Let's go!"

An important part of your management job is to keep your associates motivated and sold on three things:

1. Their ability and talent;

2. Their future and opportunity for personal growth; and

3. Your confidence in them and the contribution they will make.

This style of management is what the times demand!

Learning to Motivate

The best way to motivate your associates is to show them you are conscious of their needs, ambitions and concerns.

Your goal is not to get people to like you. You are not running a popularity contest. You are building a master agency. Here are actions to take if you wish to keep your associates highly motivated. Use them if you think your performance as a motivator is not what you believe it could be.

THE PRINCIPAL ELEMENTS OF MORALE ARE PRIDE IN THE OUTFIT AND CONFIDENCE IN YOUR LEADERSHIP.

General George Patton

Proven Motivators

1. **EXHIBIT PERSONAL DILIGENCE.** We have never known a successful motivator who was not highly motivated. You motivate by example. The best motivators are those who themselves are hard working, almost to the point of total commitment to achieving excellence in their leadership roles.

2. **EXAMINE "FACE VALIDITY."** The influence of your example is powerful. And, it all begins with appearance and demeanor. What does your appearance and demeanor convey? Confidence? Focus? Professionalism? Coach Tom Landry personified the leader-type "face validity" and his players were always highly motivated.

3. **BUILD TRUST.** Relationship-building should be considered the base upon which all personal motivation takes place.

4. **COMMUNICATE STANDARDS.** Standards usually tell your associates what is expected of them. When individuals know they are being evaluated according to a single, fair standard, they have a target to motivate them.

5. **LET THEM KNOW WHERE THEY STAND.** As we said previously, do this consistently by monitoring and measuring with your performance reviews. The positives or negatives you hold in the back of your head do your associates no good unless they know what you are thinking. Make your associates aware of your awareness. Let them know you are looking for ways to help them improve.

6. **KEEP YOUR ASSOCIATES INFORMED.** You evidence you are concerned when you inform them in advance of things where they are likely to have a direct interest.

7. **HELP YOUR ASSOCIATES GROW.** If you are an effective motivator, you'll go out of your way to help your associates get better. You

must be attuned to the fact that each individual is concerned about his or her future. Everyone must feel that you, too, are concerned about his or her growth.

8. **RECOGNIZE ABILITIES.** People will tend to perform better when they feel good about themselves. Keep them sold on their talents.

9. **BUILD ON STRENGTHS.** Keep them working on those things they do best.

10. **BUILD INDEPENDENCE.** Encourage them to show initiative, to think critically and to ask challenging questions. One of the best ways to motivate individuals is to help them achieve their fullest potential through independence.

11. **GIVE APPROPRIATE PRAISE.** Properly handled, praise will become one of your best motivating factors. It's especially helpful when you compliment someone in an area where there is visibility. In other words, where they feel they ought to be making solid progress. It's also a good idea to save your praise for a particularly challenging job that is handled in a superior manner.

12. **GAIN RESPONSIBLE COMMITMENTS.** Motivation to accomplish results tends to increase as people are given the opportunity to participate in the goal-setting process. Time devoted to securing participation is a good investment. It develops increased interest and enthusiasm in getting the job done.

13. **TAKE RESPONSIBILITY FOR YOUR ASSOCIATES.** If you wish to motivate associates, then you must assume some responsibility for what happens to them. This is all a part of caring for your people. The leader who is concerned has a personal involvement in the success of the associate. If the producer fails, then a part of the manager also fails. Caring usually creates a bond of responsibility between manager and producer.

Frank Stanton, president of the Columbia Broadcasting System, frequently challenges an associate with the question, "Is this the best job you and I can do together?" The way the question is phrased shows the subordinate that first, Stanton assumes partial responsibility for the success of the project, and second, that Stanton really cares about it.

14. **ENSURE REWARDS.** People will be motivated to accomplish the results you want to achieve to the extent that you show interest in the results they want to achieve. Set them up for success.

15. **EXPECT THE BEST.** The more you demonstrate belief in people, the greater their drive to excel and to make you look good.

Motivation At Its *Very* Best

"I'M JUST A PLOW HAND FROM ARKANSAS, BUT I HAVE LEARNED HOW TO HOLD A TEAM TOGETHER. I'VE LEARNED HOW TO LIFT SOME INDIVIDUALS UP, HOW TO CALM DOWN OTHERS, UNTIL FINALLY THEY'VE GOT ONE HEARTBEAT TOGETHER, A TEAM.

"THERE ARE JUST THREE THINGS I'D EVER SAY:

- IF ANYTHING GOES BAD, I DID IT.

- IF ANYTHING GOES SEMI-GOOD, THEN WE DID IT.

- IF ANYTHING GOES REAL GOOD, THEN YOU DID IT.

THAT'S ALL IT TAKES TO GET PEOPLE TO WIN FOOTBALL GAMES FOR YOU."

Paul "Bear" Bryant, Legendary Football Coach, University of Alabama

LEAD AS IF YOU'LL BE HELD ACCOUNTABLE, BECAUSE YOU WILL. MY CODE HAS ALWAYS BEEN TO WORK LIKE THIS IS THE LAST JOB I'LL EVER HAVE AND LIVE LIKE IT'S THE LAST DAY OF MY LIFE.

Bobby Bowden,
Head Coach, Florida State University

Exhibit 10.4 / *LAWS OF LEADERS WHO LEAD*

Laws of Leaders Who Lead

Law #1
Reputation Cultivation

Find the way to make good on all commitments.
This is motivating by example.

Law #2
Winning

Be a connoisseur of talent. You win with highly motivated talent.

Law #3
Relationship-building

Sell your associates on their abilities, their futures,
and the confidence you have in them.

Law #4
Effectiveness

Never confuse activity with accomplishment. Applaud results.

Law #5
Maximization

Consistently monitor and measure those few things that matter.
What matters will improve.

Law #6
Personal Growth

Read and inwardly digest one book each month. Motivators are readers.

Law #7
Longevity

Enjoy the rewards that can be yours by focusing on
and excelling in the things you can control.

Leaders attract listeners and followers; they may not be the boss. Our competitive world today offers two possibilities. You can lose. Or, if you want to win, you can embrace these laws and be a leader who leads.

VAL'S VIEWS ON MOTIVATING

Motivation to accomplish agency sales results tends to increase as producers are given recognition for their contribution. Producers will work hard when they get continuing recognition for their efforts.

When you give credit to producers who have earned it, you are making clear that you consider them important members of the organization. Recognition must be sincere.

The motivational impact is multiplied when you give recognition in public. Be sure to let your associates have all the credit.

Celebrations ignite sales people. Our monthly Celebrity Lunch has become a high point on our agency calendar. Associates qualify by having $12,000 MDRT credits or ten paid cases. We average 30 – 40 qualifiers each month. We recognize our associate-of-the-month, and other leaders. We take this opportunity to report agency results and create an atmosphere of high achievement. We generally have a guest speaker to close the celebration on a high note.

Excitement is contagious. Look for ways to have an epidemic in your agency on a regular basis.

Chapter Thoughts and Ideas
I'm Using or Planning to implement

√ Keep yourself available and visible

√ Prepare sales meetings that excite

√ Promote "Summer Show of Strength"

√ Display Agency Wall of Fame

√ Stage January Kick-Off meeting

√ Send out "Flash News Bulletins"

√ Make awards dinner a great occasion

√ Internalize "Laws for Leaders"

Concluding Thoughts

One of our favorite restaurants on the West Coast is Scott's, on the water at Oakland. Scott's has an engaging and effective leader in Michael Stagg, its manager. Michael is one of those guys who never "turns off the light." He's working at customer relationship management and selling all the time.

One time we were enjoying the catch of the day. Michael came by to share with us a quote chiseled into the base of the Jack London statue outside Scott's front door. "This is something you'll like, and can share with your audiences," he said. Michael was right about that one—and the Alaskan Haddock recommendation, too. Here are the words of Jack London.

I WOULD RATHER BE ASHES THAN DUST!
I WOULD RATHER THAT MY SPARK SHOULD
BURN OUT IN A BRILLIANT BLAZE THAN IT
SHOULD BE STIFLED BY DRY ROT.
I WOULD RATHER BE A SUPERB METEOR,
EVERY ATOM OF ME IN MAGNIFICENT GLOW,
THAN A SLEEPY AND PERMANENT PLANET.
THE PROPER FUNCTION
OF MAN IS TO LIVE, NOT TO EXIST.
I SHALL NOT WASTE MY DAYS
IN TRYING TO PROLONG THEM.
I SHALL USE MY TIME.

Jack London
1876–1916

And it was Carlyle who wrote:

> ONE LIFE – JUST A LITTLE GLEAM OF TIME
> BETWEEN TWO VAST ETERNITIES.
> NO SECOND CHANCE FOR US, FOREVERMORE.

This is reason enough to use these ten systems to consistently meet the challenge of building a superior organization that will outlive you.

Finally, always remember the Latin proverb:

> IF THERE IS NO WIND, ROW.